The Master Musicians Series

RICHARD STRAUSS

THE MASTER MUSICIANS SERIES

Richard Strauss

by Michael Kennedy

With eight pages of plates and
music examples in text

J. M. DENT & SONS LTD
LONDON

First published 1976
© Text, Michael Kennedy, 1976

Made in Great Britain
at the
Aldine Press, Letchworth, Herts
for
J. M. Dent & Sons Ltd
Aldine House, Albemarle Street, London

This book is set in 11 on 12 point Fournier 185

Hardback ISBN: 0 460 03148 1
Paperback ISBN: 0 460 02176 1

Preface

Richard Strauss's music is more popular with the public than it has ever been, but it still divides critical opinion into friendly and hostile camps. It always will; it is that kind of music. You can take it or leave it, but if you leave it you will miss a great deal of pleasure. Strauss himself summed it up in his reply to a young man who confessed that, try as he might, he could not bring himself to like *Rosenkavalier*. 'What a shame for you,' said Strauss. Now that Elgar and Mahler have been rehabilitated, Richard Strauss remains the most misunderstood and misrepresented great composer of the last hundred years, Schoenberg included.

Nobody writing about Strauss in English can fail to acknowledge the debt owed to Norman Del Mar's masterly three-volume survey of the works and to William Mann's critical study of the operas. They have been able to go into detail inappropriate to this series, and I unreservedly recommend readers who seek more information on the works to consult these fine books. Certain of Strauss's works which Norman Del Mar and William Mann feel unsure about I happen to admire, so I have allowed my enthusiasm to rise above the 'received opinions'.

Strauss the man is equally controversial. He was the subject, or object, of a grossly distorted television film by Mr Ken Russell, and he has been pilloried by Mr George R. Marek in a book because he did not involve himself in the realms of higher statesmanship during two world wars. The facts speak for themselves, and I have tried to present these facts without bias so that Strauss's position may be judged fairly.

Preface

In assembling illustrations I am grateful to the following for their help: Boosey & Hawkes, the Mansell Collection, the *Radio Times* Hulton Picture Library, Dr Franz Strauss and the Richard Strauss Archive at Garmisch.

I gratefully acknowledge permission to reprint extracts from Strauss's correspondence with Hofmannsthal, thanks to the courtesy of William Collins, Sons & Co. Music examples are reproduced by kind permission of the publishers: Universal Edition (London) Ltd (Ex. 1); Steingräber Verlag (U.K. agents: Bosworth & Co. Ltd) (Ex. 2.); Peters Edition London, New York and Frankfurt (Exx. 3–8); Musikverlag S.E.C. Leuckart (U.K. agents: Novello & Co. Ltd.) and Boosey & Hawkes, Music Publishers Ltd (Exx. 10–28).

March 1975.   M. K.

For Harold and Hannelore,
with my love,
remembering Salzburg 1969

Mein Herz und Seel' wird bei Ihr bleiben
wo Sie geht und steht, bis in alle Ewigkeit.
26th September 1974

Contents

Contents

List of Illustrations

'Haven't I the right, after all, to write what music I please? I cannot bear the tragedy of the present time. I want to create joy. I need it.'

Richard Strauss, in 1924.

'I wish you well, better than most people have done in your life. You have not looked for many friends, and have not had many.'

Hugo von Hofmannsthal to Strauss, in 1918.

1 Munich childhood

The long lifetime of Richard Strauss, from 1864 to 1949, spanned almost a century of an unparalleled period in the history of mankind. Music, no less than science, progressed through major developments and cataclysms. Strauss grew up beneath the giant shadow thrown across European art by Wagner; a glow from the fading rays of the Wagnerian sunset was still warming him in his own long twilight. Not for him Stravinsky's indefatigable self-renewal nor Schoenberg's impassioned intellectual theorizing: he remained consistently within his own capabilities, which he knew exactly, their extent and their limitations. 'I'm the only composer nowadays,' he wrote in 1916, 'with some real humour and a sense of fun and marked gift for parody.' If his music lacks mystical and spiritual depth—and it does, except in one late work—it has worldly, human rapture and insight, realism and humour. From first to last he put his trust in tonality, melody, dramatic instinct and a vein of fantasy which belongs to all the greatest story-tellers. In his young manhood he was regarded by many as the very arch-fiend of modernism and cacophony; in his old age he was debunked as an irrelevant survivor of a vanished epoch. Yet uninterruptedly since the first decade of the twentieth century several of his operas have held the stage of the world's leading opera-houses, and no symphony orchestra can plan rewarding programmes without his symphonic poems in its repertoire. To adapt a saying by Benjamin Jowett, you must believe in Strauss whatever the pundits may tell you.

Richard Georg Strauss was born in Munich at 2 Altheimer

Richard Strauss

Eck, on 11th June 1864. He was the first-born of Franz Joseph
Strauss (1822–1905), principal horn-player in the Munich Court
Orchestra, and his second wife, Josephine Pschorr (1837–1910),
a member of the wealthy family of brewers. Franz was a great
instrumentalist and a cantankerous man, embittered by a hard
childhood. His first wife and their two children died in a cholera
epidemic. A humble musician, he was regarded by the Pschorr
family as a poor match for one of their daughters. He courted
Josephine for seven years before their marriage in Munich
Cathedral in August 1863. Musically Franz was intensely conservative, worshipping Haydn, Mozart and Beethoven, and
detesting the later works of 'Mephisto Richard Wagner', as he
called him, marvellously as he played the horn solos in *Tristan*,
Die Meistersinger and *Der Ring des Nibelungen*. Because of his
financial independence, Franz Strauss was able to treat conductors and composers with boorish rudeness and get away with
it. His son said that 'he would have considered it dishonest ever
to revise a judgment on an artistic subject once he had arrived at
it'.[1] The worst of him is shown by his refusal—honest, in his own
lights—to join the rest of the orchestra in standing in silent
tribute to Wagner on the morrow of his death;[2] the best by his
solemn dedication to his work, for he would spend weeks preparing for difficult solos in Weber, Beethoven, Mendelssohn—
and Wagner—and would arrive at rehearsal an hour before the
rest of the orchestra to practise his part.

Temperamental and tyrannical though Franz was at home, his
marriage was happy, and Richard's childhood was untroubled.
At four and a half Richard had pianoforte lessons from August
Tombo, his father's harpist colleague, and later from Carl Niest,
and at eight Benno Walter, his father's cousin, taught him the

[1] R. Strauss: *Recollections and Reflections* (Zürich, 1949; London,
1953), 'Reminiscences of my Father'.
[2] E. Newman: *The Life of Richard Wagner*, Vol. III (New York,
1941), p. 378.

2

violin. He saw his first operas (*Der Freischütz* and *Die Zauber-flöte*) when he was six and, at the same age, had written his first compositions, a Christmas carol and the *Schneiderpolka* for pianoforte. Alongside his musical training he received a classical education. After elementary schooling from 1870 to 1874 he entered the Ludwigsgymnasium, Munich. 'I was always fonder of composing than studying,' he wrote,[1] 'but I managed to pass my matriculation examination without discredit at the age of eighteen.' He never went to an academy of music but, from the age of eleven, had a thorough education in musical theory, harmony and instrumentation from one of the court conductors, Friedrich Meyer. His father insisted on a firm grounding in the old masters. Strauss himself tells us that he heard nothing but classical music until he was fourteen. Thereafter, despite Franz's disapproval and discouragement, he came to know the Wagner operas in score and performance. His childhood was musically blessed by taking place within the influence of the Munich Opera 'and its wonderful orchestra'. But his first experiences of Wagner on the stage left him puzzled. 'The prejudices inculcated by up-bringing may have influenced me strongly,' he wrote.[2] 'It was not until, against my father's orders, I studied the score of *Tristan* that I entered into this magic work, and later into *Der Ring*.' He was bored by his first visits to *Siegfried* and *Lohengrin*. Religion seems to have played no part in his upbringing.

Throughout his teens Richard composed copiously, and several of these early works were performed. His father conducted a semi-professional orchestra known as 'Wilde Gung'l'. At its weekly rehearsals Richard learned much of the practical side of orchestration. When he was a few days short of his sixteenth birthday a gavotte he had written was played at one of its concerts. In 1880 also he composed a setting of a chorus from

[1] R. Strauss: *Recollections and Reflections*, op. cit. 'Letter on the *Humanistische Gymnasium*', 1945.
[2] R. Strauss: 'Reminiscences of my Father', op. cit.

Sophocles' *Electra* which was performed at the Gymnasium. A string quartet in A major which he wrote in 1879–80 was played in Munich on 14th March 1881 by a quartet led by Benno Walter. A *Festmarsch* in E flat major, composed in 1876, was played by 'Wilde Gung'l' on 26th March 1881 and was published as his Op. 1 later that year.[1] Four days later Hermann Levi conducted the Court Orchestra in the sixteen-year-old's Symphony in D minor. Other works dating from this time included the *Five Piano Pieces*, Op. 3, and the piano sonata in B minor, Op. 5.

For the winter and spring terms of 1882–3 Strauss attended Munich University to read philosophy, aesthetics and the history of art, but left to concentrate on music. At the age of eighteen he stood on the threshold of a meteoric ascent to national and international fame. No tale here of an unhappy, poverty-haunted childhood; no serious strife between parents and son; no struggle to adopt a career in the face of opposition. Strauss's sister Johanna, three years his junior, wrote of their childhood holidays: 'Excursions to lonely valleys among the peaks, then coffee with whipped cream and little cakes . . . There were innumerable joys and freedom which ever remained in Richard's heart.'

---

[1] The publishers were Breitkopf and Härtel, but the cost was underwritten by Strauss's uncle, Georg Pschorr.

2　'Richard the Third'

While he was at university, Richard Strauss made his first public appearance in Vienna, in the Bösendorfersaal, as pianist with the violinist Benno Walter in his own Violin Concerto, which he had composed while at school. He described himself [1] as 'never technically efficient' as a pianist because he did not enjoy practising. That performance was on 5th December 1882, and the critic Eduard Hanslick noted 'unusual talent'. A week earlier, on 27th November, his *Serenade* in E flat major for thirteen wind instruments had been performed in Dresden by the court orchestra under Franz Wüllner, the first Strauss first-performance in a city which was to hear many of them. A year later, on 26th November 1883, Hermann Levi conducted Strauss's Overture in C minor in Munich. One can imagine how the news must have travelled on the German musical grapevine that the son of that old curmudgeon Strauss the hornplayer had genuine talent as a composer. Levi and Wüllner were celebrated conductors of their day. Levi was forty-four and had been court conductor at Munich since 1872. He conducted the first *Parsifal* at Bayreuth in July 1882. Wüllner, at this date aged fifty, was in Munich from 1864 to 1877. He then went to Dresden. Clearly these fine musicians recognized something extraordinary in the work of the eighteen-year-old Strauss.

In the winter of 1883–4, Franz Strauss treated his son to a visit

---

[1] R. Strauss: *Recollections and Reflections*, 'Recollections of my Youth and Years of Apprenticeship'.

Richard Strauss

to Berlin. There Richard went to the opera, met painters, sculptors and poets, learned to play cards, and wrote his Symphony in F minor, which had its first performance in December 1884 not in Germany, nor indeed in Europe, but in New York where that astonishing talent-spotter Theodore Thomas conducted it for the Philharmonic Society, having been shown the manuscript by his old friend Franz Strauss while on a visit to Europe. The most significant factor in the Berlin visit, however, was Strauss's first meeting with the great conductor and pianist, Hans von Bülow, who had been court conductor at Munich from 1864 to 1869 and was now at Meiningen, where within a few months of his appointment in 1880 he had made the orchestra into a superb instrument, the first virtuoso orchestra of modern times even though it contained only forty-eight players compared with the Vienna Philharmonic's ninety. The Meiningen's strength was in the marvellous precision of its ensemble playing rather than in its beauty of tone. There was no opera at the Meiningen court, so Bülow was free to rehearse the symphonic repertoire with a thoroughness undreamed of elsewhere.

Strauss's first publisher, Eugen Spitzweg, a friend of Bülow, sent the wind *Serenade*—which Strauss later in life described as 'nothing more than the respectable work of a music student'[1]— to Bülow, who included the work in his orchestra's touring repertoire. 'An uncommonly gifted young man,' Bülow wrote to the impresario Hermann Wolff. 'By far the most striking personality since Brahms.' Strauss heard the Meiningen Orchestra's Berlin performance of his work (which was not conducted by Bülow) and was commissioned by Bülow to write a similar piece for them. That summer he composed the four-movement *Suite* in B flat major, also for thirteen wind instruments. 'Happy days of my youth,' he reflected, 'when I could still work to order'—but this was a cynical jest. Strauss could

[1] R. Strauss: 'Reminiscences of Hans von Bülow'.

always, and did always work, to order or not. His industry compels admiration. He was not a composer who waited for the spark
from heaven to fall; he worked and worked, in the hope that something good would sometimes be the result. From 1878 onwards
his list of compositions grew at an amazing rate. He was
particularly prolific from 1881 to 1885. In addition to works
already mentioned he had composed within this period the Cello
Sonata, First Horn Concerto, the Pianoforte Quartet, many songs,
including the Nine Lieder to words by Gilm which contained his
first masterpieces in this genre, *Zueignung*, *Die Nacht* and
Allerseelen, and the Brahmsian *Wandrers Sturmlied*, a setting of
Goethe for a six-part chorus and orchestra. 'Work is a constant
and never tiring source of enjoyment to which I have completely
dedicated myself,' he wrote at this time.

Bülow's percipience in detecting Strauss's potential greatness
was all the more to his credit in view of his reaction to the first
music by Strauss which he encountered. Spitzweg in 1881 had
sent him the *Five Piano Pieces*. Bülow replied that he disliked
them profoundly—'unripe and precocious. . . . I miss the spirit
of youthful invention. . . . We have here to deal not with genius
but with the kind of talent that comes ten a penny'. But by 1884,
when Spitzweg was losing money on the several Strauss works
which his little firm of Joseph Aibl had published, Bülow bol-
stered his resolve by this advice: 'Stay with him. In five years
you will make money.' Jestingly he called his protégé 'Richard
the Third', because after Richard the First (Wagner) there could
be no Second; but the jest was apposite, and Bülow knew it.
Bülow accepted the new *Suite*, rehearsed it in Meiningen and,
showing thoughtfulness, decided to give the first performance
when the orchestra visited Munich. Moreover, he invited the
composer to conduct it. Strauss was overjoyed but pointed out
that he had never had a baton in his hand before, so when could
he rehearse? Bülow replied that the orchestra had no time for
rehearsals on tour. On the day of the concert, 18th November

7

1884, Strauss went to Bülow's hotel where he found the great man 'in a dreadful mood', raving against Munich, which had driven out Wagner and himself. Bülow did not attend the performance. Chain-smoking, he paced furiously up and down the conductor's room. When Strauss returned, his father looked in to thank Bülow.

> Like a furious lion he pounced upon my father: 'You have nothing to thank me for,' he shouted, 'I have not forgotten what you have done to me in this damned city of Munich. What I did today I did because your son has talent and not for you.' Without saying a word my father left. . . . This scene had, of course, completely spoiled my début for me. Only Bülow was suddenly in the best of spirits.[1]

In the first quarter of 1885 Wüllner conducted (in Cologne) the first European performance of Strauss's F minor Symphony, and at Meiningen Bülow conducted the first performance of the Horn Concerto. At this time also, Bülow's assistant conductor, Franz Mannstädt, was appointed conductor of the Berlin Philharmonic. Through Spitzweg, Bülow—having rejected Felix Weingartner—offered Strauss the post—'the most joyous surprise imaginable', Strauss wrote to Bülow on 26th May. Perhaps, he suggested, he could occasionally conduct preliminary rehearsals, but the big attraction was to be able to attend all Bülow's rehearsals and 'to study closely your interpretation of our symphonic masterpieces'. In preparation, he went in July to the Raff Conservatoire in Frankfurt to attend Bülow's lectures on Beethoven's pianoforte works.

On 1st October 1885, three months after his twenty-first birthday, Strauss took up his new post—assistant to the greatest conductor of the day, with a virtuoso orchestra on which to learn. Every morning he attended Bülow's rehearsals:

> Ever since that time the memory of the works he then conducted, all of them by heart, has never been effaced from my mind. In par-

[1] 'Reminiscences of Hans von Bülow.'

8

ticular, I found the way in which he brought out the poetic content of Beethoven's and Wagner's works absolutely convincing. . . . Everything was of compelling necessity, born of the form and content of the work itself.[1]

For a fortnight this apprenticeship continued, 'a good grounding in conducting, at least in theory', Strauss wrote. Bülow conducted both performances and rehearsals by heart; at the latter he gave Strauss the scores, frequently asking him searching questions. Practical work began on 15th October when, for Strauss's public début, Bülow invited him to play the solo part in Mozart's C minor pianoforte concerto (K.491) and then to conduct his own F minor Symphony. In the audience was Brahms, who was in Meiningen for rehearsals of the Fourth Symphony, which was to have its first performance on 25th October. He commented: 'Quite pretty, young man.' He added what Strauss called a 'memorable piece of advice':

'Take a good look at Schubert's dances, and try your luck at inventing simple eight-bar melodies.' . . . I also remember clearly a further criticism made by the great master: 'Your symphony is too full of thematic irrelevances. There is no point in this piling up of many themes which are only contrasted rhythmically on a single triad.' It was then that I realized that counterpoint is only justified when poetic necessity compels a temporary union of two or several themes contrasted as sharply as possible.[2]

The performance of the Brahms symphony was to be a turning-point for Strauss. He noted the contrast between Bülow's enthusiasm and conscientiousness and the composer's indifference towards the dynamics and presentation of his work. Nevertheless the second performance of the symphony a few days later at Frankfurt led to a bitter quarrel between Bülow and Brahms because Brahms elected to conduct it himself. Bülow,

[1] For a less adulatory view, see Weingartner's *On Conductors*.
[2] 'Reminiscences of Hans von Bülow.'

9

who was naturally impulsive and was becoming a little tired of Meiningen, where players he had trained kept leaving for posts elsewhere, resigned. Strauss, after a month's training and very little practical experience, became his successor on 1st November 1885. Yet conductors are born, not made, and Strauss was a born conductor. He was immediately at ease and in command on the rostrum—just as Gustav Mahler was, with even less training and preparation for the task. As Felix Mottl said: 'One stands up and can do it.'

The Duke of Sachsen-Meiningen, Georg II, made every effort to persuade Bülow to return. He failed, and began to lose interest in the orchestra now that he had no star conductor. He proposed to reduce the number of players, but offered Strauss an extension of his contract. Strauss at this juncture received the offer of the post of third conductor at Munich. Rather half-heartedly, he signed a three-year contract to run from 1st August 1886 and left Meiningen during April.

The six months at Meiningen were potent in several ways in their influence on Strauss. First, there was Bülow, whose magic was such that working with him for only a month left an indelible impression. There was a memorable evening together in his home when Bülow played Johann Strauss waltzes—'the most endearing of all God-gifted dispensers of joy', Strauss called his namesake.[1] How could he have written the *Rosen-kavalier* waltzes without the example of 'this wonderful phenomenon'? Then there was the theatre at Meiningen. Not only did the Duke make history with his court orchestra, he was equally enlightened about plays. With a small company of gifted players, he staged productions in which every rôle was carefully studied, cast and rehearsed. Close attention was paid to details of production. Strauss attended as many performances as he could: his profound sense of theatre was developed there. When he left

[1] R. Strauss: 'On Johann Strauss'.

Meiningen a member of the ducal entourage told him that they were sorry to be losing 'the best cheer leader we've had in our theatre for a long time'.

Yet the most far-reaching influence came not from Bülow but from one of the violinists in the orchestra, Alexander Ritter. He was fifty-two in 1885 and had been at school with Bülow. He was the son of Julie Ritter, a generous patron of Wagner, and became a conductor and composer of minor rank. He married Wagner's niece Franziska, came to know Wagner well and was a member of Liszt's circle at Weimar. With his enthusiasm for the music of Berlioz, Liszt and Wagner and his dislike of the music of Brahms, he was firmly entrenched in the *avant-garde* camp of *Zukunftsmusik* (the music of the future), but he struck hard times and ran a music shop. It was from this that Bülow rescued him to play at Meiningen. When Strauss arrived in Meiningen, Ritter's interest in his benefactor's protégé was aroused, especially when he discovered that Strauss's upbringing had been thoroughly conservative. He invited the young man to his home. Strauss described the effect in these words: 'His influence on me was in the nature of the storm-wind':

I scarcely knew Richard Wagner's writings at all. Ritter, with patient explanations, introduced me to them and to Schopenhauer; he made me familiar with them and proved to me that the road led from the 'musical expressionist' Beethoven . . . via Liszt who, with Wagner, had realized correctly that Beethoven had expanded the sonata form to its utmost limits . . . and that in Beethoven's epigones and especially in Brahms, sonata form had become an empty shell. . . . New ideas must search for new forms—this basic principle of Liszt's symphonic works, in which the poetic idea was really the formative element, became henceforward the guiding principle for my own symphonic work.[1]

Ritter's anti-Semitism was particularly strong, but Strauss did

[1] 'Recollections of my Youth and Years of Apprenticeship.'

not need instruction from this teacher in this field. His father was at one with Wagner on this subject alone, and Richard grew up listening to Franz inveighing against Hermann Levi's choice of tempi and shouting at Richard, when he erred similarly, 'Why this Jewish haste?' This was the conventional, thoughtless anti-Semitism typical of the German *petite bourgeoisie*. It may be compared with some Englishmen's 'hatred' of 'those damned foreigners'. Yet Englishmen who speak like that often have strong personal liking and admiration for individual foreigners, just as Strauss had strong liking and admiration for individual Jews. Some would say that the gas-chambers were the logical result of even such casual racial prejudice, but only a fanatic would press the charge against Strauss. It should be remembered, too, that many opera houses and orchestras were controlled by Jews: to label a rival 'anti-Semitic' was sometimes a device intended to harm a career or forestall an engagement.

During the months at Meiningen, Strauss had little time for composition. While he was there he played the pianoforte part in his already completed Pianoforte Quartet and dedicated it to the Duke when he heard that it had been awarded first prize in a competition organized by the Berlin Tonkünstlerverein. He composed a Scherzo for piano and orchestra for Bülow to perform, but Bülow said it was unplayable. A few weeks later Strauss himself tried out the piece, thought it was 'pure nonsense', and laid it aside. Four years later he looked it out and re-titled it *Burleske*. It contains passages which show that the mature Strauss was on the brink of emerging in 1885, acquaintance with Liszt and Wagner notwithstanding.

3   Tone-poet

Strauss said that his 'first hesitant attempt' at a new 'expressionist' style of composition was in the suite *Aus Italien*. He had long wished to visit Italy and, spurred by a suggestion from Brahms, went there in the three summer months of 1886 between the end of his Meiningen engagement and the start of his Munich contract. Financed by his father and his uncle Georg Pschorr, he visited Verona, Bologna, Rome, Naples and Florence. He saw the great sculptures and pictures—Raphael's St Cecilia moved him to tears—he saw the ancient ruins on the Campagna, he heard Verdi's *Aida* (*'Indianermusik'*) and *Requiem* ('pretty and original') and Rossini's *Il barbiere di Siviglia*. (He wrote to his father: 'I will never be converted to Italian music.') The shopkeepers overcharged him, he said; but, like so many composers before (and after) him, he fell under Italy's spell and the impressions he formed he put down in sketches for a 'symphonic fantasy' which he completed and orchestrated during the autumn and winter of 1886. On his way home to Munich he stayed in Bayreuth and attended performances of *Tristan und Isolde* and *Parsifal*.

The next three years were to be crucial in Strauss's life. Within their span he emerged as the composer we know, his fame spread, his name was surrounded by controversy, and he learned to reconcile the conflicting demands of a career as conductor and composer. His experiences as third conductor of the Munich Opera were far from pleasing, however. Wagner's King Ludwig of Bavaria died in June 1886 and with his removal the

13

opera house lost much of its prestige. Hermann Levi was a sick man much of the time and the second conductor, Franz Fischer, was described by Strauss as 'a real criminal on the rostrum'.[1] In addition the Intendant since 1867, Karl von Perfall, now sixty-two years of age, was hostile to Strauss's music. Understandably, the third conductor was given only what were considered to be the least interesting operas. Under the Munich régime of 1886 these included not only works by Boieldieu, Marschner and Cherubini, but Verdi's *Un ballo in maschera*, Bizet's *Carmen* and Mozart's *Così fan tutte*. Conducting Verdi compelled Strauss to revise his opinion of Italian music; the Mozart became one of his greatest interpretations and the credit for its revival in modern times is largely his. He understood its unique place among Mozart's dramatic works through its psychological exploitation of a hypothetically ridiculous situation.

The first opera Strauss conducted was Boieldieu's *Jean de Paris*, which he liked sufficiently to conduct it in Vienna nearly forty years later. In the three years he conducted only forty-three performances. He might, perhaps, have had more if he had not been absent frequently as guest conductor of his compositions. The impetus for these invitations stemmed from the excitement aroused by the first performance of *Aus Italien* in Munich on 2nd March 1887, conducted by Strauss. It is difficult today to understand, or to have much sympathy with, the controversy that raged in the last quarter of the nineteenth century over the relative merits of 'absolute' classical music (Brahms) and *avant-garde* programmatic music with its literary, poetic and pictorial associations (Liszt and Wagner). Munich on the whole was reactionary and thought that young Strauss, to judge from his early works, was a Brahmsian. *Aus Italien* seemed to prove otherwise, and there was uproar. Franz Strauss, distressed, went to the artists' room where he found his son sitting on a table

[1] R. Strauss: 'Reminiscences of my Father'.

swinging his legs gleefully. Richard then wrote to a girl friend, Lotti Speyer: 'Some people applauded lustily, others hissed loudly, but finally the applause won the day . . . I was immensely proud. This is the first work of mine to have met with opposition from the mob, so it must be of some importance.' He asked his hero, Bülow, to accept the dedication of 'this symphonic fantasy embellished by local opposition'. Bülow agreed. It is likely that even then he perceived what, with hindsight, we now know: that Strauss was not the prologue to a new era but the epilogue of an old. The opposition to Strauss would appeal to Bülow, who knew from experience that the 'revolutionary' young man is attacked by the entrenched vested interests not because they genuinely believe he is a bad artist but because they are frightened by him and by the threat he represents to the established order. But Bülow's percipience was not attributable to any special sympathy on his part for the *avant-garde*. He regarded Mahler's music, for example, with horror, and he was lukewarm at first about Strauss's *Macbeth* and *Don Juan*; but *Aus Italien* is a transitional work, 'the connecting link between the old and the new methods', as Strauss said. Conductors were eager to perform it; its first and third movements were performed in London on 28th November 1889 under Henschel, the first orchestral music by Strauss to be played in England.

His conducting engagements during 1887 took him to Frankfurt, Hamburg and Cologne. From Leipzig, where he conducted his F minor symphony in October, he wrote to Bülow: 'I made a new and very attractive acquaintance in Herr Mahler [aged twenty-seven at this time], who seemed to me a highly intelligent musician and conductor—one of the few modern conductors who know about tempo rubato.' So began his generally friendly relationship with his great contemporary, whose music he consistently championed.

Even more significant was the beginning of the most important relationship of his life. He took a holiday in late August of 1887 at the village of Feldafing, where his Pschorr relatives had a villa. Living near by were General de Ahna and his two daughters. Ahna was a music-lover and an amateur singer good enough to give recitals locally at which he sang Wagner extracts. His elder daughter, Pauline, who was twenty-five, two years older than Strauss, had studied singing as a soprano at Munich University but had not made any progress professionally. This family were thrilled to meet the much-talked-about young conductor-composer; he was enchanted by Pauline and agreed to give her lessons. This was not merely a ruse to see her more often: he realized the potentialities of her voice and told her she had the talent to become a star—and he was to be proved right. He fell in love with her, with startlingly beneficial effect upon his music. Strauss, an ardent spirit, was by no means unsusceptible to women and his boyish love affairs caused his parents some concern. They were most worried by his relationship—before he went to Meiningen—with Dora Wihan, wife of the Munich court orchestra's principal cellist.[1] Dora was four years older than Strauss and very beautiful. It is likely that they were in love.

During 1887 he composed several songs, including the justly famous *Ständchen*, and a Violin Sonata. But the work which principally occupied him was a symphonic poem, *Macbeth*. He was convinced, as we have seen, that his future lay in pro-gramme music, notwithstanding the disapproval which this genre had incurred from purist and academic musical opinion since the days of Vivaldi's *The Four Seasons*. In the 1880s the symphonic poem was at its peak. The term itself was Liszt's invention for the twelve he wrote, but Mendelssohn's and Berlioz's large-scale overtures had been symphonic poems. Liszt's example was followed by Smetana, Saint-Saëns, Tchaikovsky, Dvořák, Franck and many others. Strauss took the form at the flood, as it were, devised his own name for it—tone-poem

---

[1] Hanuš Wihan, to whom Dvořák's Cello Concerto and Strauss's Cello Sonata are dedicated. He and Dora were eventually divorced.

—and imparted to it new life and urgency. His approach to programme music can be summed up in words he wrote in 1896: 'I am a musician first and last, for whom all "programmes" are merely the stimulus to the creation of new forms, and nothing more.'

Strauss completed *Macbeth* in 1888 and sent the score to Bülow, describing it as the 'most independent and purposeful work' he had so far composed. He drew attention to its 'violent and gruesome content'. Bülow was not impressed. To the publisher Spitzweg he called it 'Macbethian soup from the witches' kitchen', but to the composer he helpfully suggested revisions. Meanwhile, inspired by his love for Pauline, Strauss had begun another tone-poem dealing with the perennially fascinating figure of Don Juan. He wrote to Bülow in 1888: '*Macbeth* rests peacefully in its grave in my desk where, no doubt, *Don Juan* will shortly keep it company.' He told Ritter that he was dissatisfied with the scoring: 'There are too many inner parts ... the principal themes do not stand out as clearly as I intended.'

During the early part of the summer of 1888 he again went to Italy. In Bologna he heard *Tristan und Isolde* and for the first time became fully aware that 'it is a most beautiful *bel canto* opera'. He longed to conduct it, and this longing no doubt deepened the depression he was experiencing in his Munich Opera post where Perfall frustrated and Levi antagonized him. It was obvious that an explosion would occur and it is remarkable that it did not come earlier than the winter of 1888–9, when Perfall allocated him the revival of Wagner's *Die Feen*. Just before the final dress rehearsal Perfall ruled that Fischer would now take over because such an important revival could not be entrusted to the third conductor. On Bülow's recommmendation Strauss saw Hans von Bronsart, Intendant of Weimar Opera, and the conductor there, Eduard Lassen, men of integrity and musical idealism. They appointed Strauss as assistant conductor from 1st October 1889. In addition, Bülow obtained him a post during the summer of 1889 as a musical assistant at Bayreuth. There he heard performances conducted by Mottl and Richter and, most important of all, was shown favour by Cosima Wagner and invited to Wahnfried. Pauline de Ahna was with him, and Cosima gave advice to Strauss and his pupil on the interpretation of *Lohengrin* and *Tannhäuser*. He was overjoyed to have put the Munich experience behind him.

A first-hand account of Richard's outlook at this time is in a letter he wrote to Dora Wihan on 9th April 1889. It is also a useful guide to the dating of progress on certain works:

Just think! I have joined the ranks of the Lisztians! In short, it is hard to imagine a more progressive viewpoint than the one I now hold. I feel wonderful; a new clarity has overcome me .... I am employed in Bayreuth as 'assistant', piano rehearsals, etc. Recently I made the acquaintance of Frau Wagner, who is quite interested in me.... Where am I going? ... to Weimar.... What a splendid change from Munich! To the city of the future, Weimar, to the post where Liszt worked so long! I have great hopes.... Lassen is old and tired [he was fifty-nine] and looks forward to relief from his labours. ... As to the libretto of my opera, I have the first act and part of the second act, to the end of the big love scene, tentatively ready. (That means until I revise it again.) Ritter likes it very much. In addition I have sketched out a new tone-poem, to be called (probably) *Tod und Verklärung*.[1]

Ritter's hold, it can be seen, was still strong; in 1887 he gave Strauss a newspaper article about Austrian medieval secret societies. Strauss was attracted to the subject and promptly invented the name of his hero, Guntram. So during these Munich years he had on the stocks, simultaneously, three tone-poems and an opera libretto. This was the energetic young man who set out hopefully for Weimar. A photograph taken at this time shows him smartly dressed, sitting with arms folded. His hair is bushy and naturally curly. The first traces of a moustache cover his long

[1] Text published in *Richard Strauss Jahrbuch 1959–60*.

top lip. The mouth is firm, the chin slightly weak. One has to look long and hard to see that this face will become that of the noble old man of sixty years later. But in the eyes is a look of arrogant self-confidence, the look of the man who had written, in *Don Juan*, a work of genius.

4   Weimar and Munich

When he arrived in Weimar, Strauss played *Don Juan* on the pianoforte to Bronsart and Lassen. They were so impressed that they urged him to include it in the season of concerts which was about to begin. His letters to his father describing the rehearsals capture the excitement and apprehension with which the orchestra tackled this difficult and ardent work, the fruit of his passion for Pauline (and for Dora, too, perhaps). In its demands on their technique, it was revolutionary. Strauss himself knew that the lessons he had learned at the conductor's desk were standing him in good stead. He wrote to old Franz:

> The sound was wonderful, immensely glowing and exuberant. It will make a tremendous stir here. . . . The orchestra huffed and puffed but did its job famously. One of the horn players sat there out of breath, sweat pouring from his brow, asking 'Good God, in what way have we sinned that you should have sent us this scourge!' We laughed till we cried! Certainly the horns blew without fear of death. . . . I was really sorry for the wretched brass. They were quite blue in the face, the whole affair was so strenuous.

The first performance on 11th November 1889 was a triumph. Strauss overnight became nationally recognized as the most important German composer since Wagner. 'The piece sounded magical, dear Papa,' he wrote. Bülow was present; it is ironical that this great work should have become the cause of a rift between him and Strauss. Or perhaps the real cause was Cosima

Wagner, whose influence on Strauss was intensifying. Bülow conducted the first Berlin Philharmonic performance of *Don Juan* on 30th January 1890 with immense success, but Strauss was dissatisfied with his mentor's interpretation. He wrote to his father that Bülow was mixing now with an 'ugly Jewish circle'. He had presented to Berlin 'merely an interesting piece of music, not my *Don Juan*. He no longer understands poetic music, he has lost the touch'.

Strauss conducted three other first performances of his works in 1890, two of them in one concert at Eisenach on 21st June. He had recently become friendly with the pianist-composer Eugen d'Albert, to whom he had shown the *Scherzo* for pianoforte and orchestra written for Bülow in 1886. D'Albert persuaded him to release the piece and, under the new title of *Burleske*, played it at Eisenach. Strauss was still doubtful about its merit and rejected a substantial sum offered by a publisher. After the *Burleske* he conducted *Tod und Verklärung* (*Death and Transfiguration*). Then, at Weimar on 13th October, he conducted his revised *Macbeth*. He had provided a new ending, as Bülow had wished, and had considerably revised the scoring. But after the first performance, he revised it yet again. There was no further performance for fifteen months when, on 29th February 1892, Strauss conducted the definitive version in Berlin at Bülow's invitation, an occasion which brought them closer again. The rehearsal was also the occasion for one of Bülow's most celebrated witticisms, attributed to various conductors but here authenticated by Strauss:

I had not looked at the piece for a long time and (always a little careless in that respect, since I used to rely on my reasonable skill in reading scores) had not looked at the score even before the rehearsal, so that the members of the Philharmonic Orchestra witnessed the spectacle of a composer glued to the notes of his score. This annoyed the conscientious Bülow, and afterwards he reproached me bitterly: 'You should have the score in your head and not your head in the score' (anticipating my rejoinder) 'even if you have composed the thing yourself.' [1]

Macbeth was enthusiastically received. Bülow told Strauss: 'It's quite a good piece after all.' To Spitzweg he used the phrase 'a work of genius'. Strauss, it seemed, could not put a foot wrong. Yet there were voices of dissent from the chorus of adulation, loudest among them that of the critic Hanslick, not surprisingly. He attended the first Vienna performance of *Don Juan*, conducted by Richter on 10th January 1892, and his notice included these phrases: 'Colour is everything, musical thought nothing. . . . This is no "tone painting" but rather a tumult of brilliant daubs.' A year later, *Tod und Verklärung* provoked him to call Strauss 'a brilliant virtuoso of the orchestra, lacking only musical ideas'.

But what of Strauss's conducting at Weimar? The company contained no 'star' names and the orchestra was small, but one of the young singers, who was to become a very great star—Marie Gutheil-Schoder—said in her reminiscences that Strauss made Weimar 'the centre of the musical life of Germany'. He conducted operas by Bellini, Lortzing, Marschner, Weber, Nicolai, Mozart (*Die Zauberflöte*) and Wagner (*Lohengrin, Tannhäuser, Der fliegende Holländer*). Pauline joined the company and, under his tutelage, was good enough to sing the rôles of Pamina (*Zauberflöte*), Elsa (*Lohengrin*) and Elisabeth (*Tannhäuser*). Another of his singing pupils in the company was the *Heldentenor* Heinrich Zeller. This suggests that Strauss's extraordinary understanding of the voice, particularly the female voice, was instinctive; no doubt he was helped and advised by Pauline, but there is also no doubt that he 'made' her career.

In May 1891 Strauss had pneumonia. For a time he was dangerously ill. Convalescing at the Pschorr villa in Feldafing he wrote to the critic Arthur Seidl: 'Dying may not be so bad,

[1] R. Strauss: 'Reminiscences of Hans von Bülow'.

but I should first like to conduct *Tristan*.' His passion for this opera was unabated to his last day. (In 1933 he wrote to Fritz Busch: 'Even if only *one* person pays for a seat at *Tristan* it must be performed for him, because he must be the last surviving German.') To his joy, he was allocated *Tristan* for the 1891–2 season in Weimar and spent Christmas with Cosima discussing its every aspect. The first performance, uncut, was on 17th January 1892; he wrote to Cosima afterwards describing it as the most wonderful day of his life. Pauline sang Isolde—'too early, of course', Strauss wrote,[1] 'but somehow because of her youth and great acting a particularly charming performance'.

His appetite for work was as great as ever. In one week of March 1892 his engagements were: Tuesday night, *Tristan*; 11.30 p.m. to Leipzig. Wednesday, 10 to 2.30, first rehearsal for a Liszt concert. Evening back to Weimar. Thursday, conducted *Lohengrin* in Eisenach. Return to Leipzig 1 a.m. Friday, rehearsals 10 to 1 and 3 to 6. Saturday, rehearsal and concert. Not surprisingly, the list of his own compositions shrinks during these Weimar years: it was not only Mahler who was a 'summer-composer'. Strauss's chief occupation was conducting, and in his youth he did not set aside several months of the summer, as Mahler did, exclusively for creative work. Later he followed Mahler's routine. He told several correspondents that he could only work in the summer, because the winter 'froze his brain'. He usually revised and orchestrated during winter. Between 1889 and 1893 his only compositions, once *Macbeth* and *Tod und Verklärung* were completed, were a march for the twenty-fifth anniversary of his father's 'Wilde Gung'l' orchestra, some occasional music for the golden wedding of the Grand Duke and Duchess of Weimar performed on 8th October 1892, and two songs for Heinrich Zeller. 'The theatre and cards, as well as my fiancée, claimed almost all my attention,' Strauss wrote, but something

[1] R. Strauss: 'Recollections of my Youth and Years of Apprenticeship'.

must be debited to his ill-health. He had also devoted much time to revising the libretto of his opera, *Guntram*, and began to sketch the music in the spring of 1892. But in June he had a severe attack of pleurisy and bronchitis and his life was again in danger. His Uncle Georg insisted that he should spend the winter in the sun and gave him 5,000 marks to enable him to visit Egypt.

He sailed in November 1892, making Greece his first call. 'From the moment when, coming from Brindisi, I saw from the deck of the Italian steamer the island of Corfu and the blue mountains of Albania, I have always been a German Greek.' [1] Falling in love with Greece and its ancient civilization stimulated his creative impulses and he worked steadily at his opera, revising the libretto of the third act before leaving Athens. During his convalescence and on the voyage he had read Nietzsche's works and had been particularly attracted by 'his polemic against Christianity'. Strauss's objection was to any religion which relieved its followers of responsibility for their actions by means of confession. This was relevant to Guntram's situation in Act III. The opera's 'spiritual godfather', Ritter, who had followed every move Strauss made while writing the libretto, was a Roman Catholic and saw the work as a study in religious morals and ethics. Strauss re-wrote his last act so that Guntram renounced society (symbolizing a religious order) and went his own way. Ritter was horrified, and pleaded with Strauss to throw the new third act into the fire because it was 'an immoral mockery of every ethical creed. . . . Go and read with inner enlightenment a chapter of the gospels'. Strauss was unmoved. He tried to reason with Ritter, but Ritter never forgave him and their relationship became much cooler. Yet all that Strauss had done, in essence, was to give Guntram a creed summed up in his line: 'My God speaks to me through myself.'

Working six hours a day on the short score, Strauss completed

[1] R. Strauss: 'Letter on the *Humanistische Gymnasium*' (1945).

Guntram in Cairo on Christmas Eve, writing on the manuscript 'Deo gratia! Und dem heiligen Wagner'. He then began the orchestration while staying in Luxor. This task was completed at Marquartstein in September.

At the time of his illness in the summer of 1892 Strauss was already disenchanted with his work at Weimar. In later life he wrote: 'People were very nice to me, but I recklessly squandered some of the goodwill they bore me by my youthful energy and love of exaggeration.[1] Writing to Bülow on 30th June 1892 he said that Bronsart, the Intendant, was blocking his advancement and did not agree with the way he conducted Beethoven. He also thought that Strauss's orchestral concerts included too much Liszt, Berlioz, Wagner and Strauss—and they were eventually to include Mahler's First Symphony, which the composer conducted, at Strauss's invitation, in June 1894. 'I am going to move on,' Strauss told Bülow. While he was in Egypt he received a long letter from his father containing the extraordinary news that Hermann Levi, still the chief conductor at Munich, had sought a meeting with Franz Strauss to inquire if Richard would be friendly enough to him to accept the post of associate conductor. Richard naturally hesitated: he had been glad enough to escape from Munich, why return? He applied instead to Mottl at Carlsruhe, but no position was available. While he still hesitated, Cosima advised him to accept Levi's offer. There were several good reasons to do so: he was tired of an orchestra at Weimar which had a string section of twenty-one players; Perfall was nearly seventy and Levi, with his increasingly uncertain health, might retire at any time; his proposed salary at Munich was nearly double what Weimar paid him; he would conduct major works; and, last but certainly not least, there was a chance that *Guntram* would be performed there. He agreed to accept, but

[1] R. Strauss: 'Recollections of my Youth and Years of Apprenticeship'.

negotiations were so protracted that he stayed for Weimar's 1893–4 season, which was to prove memorable for several reasons.

On 23rd December 1893 he conducted the first performance of Humperdinck's *Hänsel und Gretel*. In the new year he decided to stage *Guntram*, come what may. He had already had warning of the difficulties he could expect: Mottl, whom Strauss admired, had been anxious to give the first performance and he put the opera into rehearsal at Carlsruhe, but abandoned it when the tenor said the rôle of Guntram was impossible. Mahler, recently installed at the Hamburg Opera, also had to abandon the project. Strauss hoped for an easier time, for in the leading rôles of Guntram and Freihild he cast two of his pupils, Zeller and Pauline. Here is his own account written in 1942: [1]

Zeller suffered torments with the insanely taxing vocal part . . . became hoarser with each rehearsal and only finished the first performance with difficulty. . . . In the course of one of the last rehearsals, when I had to interrupt Zeller time and time again, we at last came to Pauline's scene in Act III, which she obviously knew. In spite of this she did not feel sure of herself and apparently envied Zeller because he had been given so many chances of 'repeating'. Suddenly she stopped singing and asked me, 'Why don't you interrupt me?' I replied, 'Because you know your part.' With the words 'I want to be interrupted' she threw the piano score . . . at my head but, to the delight of the orchestra, it landed on the desk of the second violinist, Gutheil.

Pauline ran to her dressing-room, followed by an angry Strauss. Raised voices were heard, then silence. Eventually the orchestra's leader knocked on the door and told Strauss, who opened it, that the players were shocked by Pauline's behaviour and refused to play in any opera in which she sang. To which Strauss replied: 'That pains me very much, for I have just

[1] R. Strauss: 'Reminiscences of the First Performances of my Operas'.

become engaged to Fräulein de Ahna.' [1] Two days after the first performance of *Guntram*, on 10th May 1894, the betrothal was officially announced.

The opera was mildly successful, though how its instrumentation for ninety-two players sounded on the Weimar orchestra of barely half that number can scarcely be imagined. The score was published early in 1895 and Strauss sent a copy to Verdi, as a token of his admiration for *Falstaff* (1893). He kept Verdi's courteous acknowledgment—'I perceive that your *Guntram* is a work fashioned by a knowing hand'—all his life. One to whom he could not send a score was Bülow, who had died in February 1894. Strauss last saw him the previous month. He took over Bülow's Berlin Philharmonic concerts but was not yet ready for such a post: 'Precocious though I was, I was slow in becoming a conductor and was unable to hold my own after this great man. In 1895 H. Wolff put the magnificent Nikisch in charge of the concerts and I had to be content with my 7,000 marks in Munich.' [2]

Nevertheless the outstanding event of 1894 for Strauss was his marriage to Pauline in Weimar on 10th September. Richard was phlegmatic and 'unflappable', Pauline temperamental, fiery, tactless, rude and beguiling. Lotte Lehmann described them in their home, after twenty-five years of marriage, in these significant words: [3]

I often caught a glance or a smile passing between her and her husband, touching in its love and happiness, and I began to sense something of the profound affection between those two human beings, a tie so elemental in strength that none of Pauline's shrewish trucu-

---

[1] Lotte Lehmann, in *My Many Lives*, ascribes this incident to a *Tannhäuser* rehearsal, but in view of the date of the official engagement it was obviously during *Guntram*.

[2] R. Strauss: 'Recollections of my Youth and Years of Apprenticeship'.

[3] L. Lehmann: *Singing with Richard Strauss* (London 1964).

lence could ever trouble it seriously. In fact, I rather suspect that they were always putting on a kind of act for their own benefit as well as for that of outsiders.

On their wedding day Strauss gave four songs, his Op. 27, to her, dedicated 'to my beloved Pauline'. They were *Ruhe, meine Seele, Cäcilie, Heimliche Aufforderung* and *Morgen*, four of his greatest *Lieder*. As a gift from composer to wife, they merit comparison with Wagner's *Siegfried Idyll*.

In the month before his marriage Strauss conducted for the first time at Bayreuth, with Pauline singing Elisabeth in *Tannhäuser*. He took up his post at Munich on 1st October 1894. It was to prove no happier an experience than his first period there, although there were better artistic compensations. Perfall remained hostile, but Strauss liked his assistant, Ernst von Possart, brilliant as a producer and himself a popular actor. Levi was frequently absent through illness, so Strauss at last had the satisfaction of conducting *Tristan* and *Die Meistersinger* in the city where they had first been produced. With Possart as producer, he conducted revivals of three Mozart operas—*Die Entführung aus dem Serail, Così fan tutte* and *Don Giovanni*—at a Mozart festival at the Residenztheater. 'Shining memories in my life,' he called these occasions, writing in 1928.[1]

Less happy was his second attempt to establish *Guntram*, which had one unfortunate performance at Munich on 16th November 1895. Pauline again sang Freihild, but two of the other leading singers, Milka Ternina and the tenor Heinrich Vogl, had refused to take part, the orchestra led by his cousin and former teacher Benno Walter had sent a deputation to the Intendant asking him to spare them 'this scourge of God', and the tenor Mikorey said after the performance that he would only sing another if his pension were to be increased. There was no second performance. Strauss was deeply hurt, and bitterly resented those

---

[1] R. Strauss: 'On the Munich Opera' (1928).

who had harmed the opera. To Seidl he wrote: 'It is incredible what enemies *Guntram* has made for me. I shall shortly be tried as a dangerous criminal.' He dug a grave in his garden and erected a stone inscribed: 'Here rests the honourable and virtuous young man Guntram . . . who was horribly slain by the symphony orchestra of his own father.'

Yet this was to be a rich period for Strauss the composer. On his way home from Egypt in 1894 he had begun to think of the opera he would write after *Guntram*. He had settled on the subject of the medieval folk hero, the rascally Till Eulenspiegel. He began to write a libretto, but abandoned it, realizing that he had no talent for poetry and being by this time thoroughly discouraged about opera. In the winter of 1894–5 he wrote a rondo for orchestra on the subject, completing it on 6th May 1895. He entrusted the first performance of *Till Eulenspiegels lustige Streiche* to one of his earliest champions, Franz Wüllner, at a Gürzenich concert in Cologne on 5th November 1895. It was an immediate success, its brilliance and humour endearing it to audiences then and ever since. Within four months it had had its first Viennese, American and English performances. Bruckner loved it; Hanslick called it a box of tricks.

More *Lieder* poured from Strauss at this time, and he began work on another tone-poem. This bore the name of Friedrich Nietzsche's famous poem *Also sprach Zarathustra* and embodied Strauss's homage to the genius of its author. It was completed on 24th August 1896 and Strauss conducted the first performance in Frankfurt-am-Main on 27th November. The first Berlin performance, under Nikisch, followed three days later. This work, too, was well received, but with rather more solemnity. He was then deep into composition of another large-scale orchestral work, his third within four years. This, completed on 29th December 1897, was *Don Quixote*, 'fantastic variations on a theme of knightly character'. He again gave the first performance to Wüllner at Cologne, on 8th March 1898.

Within this period, Perfall had handed over to Possart at the Munich Opera and, in 1896, Levi retired and Strauss became chief conductor. Yet by then, one suspects, the salt of Munich had lost its savour. The success of his works, especially *Don Juan* and *Till*, meant that he was much in demand as a guest conductor: he visited Russia, he conducted at the Lower Rhine Festival in Düsseldorf; in 1897 he toured in Germany as pianist with Possart, for whom he had written the melodrama *Enoch Arden*, and he undertook conducting engagements in Holland and Spain. He visited London for the first time, conducting the first English performance of *Tod und Verklärung* at Queen's Hall on 7th December, and he conducted in Paris in February and November.

It was while he was in Stuttgart performing *Enoch Arden* that his son was born on 12th April 1897. Pauline was thirty-five and had had a difficult pregnancy and delivery. Both parents were thrilled about their child, who was named Franz Alexander (the second name after Ritter, who had died on 12th April 1896) but usually known as Bubi. On his son's birthday Strauss dedicated six new songs, including *Meinem Kinde*, 'to my beloved wife'.

Early in 1898 Strauss received two offers of new posts. Felix Weingartner had vacated the position of chief conductor of the Royal Court Opera in Berlin. Hochberg, the Intendant, and Pierson, his lieutenant, offered the post to Strauss at a high salary, on a ten-year contract, summer and winter holidays, a life pension and a widow's pension—a pointer to the high regard in which he was held. A few weeks later the New York Philharmonic offered him their conductorship at double the Berlin salary but on a short-term contract. Strauss had little hesitation in accepting Berlin. 'At last,' he wrote to his parents, 'I can throw down the gauntlet to that gang in Munich who have treated me so wretchedly.'

So the future looked rosy for the Strauss family when they went to their Marquartstein villa for the summer. Richard had the sketches of a new orchestral work with him, his biggest to date. 'Beethoven's *Eroica* is so little beloved of our conductors, and is on this account now only rarely performed,' he wrote ironically, 'that to fulfil a pressing need I am composing a largeish tone-poem entitled *Heldenleben* [Hero's Life], admittedly without a funeral march, yet in E flat, with lots of horns, which are always a yardstick of heroism.'

5　A hero's life

'I had no reason ever to regret my association with Berlin; on the whole, my stay there was pure joy, and I found much appreciation and hospitality.' Thus Strauss wrote [1] in old age. Berlin between 1900 and 1914 was a contrast with the Vienna of the same period, a contrast that is curiously epitomized in the music of Strauss, Berlin Opera's conductor from 1898 to 1908, and of Mahler, Vienna Opera's conductor from 1897 to 1907. Much that was exciting, new and glorious in the arts occurred in Vienna at this period, yet the atmosphere of Austrian twilight, as Emperor Franz Joseph grew older, was everywhere, and not only twilight but corruption and decay. In Berlin, where Bismarck died in 1898, Kaiser Wilhelm ruled over a strong, buoyant, militaristic and proud nation. It was a rich city, mixing the grandiose and the sentimental in its architecture, literature and music. The prosperous middle class prospered still more, largely oblivious of the seamy streak inseparable from the social conditions of a country 'on the make'.

Critics of Strauss maintain that he was the very man for this atmosphere. But he was much too complex both as man and artist to be conveniently fitted into any one category. He had little interest in, or knowledge of, politics and was—as will be seen—pitifully naïve when they encroached upon him. First and last he was a court musician and he understood musical politics and mastered them. One has only to read Weingartner's dis-

[1] R. Strauss: 'Recollections of my Youth and Years of Apprenticeship'.

agreeable autobiography [1] to gain a strong impression of the intrigues and skulduggery rampant in European musical life and of the power exercised by the opera intendants and their henchmen. If only half of what he recounts was true, it still leaves a scarifying picture (nor, of course, is it a thing of the past). In Strauss we see constantly at work the conflicts and tensions which stemmed from his personality: the instinctive musician, overwhelmingly brilliant and intelligent—'in music one can say everything', he said, 'people won't understand you'—and the lower-middle-class man, non-intellectual and down to earth. Moreover, there was the extraordinary background of his marriage, a mystifyingly secure union with a woman who, though herself a fine singer, considered that she had demeaned herself by marrying a musician and who, on many public occasions, made derogatory remarks about her husband's music. Yet for whatever reasons, their ties were strong.

Penetrating analysis and description of Strauss at this point in his career may be found in the writings of the French author Romain Rolland, who had first met him casually in 1891 when they were fellow lunch guests of Cosima at Bayreuth, but came to know him well in Berlin and Paris from 1898. He described him in his fourth-floor flat at No. 30, Knesebeckstrasse, Charlottenburg:

Very young face; dark hair receding, very little hair on the forehead, which is rounded, full and rather handsome; very pale eyes; the moustache so fair as to be almost white. . . . Tall, but holds himself with extreme lassitude. Childish and involuntary shyness in his smile and gestures; but one feels underneath a pride which is cold, self-willed, indifferent or contemptuous of the majority of things and people.[2]

[1] F. Weingartner: *Buffets and Rewards* (Eng. trans. by Marguerite Wolff, London, 1937).
[2] Quoted from *Richard Strauss and Romain Rolland: Correspondence, diary and essays* (ed. Rollo Myers, London, 1968).

To Rolland, Strauss described Berlin's opera audience as 'nothing but bankers and shopkeepers'. But Rolland wrote in his diary, 'when the word "people" is mentioned, this disciple of Nietzsche understands—rabble. . . . The tradition and the conventionalism of the Schauspielhaus . . . disgust him'. Rolland quickly noticed the two faces of Strauss. He saw him as 'the typical artist of the new German empire, the powerful reflection of that heroic pride, which is on the verge of becoming delirious, of that contemptuous Nietzscheism, of that egotistical and practical idealism, which makes a cult of power and disdains weakness'. But: 'He has certain dispositions which I had not seen clearly before, and which strictly speaking belong more to the people of Munich, the South Germans: an elemental vein of the clownish humour, paradoxical and satirical, of a spoilt child, or of Till Eulenspiegel.'

Yet this 'typical artist of the new German empire' made it plain to Rolland that he was uneasy with the strictness and moral hypocrisy of Berlin, that it had been predicted that because of his outspokenness he would lose his head, and that he had something less than an adulatory opinion of the Kaiser, who had described Strauss as 'a serpent I've harboured in my bosom'. Strauss's account of his first interview with the Kaiser, recorded in Rolland's diary for 1st March 1900,[1] is often quoted, and deservedly:

The Emperor . . . frowns as he looks at him: 'You're yet another of these modern musicians?' He [Strauss] bows. 'I have heard Schillings's *Ingwelde*; it's execrable, there's no melody.' 'Forgive me, Your Majesty, there is melody but it is hidden beneath the polyphony.' He looks at him with a stern eye: 'You are one of the worst.' Another bow. 'The whole of modern music is worth nothing, there's no melody.' Same game. 'I like *Freischütz* better.' 'Your Majesty, I too like *Freischütz* better'.

[1] Norman Del Mar ascribes this conversation to November 1904, but it must have been in 1898 or 1899.

34

Rolland wrote: 'He seems to live in a rather isolated way in Berlin. . . . He does not like society, nor does his wife. They always vie with one another in not accepting invitations. . . . In Berlin he is the enemy of the conservatives' camp, of which the Mendelssohns are the patrons and Joachim the god.' What particularly worried Strauss in Berlin was the increasing puritanical attitude to art and its reflection in extended powers of censorship. Although he conducted several new operas, he felt frustrated because he had no direction of artistic policy: he was chief conductor, but the Intendant was the director. His rose-coloured recollection of 'pure joy' must be interpreted within this context.

Another criticism of Strauss—especially by English puritans —is that he knew the value of money and especially his own value in money. He was, after all, the scion of a banking family, and he saw no virtue in starving in garrets. His money-consciousness was not selfish. In 1898 he sought the aid of two friends, Friedrich Rösch, a lawyer, and the much older H. F. A. Zincke, physicist-turned-composer (under the name Hans Sommer) in founding a society with the aims of improving German copyright law, obtaining higher royalties, determining a minimum fee, and establishing an agency for the collection of royalties and fees. The society was named Genossenschaft deutscher Tonsetzer (Fellowship of German Composers). It took seven years, against opposition from publishers, politicians and composers, before the struggle was won and a performing-right society was established. In all this, Strauss was the principal champion of his colleagues' dues.

His contract at the Berlin Opera began on 1st November 1898 and he chose *Tristan* for his first appearance. In his first eight months there he conducted twenty-five different operas in a total of seventy-one performances (including a *Ring* cycle) and in his second season he was at the desk for ninety performances of thirty works. His chief assistant was Karl Mück. His international fame (and notoriety) continued to spread. Just before he began his work in Berlin he went again to 'staid and solid Amsterdam' for 'the greatest triumph of my career' (as he wrote to his father). In 1895 the twenty-four year old Willem Mengelberg had become conductor of the Concertgebouw Orchestra and rapidly made it a superb instrument. In October 1898, Strauss conducted it in *Also sprach Zarathustra*, 'the most beautiful performance . . . I have ever experienced; it had been rehearsed in sectional rehearsals for three weeks'. In gratitude, Strauss dedicated *Ein Heldenleben* to Mengelberg and the Concertgebouw Orchestra, but the dedicatees did not give the first performance, which Strauss conducted at Frankfurt on 3rd March 1899.

The new tone-poem had a mixed reception. Because it was easily identifiable as musical autobiography and there was a long section of quotations from some of Strauss's other works, the work was labelled by some commentators as 'megalomaniac'. (Why literary autobiography and pictorial self-portraiture should be considered respectable but musical autobiography be 'tasteless' is an aesthetic mystery that defies rational solution.) Also, there was the section about the 'adversaries', in other words the critics, who are depicted as spiteful, whining and pompous. Franz Strauss thought that it was 'beneath one's dignity to notice' the adversaries his son depicted, and many people still agree with him. It has also been pointed out that, apart from *Guntram*, Strauss's career had been unhindered by failures attributable to the critics. But his successes had been with the public and other conductors rather than with the critics. Hostility to the new was general, and was often venomously expressed. In writing the adversaries section, Strauss was probably thinking not only of himself but of Wagner, Liszt and Berlioz and even of some of his contemporaries, such as Mahler. The adversaries also include the philistine elements in German life which he had detested in Munich and was to find also in Berlin.

If Strauss was less than magnanimous in his attitude to

criticism, he did not lack the more important virtue of helpfulness to colleagues. In the opera house he was always willing to conduct a new contemporary work provided he could persuade the Intendant to risk it. At his concerts he several times conducted works by Mahler (though not the first performances with which he has often been credited, and credited himself); he recommended Reger to his own publisher; he interested himself in the French composers Dukas and Chabrier; he helped Schoenberg; and England must never forget that on 20th May 1902, the day after a Düsseldorf performance of *The Dream of Gerontius*, Strauss proposed a toast to 'the first English progressivist, Meister Edward Elgar', and thereafter remained a friend and admirer of Elgar.[1] From October 1901 until the summer of 1903 he was conductor of the Berlin Tonkünstler Orchestra 'in concerts of exclusively new works', thereby often giving himself in the winter a working day of six hours' orchestral rehearsals for works like *Don Juan* and Bruckner's Third Symphony, followed by *Tristan* at the opera in the evening.

Strauss wrote the last notes of *Ein Heldenleben* on 27th December 1898. It was to be his last orchestral work for over three years. Since *Guntram* he had, on his own admission, 'lost the courage to write for the stage'. Maybe. The fact remains that he was continually considering libretti. He progressed some distance with an elaborate three-act ballet scenario called *Die Insel Kythere*, based on Watteau's painting *Embarquement pour Cythère*. This occupied him for much of 1900, a year in which his published output was confined to a fine crop of songs. It was laid aside, but the music survives and is found to contain themes which he used in later works.

In 1898 he met Ernst von Wolzogen, nine years his senior, a writer who founded the *Überbrettl* movement, a rather superior

---

[1] Elgar and Strauss first met in August 1897 while Elgar was on holiday at Garmisch. Strauss conducted *Cockaigne* in Berlin early in 1902 and Elgar sent him some notes about tempi.

kind of barbed cabaret-song satire. Still seething at the way he had been treated in Munich, Strauss told Wolzogen that he wanted to 'wreak some vengeance' by composing an opera in which Munich's philistinism could be lampooned. Both men agreed to look for a suitable subject, and Strauss discovered the Flemish legend *The Extinguished Fires of Audenaarde*, in which a spurned suitor is publicly humiliated by his girl and has revenge aided by a magician, who puts out all the fires in the town and makes it known that they can only be re-lit one at a time from the flame which will spring from the girl's anus when she is exhibited naked in the market-place. Wolzogen changed the location to medieval Munich and made the hero a sorcerer's apprentice. He introduced topical allusions by aligning the sorcerer with Strauss and his master with Wagner. The libretto contains puns on the names Wagner, Strauss and Wolzogen, the music quotes Wagner, and the revised plot, set on midsummer's eve, is obviously inspired by *Die Meistersinger*, especially the hero's long monologue on the nature of art and inspiration, ending with the assertion that warmth and light spring only from women and from love.

Wolzogen called the poem *Feuersnot (Fire Famine)*. It was finished in October 1900 when Strauss began to sketch the music. He worked fast—it would be 'pure Lortzing', he told old Franz, 'supremely popular and melodious'—and finished the sketches by Christmas. Orchestration took from 1st January until 22nd May 1901, which was Wagner's birthday. 'Completed on the birthday and to the greater glory of the "Almighty",' he wrote on the last page—blasphemy enough to damn *Feuersnot* in the eyes and ears of those at whom its barbs were aimed.

Two opera houses applied to Strauss for the first performance, Mahler's Vienna and Ernst von Schuch's Dresden. He awarded it to Schuch, who at this time was fifty-five and had been in full charge at Dresden since 1882. Strauss had been profoundly impressed by Schuch's conducting of *Till* in December 1895.

He knew that Vienna would cause trouble over the licentious parts of the libretto, and when Dresden surprised him by doing likewise he refused to accept their suggested alterations. The first performance on 21st November 1901 was highly successful. 'Schuch is a marvel,' Strauss told his father. 'He has let me see my work as it really is.' In consequence there were to be eight more Dresden premières of Strauss operas over the next thirty-seven years.

The Vienna première of *Feuersnot*, two months later under Mahler, was also a success. It has been vividly described by Alma Mahler,[1] although she states, wrongly, that Mahler did not conduct 'because he had a horror of the work'. (He did conduct, moreover he conducted several revivals.) Pauline was in Alma's box 'raging the whole time. Nobody, she said, could possibly like that shoddy work . . . there wasn't an original note in it, all stolen from Wagner and many others'. Later she and Strauss had one of their famous rows, which Richard explained to Alma thus: 'My wife's a bit rough sometimes, but that's what I need, you know.'

Although he did not know it at the time, the most significant event in Strauss's operatic career had occurred before he began to compose *Feuersnot*. In the first days of March 1900, while he was conducting in Paris, he met the twenty-six year old Austrian poet and playwright Hugo von Hofmannsthal, who went to him with a suggestion for collaboration in a ballet. Strauss showed interest. In mid-November Hofmannsthal sent him the almost-completed scenario. Strauss replied from Charlottenburg on 14th December, in a letter which shows how accurately he planned his work schedule:

I shall not set it to music, much as I like it. . . . My own ballet [*Kythere*], which I pieced together last summer, though probably

[1] A. Mahler: *Gustav Mahler: Memories and Letters* (Eng. trans. by B. Creighton, ed. D. Mitchell, London, 1968).

Richard Strauss

inferior to your work, is nevertheless so much nearer to me that I shall certainly tackle it first, as soon as a little opera of mine is finished [*Feuersnot*]. And *after* this ballet (i.e. in about three years' time) the symphonic composer who has lain entirely dormant for the past two years will no doubt break through violently.[1]

This was the unpromising prelude to one of the most fruitful collaborations in the history of music.

[1] *Correspondence between R. Strauss and H. von Hofmannsthal* (Eng. trans. by H. Hammelmann and E. Osers, London, 1961).

6 Vulcan's labours

During the first years of the twentieth century Strauss was a regular visitor to Britain, conducting his works in London, Birmingham and Glasgow (he directed the Scottish Orchestra in the first complete British performance of *Aus Italien*). In June 1903 there was a Strauss Festival in London at the St James's Hall, at which he and Mengelberg conducted the Concert-gebouw Orchestra. A still valid summing-up of the enlightened British attitude to Strauss was written on 17th October 1902 by one of England's most brilliant music critics, Arthur Johnstone of the *Manchester Guardian*, who died in 1904 at the age of forty-three:

Of course the upholders of a turnip-headed orthodoxy will not hear of him, any more than they would hear of Richard I a quarter of a century ago, and he seems to have an irritating effect on all critics, except a certain very small minority. . . . He is enigmatic, Sphinx-like, a complex personality not to be conveniently catalogued. . . . Those who assert that Strauss is a mere eccentric will sooner or later find themselves in the wrong. He has in a few cases played tricks on the public, but he is nevertheless a master-composer, in the full and simple sense of those words—a master-composer just as Mozart was.[1]

The 'mere eccentric' was on the verge of upsetting the turnip heads more than ever. In April 1902 he began work on a large-scale symphonic poem. Progress was slow, by Strauss standards, and the draft sketch of what he was to call by a Latin title,

[1] A. Johnstone: *Musical Criticisms* (Manchester, 1905).

Symphonia Domestica, was not completed until July 1903 when he was staying in the Isle of Wight. The full score was finished on New Year's Eve 1903 and dedicated 'to my dear wife and our son'. It was scored for an orchestra of nearly 110 players, including five clarinets, eight horns and four (optional) saxophones. 'In the home one can't make so much noise!' old Franz Strauss protested.

Strauss reserved the first performance for his and Pauline's first visit to the United States. He was enticed to the New World at very high fees by an expatriate German musician, Hermann Hans Wetzler, who had founded his own orchestra in New York. With this short-lived orchestra Strauss made his American conducting début in Carnegie Hall on 27th February 1904. The new work was to be performed on 21st March, and Strauss told the Press that it represented 'a day in the life of my family, part lyrical, part humorous'. Nothing could have been better calculated to concentrate people's ears on extra-musical matters, and Strauss was naïve to expect otherwise.

Since that day the *Symphonia Domestica* has been the butt of heavy humour; worse, there was real hostility because Strauss had 'exploited' his private life in his music. People who contentedly read novels or attended plays and operas in which broken lives and adulterous passions were romanticized were 'shocked' or 'embarrassed' by Strauss's depiction of his blameless Bavarian home life. Also there was still so much fatuous controversy about the relative aesthetic values of programme and absolute music that Strauss, who was as sensitive and irritated about it as Mahler was, tried to cover his tracks by deleting from the printed score his numerous original headings for the various incidents, but some remained accidentally (for example the uncles' and aunts' comments on the baby: 'Just like his father', 'Just like his mother') and gave the game away. The work was politely received by the public and most impolitely by the American critics. Meanwhile the German Press denounced him for conducting two afternoon concerts in a New York department store, Wanamaker's. Such conduct was 'a prostitution of art'. Strauss replied that the concerts had been given in artistic conditions and, anyway, it was no disgrace to earn money.

The furore over the new tone-poem was a nine-day wonder, to be totally overshadowed by the response to Strauss's next work, the one-act opera *Salome*. With unerring artistic (and business) instinct he perceived that here was the perfect subject; it symbolized the decadence of late-Romantic literature and painting and mixed lust and religion against the fashionable background of orientalism. A winner, surely! Oscar Wilde's play, written in French for, but never acted by, Sarah Bernhardt, had been published in Paris in 1893. He interpreted the character of Salome in a new way: erotic desire, he decided, was at the root of her behaviour.

The first German production of the play was in Breslau in 1901. The following year *Salomé* was staged in Berlin by a twenty-nine year old producer, Max Reinhardt, and ran for 200 performances. Strauss first read the play when it was sent to him in 1902 by the Austrian poet Anton Lindner,[1] who offered to convert it into a libretto and after Strauss showed interest sent 'a cleverly versified' opening scene as a sample. Strauss did not like Lindner's contribution. He saw that Wilde's text, in Hedwig Lachmann's German translation—particularly the opening line 'How beautiful the Princess Salome is tonight'—had distinct musical possibilities, and he began sketches. In November 1902 he attended the Reinhardt production, with Gertrud Eysoldt in the title-rôle. Afterwards a friend said to him: 'Surely you could make an opera of this?' He replied: 'I am already composing it.'

The bulk of the composing was done between his return from America and 20th June 1905. The full sketch was completed during his 1904 summer holiday. He played some of it to his

[1] Strauss had set Lindner's poem *Hochzeitlich Lied* in 1897–8 as No. 6 of the *Sechs Lieder*, Op. 37.

father, who commented: 'It's like having ants in your pants.' It was the last new music by his son that Franz heard. He died, aged eighty-three, on 31st May 1905. A few days before that, Strauss was in Strasbourg with Mahler and his wife, Alma, and played *Salome* to them in a pianoforte showroom. The score was then completed except for the Dance of the Seven Veils. Mahler asked if it was not risky to write it later 'when you're not in the same mood'. Strauss replied light-heartedly: 'I'll soon fix that.'

He again offered the first performance to Schuch at Dresden. At the first read-through in the summer of 1905 the soloists returned their parts to the conductor except for Carl Burrian (Herod), who already knew his by heart. The Salome, Marie Wittich, caused the most trouble. 'I won't do it, I'm a decent woman,' she kept saying. She was excessively fat, but had the voice for a part which Strauss had described as 'the sixteen-year-old princess with the voice of Isolde'. The first performance was on 9th December. It was a roaring success, and this news spread to all major opera houses, fifty of which had each staged several performances within two years. By the end of 1907 there had been fifty Berlin performances. *Salome* encountered its worst censorship trouble in Vienna, as Mahler had warned Strauss that it would. Mahler offered his resignation but to no avail; this work was not performed in Vienna's great opera house until 1918. The rest of Austria was more amenable and Mahler saw *Salome* at Graz on 16th May 1906. He saw it again twice in Berlin in January 1907 with Emmy Destinn as Salome. His opinions are fascinating: 'It is emphatically a work of genius, very powerful, and decidedly one of the most important works of our day. A Vulcan lives and labours under a heap of slag, a subterranean fire—not merely a firework! It is exactly the same with Strauss's whole personality. . . . It is one of the greatest masterpieces of our time.' [1]

[1] A. Mahler: *Gustav Mahler: Memories and Letters.*

Toscanini conducted the first Italian performance. In New York in 1907 there was such an outcry after the first Metropolitan performance—'moral stench . . . loathsome . . . abhorrent'—that further performances were cancelled and the work disappeared from that theatre until 1933. At Covent Garden in 1910, when Beecham conducted, some alterations were made in the text to appease the Lord Chamberlain and were ignored in performance without anyone noticing. The total effect was that Strauss became unquestionably the most famous living composer, notwithstanding Puccini. And not only famous. The Kaiser commented: 'I really like this fellow Strauss, but *Salome* will do him a lot of damage.' Strauss drily comments in his reminiscences: 'The damage enabled me to build the villa in Garmisch.'

In the winter of 1903–4 Max Reinhardt followed Wilde's *Salomé* with 'a new version' of Sophocles' *Electra* by Hugo von Hofmannsthal. Strauss sounded the playwright on the possibility of his adapting it as a libretto. Hofmannsthal completed the task in 1905. Three months after *Salome* had been launched, he wrote from his home at Rodaun, near Vienna, to ask if Strauss had made any progress. Strauss was by now having doubts whether he could tackle so similar a subject so soon after *Salome*. Perhaps they could do something else first. He added these remarkable words: 'I would ask you urgently to give me first refusal of anything composable that you write. Your manner has so much in common with mine; we were born for one another and are certain to do fine things together if you remain faithful to me.'

Hofmannsthal persisted that *Elektra* ought to be their first collaboration and a contract was signed whereby he received 25 per cent of the royalties on their joint work. They never quarrelled over their business arrangements. Strauss's 'mercenary' nature is often pilloried, but in a letter to his collaborator on 5th June 1906 he set out his views in a manner that commands respect:

45

One does not need to be a businessman to wish to derive decent remuneration after sitting up with a long opera score night after night for two or three years. Once the pleasure of creation has passed, then the annoyance of performances and those blessed criticisms begin, and only a good stipend can compensate one for that. . . . I merely say out loud what other 'idealists' think to themselves.

By mid-June of 1906 Strauss had begun to compose *Elektra*, 'making rather heavy weather'. Work on it stretched over the next two years, being completed on 22nd September 1908. 'You are the born librettist,' he told Hofmannsthal after receiving the Recognition Scene. 'The end is juicy,' he wrote to Schuch at Dresden. 'The principal rôle must now undoubtedly be given to the most dramatic soprano you have.' They chose Annie Krull. Strauss found Schuch's treatment of the teeming orchestral score too subdued and colourless during rehearsals but admitted that the first performance was perfectly balanced. (Otto Klemperer has said that Strauss himself made *Elektra* sound 'like an opera by Lortzing'.[1]) The first performance, in Dresden on 25th January 1909, was no more than a *succès d'estime*. Many people echoed the opinions of Ernestine Schumann-Heink, the first Klytemnestra, who declared in New York that the opera was 'a horrible din'. Nevertheless, being by Strauss it was eagerly sought by other opera houses. Vienna staged it on 24th March, and Milan shortly afterwards; Beecham conducted it in London in February 1910, with Edyth Walker as Elektra.

The Covent Garden performances, played to excited full houses, led to a famous controversy. Ernest Newman, reviewing *Elektra* in *The Nation* on 26th February 1910, allowed that Strauss was 'the greatest living musician' but that 'much of the music is as abominably ugly as it is noisy. . . . One still clings to the hope that the future has in store for us a purified Strauss, clothed and in his right mind, who will help us to forget the

---

[1] P. Heyworth: *Conversations with Klemperer* (London, 1973), p. 44.

present Strauss—a saddening mixture of genius, ranter, child and charlatan'. Newman was answered by Bernard Shaw, who described these remarks as 'ridiculous and idiotic'. He added that the power of 'the passion that detests and must and finally can destroy that evil' was what made the work great 'and makes us rejoice in its horror'.[1]

Strauss himself conducted two of the first nine London performances, on 12th and 15th March 1910. The critic of the *Daily Mail*, probably Richard Capell, described him brilliantly: 'His thin long hand held the tapering baton like a pen. His head was immobile; only his eagle eyes flashed from time to time. . . . His elbows seemed riveted to his body. . . . The baton did not cleave the air with fantastic arabesques; he seemed a mathematician writing a formula on an imaginary blackboard, neatly and with supreme knowledge.' When Strauss conducted *Elektra* in Vienna in June 1909 it was his first appearance at the Court Opera there. Vienna was to be the scene of his next and most famous opera. He had had enough of horror and tragedy. 'Next time I'll write a Mozart opera.'

In later years Strauss sometimes affected to be bored with his early 'green horror'. But the conductor Karl Böhm has a touching memory of the old composer at a rehearsal of *Elektra*: 'Strauss was sitting in the stalls with my wife; about fifteen minutes from the end he grabbed her hand and wouldn't let go. When we had finished she asked him what was wrong, and he simply said: "Did I write that music? I'd almost forgotten it."'

[1] G. B. Shaw (ed. D. H. Laurence): *How to become a Musical Critic* (London, 1960), pp. 257–67.

7   Comedy for music

In thinking about providing Strauss with a comedy, Hofmanns-
thal re-read Beaumarchais's *Le Mariage de Figaro* and other
French novels and plays, notably Louvet de Couvray's *Les
Amours du Chevalier de Faublas*. He wanted to give Strauss
characters with the psychological interest of Figaro, Susanna,
Cherubino and the Countess. In February 1909 he stayed in
Weimar with Count Harry Kessler, diplomat and journalist.
They worked out the action of a comedy, taking some of the
names and situations from Couvray's novel. Hofmannsthal out-
lined a scenario. It contained these points:

> Sophie, with the pretty Faublas, tells of her forthcoming marriage.
> She is astonished that he is troubled by it. . . . The Intriguers. . . . Bed-
> room of the Marquise. Night of love. Pourceaugnac announced.
> Faublas remains in disguise. . . . Hairdresser, servants etc. . . . While
> the Marquise has her coiffure dressed, P. invites the chambermaid to
> supper. . . . Room at the inn. . . . The Marquise appears. . . . The dis-
> guised Faublas reveals himself.

Hofmannsthal wrote to Strauss from Weimar on 11th
February: 'I find the scenario enchanting. . . . It contains two
big parts, one for baritone and another for a graceful girl dressed
up as a man, *à la* Farrar, or Mary Garden. Period: the old Vienna
under the Empress Maria Theresa.' Strauss replied: 'We'll go
ahead with this. . . . You go straight home and send Act I as soon
as you can.' So began what the world knows as *Der Rosenkavalier*, although its authors did not give it that title until it was

completed. Faublas became Oktavian, Pourceaugnac the Baron Ochs and the Marquise the Feldmarschallin. Both men worked enthusiastically at astonishing speed, as extracts from their marvellous correspondence show:

Strauss (in Garmisch), 21st April 1909: 'Am impatiently waiting for the next instalment. The opening scene is delightful: it'll set itself to music like oil and melted butter; I'm hatching it out already. You're da Ponte and Scribe rolled into one. . . .'

Hofmannsthal (in Rodaun), 24th April: 'Do try and think of an old-fashioned Viennese waltz, sweet and yet saucy, which must pervade the whole of the last act.'

S. 4th May: 'The final scene [Act I] is magnificent: I've already done a bit of experimenting with it today. I wish I'd got there already. But since, for the sake of symphonic unity, I must compose the music from the beginning to the end I'll just have to be patient. . . . I'll need very good actors again; ordinary operatic singers won't do.'

16th May: 'My work is flowing along like the Loisach: I am composing everything—neck and crop.[1] I am starting on the Levée tomorrow.'

H. 12th June: 'Everything you played to me from the first act of the opera is most beautiful, and has given me great and lasting pleasure. I have now re-read Act II and am absolutely determined to make drastic changes in the last five minutes. . . . I know already how to do it.'

On 9th July Strauss wrote a long letter criticizing Act II severely and suggesting in considerable detail a complete revision of the action. From Ochs's return after signing the marriage contract to the end of the act is entirely in accordance with Strauss's new ideas. Reconstruction of this act occupied most of the remainder of 1909, and Hofmannsthal decided to put completion of Act III aside for some months to 'mature and

---

[1] He was not exaggerating. In one scene he 'composed' one of Hofmannsthal's stage directions.

enrich' it. During the winter of 1909–10 it was decided that Alfred Roller, the great stage designer whose work with Mahler in Vienna had revolutionized opera presentation, should provide the settings and costumes. On 23rd April 1910 Strauss wrote: 'I am in Garmisch and am in agonies waiting for Act III! The full score of Act II is already with the printer! . . . Roller's costume sketches are magnificent!' Strauss began composing Act III in May. At this stage he still favoured the title *Ochs auf Lerchenau*.

On 6th June Hofmannsthal wrote to say that he had completed the act. Significantly he added: 'The Marschallin is the central figure for the public, for the women above all, the figure with whom they feel and *move*.' Strauss was conducting *Elektra* in various cities, including Vienna, and at Strauss Weeks in his native Munich and Frankfurt.[1] It was not until 1st July that he briefly wrote 'Received end of *Rosenkavalier*: seems perfect to me.' This is the first indication that the opera's title had been decided. On 30th August Hofmannsthal had sudden misgivings about the end, after Ochs's exit—'a definite falling-off in interest'. He sent Strauss some cuts. Strauss's reply was masterly: 'That it sounds a bit flat in reading is obvious. But it is at the conclusion that a musician, if he has any ideas at all, can achieve his best and supreme effects—so you may safely leave this for me to judge. . . . From the Baron's exit onwards, I'll *guarantee* that, provided you undertake to guarantee the rest of the work.'

On 26th September Strauss completed the full score of what, recognizing the supreme quality of the libretto, he insisted that the publisher should describe as a 'Comedy for Music in three acts by Hugo von Hofmannsthal: music by Richard Strauss'. He had begun negotiations for its production at Dresden when he saw Count Seebach, Intendant of the Court Theatre there, earlier in 1910. Seebach objected to certain passages. The curtain could not rise on the Marschallin in bed; Ochs could not refer to

[1] In Munich he conducted *Feuersnot*, *Salome* and *Elektra* and several of his orchestral works. A plaque was fixed to his birthplace.

tumbling girls in the hay; a Neapolitan general became a Russian general, etc. Strauss and Hofmannsthal devised a series of alternatives which appeared either in libretto, vocal score or full score but never in all three.

When Strauss went to an early rehearsal he was dismayed by the inadequacy of Georg Toller's production. So he asked Max Reinhardt to supervise the carrying out of his own ideas, but told nobody he had done so. Toller was furious. 'I couldn't possibly have foreseen that so intelligent a man as Toller would not have been simply delighted to have been helped by a Reinhardt,' Strauss wrote to Schuch with surpassing naïveté, 'just as even today I would be ready to learn like a schoolboy from you or Mahler or anybody else without a thought of being knocked off my pedestal'. Seebach insisted that Reinhardt should give his advice from the stalls, but later relented and allowed him on the stage. But only Toller's name was printed in the programme.

Even more important was the casting. For Ochs, Strauss always had in mind the great Vienna Opera bass, Richard Mayr, but he could not be released from his commitments there. The alternatives were Paul Bender, of Munich, or Dresden's Carl Perron, who was fifty-three and had created the rôles of Jokanaan in *Salome* and Orestes in *Elektra*. Perron was chosen, but Strauss authorized cancellation of the première if Reinhardt and Hofmannsthal could not groom him for the part. The first performance, on 26th January 1911, was a dazzling success, and Strauss and Hofmannsthal gave Reinhardt principal credit for realization of the work as a true 'comedy for music'. Fifty performances were given in Dresden within a year, all sold out. Special trains were run from Berlin. So great had been the work's advance publicity that other opera houses were ready with their productions as soon as Dresden's right to the première had been fulfilled. It was produced in Nuremberg on 27th January and Mottl conducted it in Munich a few days later. In Hamburg, under Gustav Brecher, Edyth Walker sang Oktavian and the

Sophie was Elisabeth Schumann, whose understudy in the rôle was Lotte Lehmann, eventually to be the greatest of Marschallins and, before that, to sing both Sophie and Oktavian. In Milan, where Tullio Serafin conducted, hisses and whistles greeted the second act because waltzes were tolerated only in ballet by the Scala audience—a turmoil renewed in the third act.

On 8th April 1911 Franz Schalk conducted the Vienna première, with Mayr as Ochs, Gertrud Förstel as Sophie, Marie Gutheil-Schoder as Oktavian and Lucie Weidt as the Marschallin. The audience acclaimed it; the Viennese critics gave a display of stupidity well in keeping with their long tradition in this respect (only rivalled over the years by New York critics): 'A joke against the public . . . banal tunes . . . will not retain a place for long in the repertoire of our Court Opera . . . cheap, low-class wit . . . morbid and unnatural.' Nevertheless, in the remaining eight months of 1911, *Der Rosenkavalier* was performed thirty-seven times in Vienna. London and New York first heard it in 1913. Its popularity has never waned and there is no sign that it will.

Strauss first conducted *Rosenkavalier* in Cologne on 17th June 1911. He discovered that, as soon as he had left Dresden, Schuch had begun to make 'infamous cuts'. Strauss therefore infuriated him by pointing out that he had overlooked a good long cut in Act III where the action was held up for several minutes. He was referring to the greatest music in the opera, the Trio! In puritanical Berlin—where Strauss had resigned as court opera conductor in 1910 and was now principal guest conductor—the opera was not produced until 14th November 1911. When a friend from Dresden remarked that it had seemed shorter in Berlin, Strauss replied: 'Because there were fewer cuts.'

8 Airy-fairy

As early as 1906 Strauss and Hofmannsthal had discussed an opera on the subject of *Semiramis*, from a play by the seventeenth-century Spanish poet Pedro Calderón de la Barca. Strauss was greatly interested by this subject. On 20th February 1908 he asked for 'something tangible' by 1st June. 'Don't forget plenty of ballet, martial music and victory marching: these, apart from the erotic elements, are my strong suit.' No doubt he saw the opportunity for another *Aida*, having noted the success of that opera with the Berlin public in 1907 in a spectacular production. On 8th October 1910, when *Rosenkavalier* was finished, he wrote: 'The time has now almost come to think of *Semiramis*!' Hofmannsthal replied: 'No intellectual or material inducements could extract from me a play on this subject, not even a most determined effort of will.' It is possible that those dismissive words were fatefully crucial in their effect on Strauss's musical development.

Hofmannsthal then settled on *Das steinerne Herz*, based on a fairy-story by Wilhelm Hauff. 'Cheers for *Das steinerne Herz*!' Strauss wrote on 5th January 1911. 'Plenty of native atmosphere, please: German forest. Thunderstorm as Holländer-michel fells his trees: this is how the thing might start.' Henceforward can be seen ever more plainly the conflict between Hofmannsthal the intellectual and Strauss the practical man of the theatre. To put it crudely, 'airy-fairy' versus 'down-to-earth'. 'What a confounded fool I was to tell you the title and the subject,' the poet replied. His idea of an adaptation was to be 'real and symbolical'. No *Freischütz* forest, peasants or scenic effects.

Hofmannsthal's next letter, on 20th March, contained the germ of two operas:

If we were to work together once more on something (and by this I mean something important, not the thirty-minute opera for small chamber orchestra which is as good as complete in my head; it is called *Ariadne auf Naxos* and is made up of a combination of heroic mytho-logical figures in 18th-century costume . . . and, interwoven in it, characters from the *commedia dell'arte* . . . representing the buffo element which is throughout interwoven with the heroic) . . . it would have to possess colourful and clear-cut action. I have something definite in mind. . . . It is a magic fairy-tale with two men confronting two women, and for one of the women your wife might well, in all discretion, be taken as a model. . . . Anyway she is a bizarre woman with a very beautiful soul, *au fond*, strange, moody, domineering and yet at the same time likeable.

Two months later the magic fairy-tale had a title, for Strauss refers to *Frau ohne Schatten*. He was so anxious for work that he had even been in touch with Gabriele d'Annunzio about possible collaboration 'on an entirely modern subject'. Hofmannsthal put the damper on *Die Frau ohne Schatten*: he could not hurry such a subject. But he had a new idea for Molière, having seen *Le Bourgeois Gentilhomme* while in Paris. He planned a mixture of play and opera, the first part to be his adaptation of *Le Bourgeois Gentilhomme* (*Der Bürger als Edelmann*) with some incidental music for the dances, the second, *Ariadne auf Naxos*, with Strauss's music. He sent an outline on 19th May 1911. Strauss replied next day. Upset by Mahler's death two days earlier, he was offhand: 'The first half is very nice . . . the second half is thin. . . . For the dances of the Dancing Master, tailors and scullions, one could write some pleasant salon music.'

This novel entertainment was designed by Hofmannsthal as a challenge to the genius of Max Reinhardt. He was horrified when

Strauss fixed on the *commedia* character of Zerbinetta, in the *Ariadne* half, as a star rôle for a coloratura soprano like Selma Kurz or Tetrazzini—he did not visualize a rôle for fat women, he wanted exquisite young voices, nothing remotely 'grand opera'. Yes, replied Strauss, you could get away with that while Reinhardt is in charge, but what about other theatres? They will need some star singing parts to make their profit,

for the plot as such holds no interest and interesting costumes won't turn the scale either. Personally I am not particularly interested by the whole thing: that was why I asked you to spur your Pegasus a bit, so that the ring of the verses should stimulate me a little. You probably know my predilection for hymns in Schiller's manner and flourishes *à la* Rückert. Things like that excite me to formal orgies, and these must do the trick where the action itself leaves me cold. Soaring oratory can drug me sufficiently to keep on writing music through a passage of no interest.

Such blatant honesty offended Hofmannsthal, who wrote the first of a series of long letters explaining the psychological motives of his characters. 'When two men like us set out to produce a "trifle" like this, it has to become a very serious trifle,' he wrote portentously. In a further letter he explained 'the underlying meaning', with references to 'Death and Life at once' and 'the monologue of a lonely soul'. Strauss's reply was a delicious mixture of syrup and aloes:

Your letter . . . is so beautiful and explains the meaning of the action so wonderfully that a superficial musician like myself could not, of course, have tumbled to it. But isn't this a little dangerous? . . . If even I couldn't see it, just think of the audiences and—the critics. . . . Surely the symbolism must leap out alive from the action?

Strauss, pulling all available strings in Berlin, obtained permission for the entire personnel of the Kleines Deutsches Theater to work in Stuttgart under Reinhardt, and he would himself select the orchestra of thirty-seven players. The Stuttgart theatre was new and well equipped. Rehearsals began in June, and Strauss began to be enthusiastic. 'The score is going to sign-post a new road for comic opera. . . . It is a real masterpiece of a score: you won't find another like it in a hurry.' Further rehearsals were in October; Strauss, nurtured in drama at Mein-ingen, now saw the real possibilities. 'Tremendously effective. Molière is unspeakably funny,' he reported to Hofmannsthal. What he did not report was that all was not well at Stuttgart, where neither the resident actors and singers nor the theatrical management and staff welcomed the arrival of Reinhardt's Berlin company. Since they had undertaken all the preliminary rehearsals (which had convinced Strauss of the work's worth) and were to take over after the first performance, they had some cause for annoyance and Strauss did not help by telling the resident producer, who queried a technical point, 'Reinhardt will settle all that.' At the dress rehearsal, vital members of the stage staff went to work on another production in another theatre, leaving *Ariadne* in 'a mess', to quote Strauss, who lost his temper and insulted various people.

The première on 25th October was also a disaster. For one thing, as Strauss said, 'the playgoing public had no wish to listen to opera, and vice versa. The proper cultural soil for this pretty hybrid was lacking'. The evening was protracted to nearly five hours because the King of Württemberg held receptions lasting fifty minutes each in the intervals during and after the play. By the time the opera was reached, the audience not surprisingly 'was somewhat tired and ill-tempered'. Strauss conducted. For the rôle of Ariadne he had engaged a Czech soprano of great physical beauty whom he had heard sing in Offenbach in Munich, Mizzi Jeritza. As Maria Jeritza she was to become one of the immortal Strauss and Vienna singers.

So Strauss and Hofmannsthal tasted failure. This, we may be sure, was not unwelcome to their enemies. There was in Ger-many and elsewhere immense envy, amounting to hatred, of

Strauss's success. (England, in the 1950s, provided an exact parallel in the widespread hostility to Benjamin Britten.) His devotees, like Wagner's and Britten's, made the situation worse by their exaggerated language, but there was a malignant note in much of the written criticism. Though neither man could know it, *Rosenkavalier* had marked their high noon. Never glad confident morning again for Richard Strauss, only qualified, relative success and the implication that he was living off his artistic capital.

Strauss and Hofmannsthal broached the question of revisions of *Ariadne* during a meeting in Berlin. It soon emerged that Hofmannsthal was considering jettisoning the Molière play and turning the evening into a complete opera, with Prologue. On 9th January 1913 he wrote:

This Vorspiel [Prologue] then, with the established characters (Composer, Dancing Master, singer, tenor, Zerbinetta and others) is to take place not *on* the *Ariadne* stage, but behind it, in a hall where the dressing rooms have been improvised. The scene of the action to be described as: the big country-house of a rich gentleman and patron of the arts. The Maecaenas (Jourdain) himself remains unnamed, allegorical, in the background. . . . More strongly even than before, the focal point will be the musician's destiny, exemplified by the young Composer.

On 12th June, Hofmannsthal sent Strauss the 'new definitive Vorspiel' in which the figure of the Composer had been developed as 'tragic and comic at the same time, like the musician's lot in the world. . . . Please take to it kindly.'

This was what Strauss did not do. He did not like the new Prologue. The part of the Composer was 'downright distasteful. . . . I have an innate antipathy to all artists treated in plays and novels, and especially composers, poets and painters. Besides, I now cling so obstinately to our original work. . . . To me its original version is still the right one and the second no more than a makeshift.' This was somewhat ingenuous, since the idea of the

Richard Strauss

Vorspiel had been first suggested by Hofmannsthal in July 1911 as a prose scene preparing the ground for *Ariadne*. 'That's excellent,' Strauss had then said. 'It can become a hit provided you develop the parts of composer and Dancing Master. . . . It could become a companion piece to *Meistersinger*: fifty years after . . . Zerbinetta might have an affair with the Composer, so long as he is not too close a portrait of me.' But that was written before failure. On 2nd January 1914 Hofmannsthal saw *Ariadne* in Munich. 'It was an enchanting evening for me,' he wrote next day. 'You are quite right: we shall change nothing, not one thing.' And there, for a time, the matter rested.

Part of Strauss's disinclination to interest himself further in *Ariadne* arose from his desire for something large scale. He kept asking about the progress of *Die Frau ohne Schatten*. Hofmannsthal still would not be hurried; on 8th March 1912 he produced another red herring. He had a fit of conscience that the subjects he had offered Strauss since *Elektra* had neglected to cater for the composer's 'mastery over the dark, savage side of life', and he suggested a thirty-five minute 'tragic symphony' on the subject *Orestes and the Furies* as a ballet for Nijinsky. (This was the heyday of the Diaghilev Ballet, for which Ravel and Stravinsky, among others, had composed scores.) Strauss was not interested, but Hofmannsthal believed that 'such a symphonic piece . . . might not be wholly unwelcome to you as an interim work. . . . Together with Kessler . . . I have produced a short ballet for the Russians, *Joseph in Egypt*, the episode with Potiphar's wife; the boyish part of Joseph of course for Nijinsky.'

Strauss rose to this bait, having been delighted by the Russian Ballet in Berlin. But on 11th September he wrote:

The chaste Joseph himself isn't at all up my street, and if a thing bores me I find it difficult to set it to music. This God-seeker Joseph— he's going to be a hell of an effort. Well, maybe there's a pious tune for good boy Joseph lying about in some atavistic recess of my appendix.

58

Hofmannsthal, prig that he was, was offended. He thought Strauss would need to look for Joseph's music 'in the purest region of your brain'. He sent him a long lecture on Joseph's 'meaning' in mystical terms. It is extraordinary that he should have believed that Strauss could be fully inspired by a religious theme: perhaps *Salome* misled him, though he must have known that Jokanaan was the weak point in that opera. When Strauss played him some of the Joseph themes on 12th December 1912, he wrote arrogantly next day:

> In every task before us the final criterion can only be sensitivity in the matter of style, and of this I must consider myself guardian and keeper for the two of us. . . . There may be something absolutely right in these themes for *Joseph* . . . but as they stand they are, or strike one as, dressed up, dolled up, pastoral, *impossible* for this atmosphere, and they put one off fatally.

Strauss, as always, took this in good part and promised to do better. The subject then vanished from their correspondence until July 1913 when Strauss wrote that he had 'at last' completed the sketch of Joseph's dance. In September he reported that he was 'now at this job without interruption and shall do my best to get it ready for Paris in June: 100 pages are already scored, but it's a big and laborious job'. In fact he completed the score—for 112 players—on 2nd February 1914 and the first performance of *Josephslegende* was given at the Paris Opéra on 14th May, with Strauss conducting. The rehearsals were a nightmare because of the French players' system of sending substitutes if they were giving private lessons. He admits in his memoirs that he 'became very impatient'. Stravinsky, who was there, said Strauss's manner to the orchestra was 'not admirable' but 'every corrective remark he made was exact: his ears and his musicianship were impregnable'.[1]

---

[1] *Stravinsky in conversation with Robert Craft* (London, 1962), pp. 89–90.

The rôles of Joseph and Potiphar's wife were taken by Leonid Massine and Maria Kusnetzova, with choreography by Fokine and sets and costumes by Bakst, who placed the action in sixteenth-century Venice in the style of Veronese. Nijinsky's absence—the result of his rift with Diaghilev when he married—was a major blow, but the première was nevertheless an opulent occasion. Strauss went to London for the first English performance at Drury Lane, conducted by Beecham, on 23rd June. 'A great success,' he wrote to Hofmannsthal, 'in spite of the fact that most of the press was angry and even the most sophisticated Englishwomen found the piece indecent. . . . Joseph's dance still inadequate and hence boring.' Beecham found the score 'heavy and plodding'; and Ernest Newman described listening to the music as 'like attending the funeral of a lost leader'. While in England, Strauss went to Oxford to receive the University's honorary degree of Doctor of Music, a tribute timed to celebrate his fiftieth birthday on 11th June. His native Munich marked this anniversary by naming a street after him. Hofmannsthal reported 'decisive progress' with *Die Frau ohne Schatten* in January 1913. 'The profound meaning of this plot, the effortless symbolism of all the situations, its immensely rich humanity, never fail to fill me with delight and astonishment.' In the spring Strauss and Hofmannsthal made a car journey through Italy during which they discussed their new project. Strauss for the first time was given a real inkling of this subject which Hofmannsthal had told him 'would be related to *Zauberflöte* as *Rosenkavalier* is to *Figaro*'. The four main characters were to be the Oriental fairy-tale Emperor and Empress (she is the woman without a shadow, i.e. childless and infertile) and the earthly dyer Barak and his wife. 'In the upper sphere,' said Hofmannsthal, 'we shall have heroic recitative throughout . . . while below there is real conversation such as only the Master of *Rosenkavalier* can compose.'

But this time the recitative and conversation were not concerned with amorous intrigues in eighteenth-century Vienna but with supernatural powers, falconry, an empress who could change her shape at will, an emperor under threat of being turned to stone by his wife's father, the magician Kaikobad; with the machinations of an evil nurse, with the symbolism of childlessness, of the trials placed upon the good Barak and his passionate but shrewish wife; with unborn children and the Golden Water of Life. Hofmannsthal sent Strauss half of the first act as a New Year gift for 1914. 'Simply wonderful,' was the composer's verdict; and he began his customary suggestions for cuts and improvements. But whereas in *Rosenkavalier*, as the full correspondence shows, Strauss was the dominant partner, literally calling the tune, in *Die Frau ohne Schatten* it was the poet who applied most of the pressure:

Only one thing you must not, must never forget: the Empress is, for the spiritual meaning of the opera, the central figure and her destiny the pivot of the whole action. . . . You should never for a moment lose sight of it, for otherwise the third act will become impossible, where it can and ought to be the crowning glory of the whole work . . . it is to lead us where music and poetry, without clipping each other's wings, and truly hand in hand for once, shall float lightly over the gardens of paradise.

Strauss completed the sketch of Act I on 20th August 1914; on 8th October he told Hofmannsthal: 'You've really pulled off your masterpiece here. . . . If I succeed in getting Act II ready this October I shall leave the whole thing till next Easter and then tackle the end with fresh vigour. During the winter I'll score my *Alpensinfonie*!' On the 27th he reported the second act finished 'to schedule'. By then Europe had been at war for nearly three months.

9 The crisis

Strauss was in Italy when the Sarajevo assassination occurred. A few weeks later, at Garmisch, he learned that a considerable portion of his savings over thirty years which he had deposited in London with the financier Sir Edgar Speyer had been confiscated by the British. The sum involved is said to have been £50,000. 'For a week I was very depressed,' he wrote,[1] 'then I carried on with *Die Frau ohne Schatten*, which I had just begun, and started again from the beginning to earn money by the sweat of my brow when I had just entertained hopes of devoting myself exclusively to composition from my fiftieth year onward.' He clearly regarded the war as a nuisance, its chief effect being financial inconvenience to himself. His attitude to world affairs was uncomplicated and selfish. Rolland, for example, recorded in 1900 Strauss's 'absolute indifference' to the Boer War. About the First World War, in which his own country was involved, he was almost as casual.

Hofmannsthal went at once into the army. 'Really,' Strauss wrote to his librettist's wife on 31st July 1914,

poets ought to be permitted to stay at home. There is plenty of cannon fodder available: critics, stage producers who have their own ideas, actors who act Molière, etc. I am convinced there will be no world war, that the little altercation with Serbia will soon be over, and that I will receive the third act of my *Frau ohne Schatten*. May the devil take the damned Serbs.

[1] R. Strauss: 'Reminiscences of the First Performances of my Operas'.

But when the war began in earnest he took a patriotic pride in Germany's successes. 'These are great and glorious times,' he wrote on 22nd August to Gerty von Hofmannsthal, 'one feels exalted, knowing that this land and this people . . . must and will assume the leadership of Europe.' Yet he was cautious. Richard Specht, writing in the Budapest *Pester Lloyd* on 12th September, reported that when signatures were being collected for the famous manifesto of German artists and intellectuals, Richard Strauss refused to give his, explaining that 'declarations about things concerning war and politics were not fitting for an artist, who must give his attention to his creations and to his work'.

Strauss allowed himself some jingoistic outbursts in his letters to Hofmannsthal in October 1914, complaining of Reinhardt staging Shakespeare and Frankfurt performing French opera. No need to scoff at him for such silliness: in England, Wagner was excluded from the Royal Philharmonic Society's programmes and Strauss's *Don Juan* was dropped from a Promenade Concert on 15th August 1914. Sixty years later the State of Israel still refuses to perform the music of Richard Strauss. Strauss was revolted by hypocrisy, hence this to Hofmannsthal in February 1915, when he bemoaned the kind of people

for whom this great epoch serves merely as a pretext for bringing their mediocre products into the open, who seize the opportunity to decry real artists as hollow aesthetes and bad patriots, who forget that I wrote my *Heldenleben*, the *Bardengesang*, battlesongs and military marches in peacetime, but am now, face to face with the present events, keeping a respectful silence.

Hofmannsthal was quickly given a diplomatic post to keep him away from the front line. On 12th January 1915 he told Strauss he had resumed work on Act III of *Die Frau ohne Schatten*. It was delivered in April. 'Magnificent,' said Strauss, 'only in its quest for brevity it has become too sketchy.' Hofmannsthal had not yet heard a note of the music: Strauss played the first two acts to him on 25th April in Vienna. 'Really wonderful,' the poet told his friend Eberhard von Bodenhausen. But Strauss was far from satisfied with the Act III libretto and raised query after query which Hofmannsthal, busy with war work, did not answer with his usual speed. Progress faltered and halted. Meanwhile Strauss had completed scoring his *Alpensinfonie*, for a mammoth orchestra, on 8th February 1915. Composition had spread over four years; during this period his great Dresden interpreter Schuch had died (May 1914) and Strauss dedicated the symphony to the Dresden Intendant, Count Seebach, and to the Dresden Court Orchestra who, under Strauss, gave the first performance —but in Berlin—on 28th October. At the final rehearsal he remarked: 'At last I have learned to orchestrate. I wanted to compose, for once, as a cow gives milk.'

With *Die Frau* at a standstill, Strauss cast around for something to do. The revision of *Ariadne*! The original version was performed in Berlin in January 1916 and Strauss and Hofmannsthal saw it. They decided to adapt the piece as an opera, dropping the Molière play and substituting the new Prelude (*Vorspiel*) Hofmannsthal had written in 1913. The first performance was planned for October 1916 in Vienna. In April Strauss lobbed a grenade at his collaborator:

The part of the Composer (since the tenors are so terrible) I shall give to Mlle. Artot.[1] Only you'll have to consider now how we might further fill out the part for her with, say, a little vocal number; or perhaps you could write an additional pretty little solo scene for the Composer at the end. . . . I can only win Mlle. Artot for our piece if I can offer her a kind of small star part.

The use of a woman singer as the Composer had been suggested to Strauss by the Berlin conductor Leo Blech. Hofmannsthal was appalled.

[1] Lola Artot de Padilla, a Franco-Spanish soprano who had been Berlin's first Oktavian.

Your opportunism in theatrical matters has in this case thoroughly led you up the garden path. . . . To prettify this particular character, which is to have an aura of 'spirituality' and 'greatness' about it . . . strikes me as, forgive my plain speaking, odious. . . . Oh Lord, if only I were able to bring home to you completely the essence, the spiritual meaning of these characters.

Strauss was unimpressed. 'You almost act as if I had never understood you,' he replied.

'Do whatever you like about the ending, only do it soon, please! But as for Artot . . . I am not going to budge on this point, for artistic as well as for practical reasons. A tenor is impossible . . . a leading baritone won't sing the Composer: so what is left to me except the only genre of singer not yet represented in *Ariadne*, my Rofrano [Oktavian] . . . as a rule she is the most talented woman singer in the theatre.'

He and Blech were right. As in the case of Oktavian, it would be almost impossible to find for the Composer a male singer who combined the necessary youthful looks with the histrionic and vocal experience.

Hofmannsthal found the music for the *Vorspiel* 'enchanting . . . like fireworks in a beautiful park one enchanted, all too fleeting summer night'. The first performance of the revised *Ariadne auf Naxos* was given in Vienna on 4th October 1916 conducted by Franz Schalk, who had been one of Mahler's assistants (though Mahler had a poor opinion of him). Maria Jeritza sang Ariadne, Selma Kurz was Zerbinetta and Lotte Lehmann, stepping in on Strauss's insistence during rehearsals when Marie Gutheil-Schoder fell ill, had her first major success as the Composer. Leo Blech conducted the first Berlin performance on 1st November. In neither city, nor in others, was the work a success.

There are hints here that at this period Strauss was deeply conscious that he stood at an artistic crossroads. Some explanations of the generally assumed decline in his creativity have over-simplified it by relating it to the destruction in 1918 of the German superiority symbolized by the Kaiser's pre-1914 Berlin. This is facile; and in any case some critics had been 'writing off' Strauss since 1904 and earlier. It is also too easy to say that Strauss had 'gone soft', that all he wanted was to live comfortably in his villa composing out of habit rather than from compulsion. True, he sometimes took the line of least resistance; true, he could give the impression of indolence, but there is no reason to suppose that he became a less serious, dedicated and industrious artist. He involved himself as much as ever in all matters musical; and, knowing that he was in his fifties, he looked into his heart. Always a realist, he knew—or thought he knew—what was good for him and what he was good for. This crisis he did not treat emotionally and dramatically, but factually and with wry humour. It highlights the astonishing temperamental differences between Strauss and Hofmannsthal.

What a contrast they make! The German composer easy-going, comfortable, preferring to turn away wrath with a joke, at ease with practical musicians and temperamental singers; the Austrian poet aloof, stiff, subject to fits of depression, intensely well read, more than slightly snobbish, a great propagandist for his own work, mixing in all the intellectual coteries in the arts and on the fringe of politics. Both men were wealthy, but whereas Strauss lived in comfort, Hofmannsthal allowed no up-to-date equipment to mollify the spartan régime in his small rococo castle at Rodaun—no twentieth-century bathroom and no central heating, even though, like Strauss, he detested cold weather.

Strauss tried hard to signal to him in 1916 that he wanted to change direction in their choice of subjects:

I have two things in mind: either an entirely modern, absolutely realistic domestic and character comedy . . . —or some amusing piece of love and intrigue. . . . Say a diplomatic love intrigue in the setting of the Vienna Congress. . . . You'll probably say Kitsch! But then we musicians are known for our poor taste in aesthetic matters, and besides, if *you* were to do a thing like that it wouldn't be Kitsch.

This flattery failed. Hofmannsthal confessed to 'a good laugh' over these 'truly horrid' proposals. He added:

You have every reason to be grateful to me for bringing you (as now once again with *Die Frau ohne Schatten*) that element which is sure to bewilder people and to provoke a certain amount of antagonism, for you have already too many followers, you are already all too obviously the hero of the day, all too universally accepted. By all means get angry with me and keep harping for a while on this 'incomprehensibility', it is a mortgage to be redeemed by the next generation.

Strauss was undeterred:

I have a definite talent for operetta. And since my tragic vein is more or less exhausted, and since tragedy in the theatre, after this war, strikes me at present as something rather idiotic and childish [so much for the 'insensitive' Strauss], I should like to use this irrepressible talent of mine—after all, I'm the only composer nowadays with some real humour and a sense of fun and a marked gift for parody. Indeed, I feel downright called upon to become the Offenbach of the 20th century, and you will and must be my poet. . . . Our road starts from *Rosenkavalier:* its success is evidence enough, and it is also this genre (sentimentality and parody are the sensations to which my talent responds most forcefully and productively) that I happen to be keenest on.

Hofmannsthal's reply was never sent—he withheld it as being 'sullen and ill-inspired'—but it has survived. He accused Strauss of failing to enter into his ideas and of treating 'quite a few things in the wrong style'. Zerbinetta's aria, for example, he had always detested. Faninal's servants in Act III of *Rosenkavalier:* their chorus had been written 'to be rattled off in burlesque fashion . . .

what you did was to smother it with *heavy* music and so to destroy utterly the purpose of the words. . . . The fun of this passage has simply ceased to exist, the very thing a man like Offenbach would have brought out'. The footmen at the end of Act I of this opera were 'quite terrible' (few will agree with this) and Ochs's exit in Act III 'offends no less gravely against the style of the whole work'.

That was written on 11th June 1916. On 28th July Strauss returned to his problem with Act III of *Die Frau*:

Characters like the Emperor and Empress, and also the Nurse, can't be filled with red corpuscles in the same way as a Marschallin, an Oktavian or an Ochs. No matter how I rack my brain—and I'm toiling really hard, sifting and sifting—my heart's only half in it, and once the head has to do the major part of the work you get a breath of academic chill (what my wife very rightly calls 'note-spinning') which no bellows can ever kindle into a real fire. I have now sketched out the whole end of the opera . . . but my wife finds it cold and misses the heart-touching, flame-kindling melodic texture of the *Rosenkavalier* trio. . . . Let's make up our minds that *Frau ohne Schatten* shall be the last romantic opera.

When he completed Act III early in September he confessed he was uncertain what was good and what was bad. 'That's a good thing, for at my age one gets all too easily into the rut of mere routine and that is the death of true art.' He harked back to the subject which had obsessed him all summer:

Guided by *Ariadne* and in particular the new Vorspiel, I hope to move forward wholly into the realm of unWagnerian emotional and human comic opera. I now see my way clearly before me and am grateful to you for opening my eyes—but now you go ahead and make me the necessary libretti . . . peopled by human beings *à la* Hofmannsthal instead of puppets. An amusing, interesting plot . . . in any form you like! I promise you I have now definitely stripped off the Wagnerian musical armour.

Hofmannsthal could not fail to respond to such candour: 'I shall do what I can to fulfil your wishes.' Whether he could respond to the Eulenspiegel element in Strauss was to determine Strauss's artistic development in a Europe which was savagely changed from the world in which their partnership had begun.

10 Vienna

A recurrent dread for Strauss seems to have been of a summer without work: he must have something to compose, even if he laid it aside to play skat. Perhaps for this reason alone he allowed Hofmannsthal to lure him into yet another version of their adaptation of Molière's *Le Bourgeois Gentilhomme*. On 24th July 1916 the librettist had written to Strauss of a meeting with Hermann Bahr, the dramatist and critic (and husband of Mahler's former mistress, the soprano Anna von Mildenburg). Hofmannsthal had mentioned Strauss's desire for a *Singspiel* work, and 'if Bahr can think of anything he will submit to you a scenario or a plot'. The letter continued:

He spoke very intelligently of you, of that mixture of the hearty, Bavarian aspect of your nature with a subtle, witty mind and in this connection described your music for the *Bourgeois* as the finest thing you had done. . . . Please, dear Dr. Strauss, do not rashly waste these pieces of music; I am sure I shall succeed in inventing a second delicate action for this comedy.

By April 1917 the first performance of the new Hofmannsthal-Molière adaptation had been fixed for a year ahead, directed by Reinhardt at the Deutsches Theater in Berlin. Hofmannsthal admitted that the adaptation had given him more trouble than he had expected. Strauss had reservations; after all, the 1912 version had had little success, and he could not see that this further elaboration would be better. He was worried by Hofmannsthal's determination to end the acts without a musical finale—he had had enough of that in the original version. 'For the love of God,' he wrote, 'not a succession of three curtains after which not a hand will stir.' Hofmannsthal's reply was gratuitously offensive: 'I undertook this whole thing solely and exclusively to create for your already existing music . . . a proper and worthy outlet. . . . This genre I shall not allow to be adulterated or bent towards operetta . . . for although you are my superior in many artistic gifts and abilities, I have the greater sense of style and more reliable taste.'

When Strauss received the full text he was markedly unenthusiastic and suggested there ought to be a fourth act. Hofmannsthal's reply, for which he later apologized, called Strauss's proposals 'beneath discussion' and asked for a decision whether he was 'free to dispose otherwise of this Molière adaptation, of which I do not intend to alter one iota'. Strauss at this point seems to have decided to shrug his shoulders. He made a few more protests and kept up a show of interest, but it is difficult to feel that he was much concerned about the work's fate. When it was produced, on 9th April 1918, it ran for only thirty-one performances. Hofmannsthal suggested that they might now try to make an opera of it and that Strauss might compose entirely new music in *Ariadne* for Zerbinetta's coloratura aria, which he still considered an 'obstacle in the way of the opera's future prospects'.

In his reply, written on 12th July 1918, Strauss put an end to the seven-year obsession with the Molière play. He was prepared to leave its future to chance in the certainty that 'a more cultured public' would one day appreciate it. 'I would suggest that we stop doctoring it. . . . I should find difficulty in applying the surgeon's knife to Zerbinetta again. Shall we write something new in the same manner and form?'

In any case Strauss was by now intent on several new projects. Hofmannsthal's mention of Bahr as a possible librettist had reminded him of Bahr's play *Das Konzert* about the marriage troubles of a musician. Strauss met Bahr in Salzburg in September 1916 and suggested an opera about a misunderstanding he and Pauline had had some years before, when Pauline had suspected him of adultery. Bahr sent a draft libretto, on which Strauss commented: 'I am sending you a succession of scenes I have thought out, little more than cinema pictures, in which the music says everything, the writer contributing only a few cue words.' Bahr enjoyed what Strauss had done so much that 'even if you were in agreement, I would on no account substitute my dialogue. . . . My suggestion is, therefore, that this time you must write your own text'. While he spent a week in hospital in Munich in the first week of July 1917, Strauss worked on the libretto of what was to become *Intermezzo*.

It is easy to sense Strauss's restlessness in these years, his feeling that, despite the completion at last of *Die Frau ohne Schatten*, nothing engaged his wholehearted interest. Partly this may have been caused by worry about his delicate son, Franz, who was nearing the age of call-up for military service (in May 1918 he was declared 'fit only for limited service at home stations' and was never called). But a deeper, more radical cause was Strauss's growing awareness that he and his music were becoming almost grotesquely out of tune with the times. In this respect he is a parallel with Elgar, whose letters at this time betray a despondency about the future of music, and of his own music, which resulted in his almost total silence for fifteen years after the composition of his last masterpiece, the Cello Concerto, in 1919. Strauss was a less hypersensitive and depressive case than Elgar but he felt equally keenly that the post-war world was alien to him. He had no curiosity about the music of the younger generation, no interest in Stravinsky, Berg, Bartók, Schoenberg, Hindemith, Prokofiev and others. (He said to the young Hindemith: 'Why do you compose like that? You don't need to—you have talent.') He saw the end of the world in which he had risen to fame, the end of the ducal courts and kingdoms with their private opera orchestras and companies, and he saw them end not only as the result of military defeat but amid a whirlwind inflation which devalued money to the point where it had no value. What was Strauss, still a rich man and still energetic, to do? Elgar took refuge in the life of a country squire and in the practical side of music, conducting and recording his own works. So did Strauss. At Garmisch he was the squire; and when the opportunity came to escape to the exciting, scheming world-within-a-world of the Vienna Opera, he seized it, just as he had escaped into the Vienna of *Rosenkavalier* after the crisis-point of *Elektra*.

In April 1918, while Hans Gregor was still director of the Vienna Court Opera, Strauss conducted *Elektra*, *Ariadne* and *Rosenkavalier* there. On 23rd May he wrote to Hofmannsthal:

I have pursued in my mind many recollections of my pleasant stay in Vienna, and in particular have discussed with my wife (who agreed sympathetically) the possibility that, in the event of Gregor's departure, I might share in a possible Schalk directorship, perhaps as co-director, in such a way that I would spend two or three winter months in Vienna over a number of years. . . . I should gladly make a personal sacrifice to prevent some Weingartner from trying his destructive hand again on that fine artistic institution.

This was written in the month that Strauss ended his long association with the Berlin Court Opera after a quarrel with the autocratic Intendant, Hülsen. Hofmannsthal made no comment until three months later, on 1st August, when, in a remarkable letter, he expressed his candid opposition, saying he believed Strauss would put his own operas' interests above the institution. He added: 'The great danger of your life, to which you surrender and from which you try to escape in almost periodic cycles, is a neglect of all the higher standards of intellectual existence.'

Strauss took no offence. He did not intend, he said, to try to fill the post as Mahler had. But he had resolved to devote five winter months for the next ten years or so to his work as a conductor. 'It has been my devoutest wish for the past thirty years to assume the *de facto* supreme direction of a big Court Opera House on the artistic side.'

In July 1918 Leopold von Andrian-Werburg was appointed Intendant of the Vienna Court Opera, the last such appointment made by the Austrian monarchy. By now Hofmannsthal was reconciled to Strauss's intentions and promoted them eagerly. In September he reported a conversation with Andrian in which he 'explained our ideas' to the Intendant, who wanted some assurance that Strauss would refrain from conducting predominantly his own works. Hofmannsthal believed that Strauss would work well with Franz Schalk, and was determined that they should recall Alfred Roller to work with them as stage designer. On the last day of the monarchy, 10th November 1918, Andrian appointed Schalk as Director, but it was already widely known—and was accepted by Schalk—that Strauss would be brought into the partnership.

In the early months of 1919 the Court Opera became the State Opera and the Republic confirmed the contract between Andrian and Strauss. His appointment was announced on 1st March. Immediately, almost the whole staff (800 members) of the Opera, with the notable exceptions of Schalk, Maria Jeritza and Selma Kurz, signed a resolution demanding his withdrawal, on the grounds that the proposed salary was too high for 'an impoverished country like the new Austria',[1] objecting that he would favour his own works, and that he was planning to give concerts with the Philharmonic in the Opera House, thus damaging the Philharmonic's subscription series under Weingartner. Their

[1] This was 80,000 kronen for seven months as director, plus 1,200 kronen on each night when he conducted. In view of the rate of inflation the sum was meaningless; it was much less than he earned in Germany, and several officials of the Opera were being paid a similar sum.

real fear, though, was that Strauss intended to purge the company of superannuated singers. Strauss's reaction was to stay in Garmisch, aloof from the controversy except for an offer (which he knew would be refused) to withdraw the première of *Die Frau ohne Schatten*. A group of Viennese intellectuals sent him an open telegram urging him to come to Vienna. Signatories included Stefan Zweig, Hofmannsthal, Georg Szell, Arthur Schnitzler, Alfred Roller, Richard Specht and Alma Mahler. The affair fizzled out, and Strauss went to Vienna in May as guest conductor at a festival to celebrate the Opera House's fiftieth anniversary when he conducted *Fidelio, Tristan, Zauberflöte, Ariadne* and *Rosenkavalier*. If this seems like a golden age, it should also be remembered that the spring of 1919 in Austria was marked by strikes, political uprisings, poverty and hunger.

The first performance of *Die Frau ohne Schatten* was given in Vienna on 10th October 1919 conducted by Schalk, with Jeritza as the Empress, Lotte Lehmann as Barak the Dyer's wife, Richard Mayr as Barak, Lucie Weidt as the Nurse and Karl Aagard-Oestvig as the Emperor. In spite of such a galaxy the opera was no more than moderately successful. There is a well-authenticated legend that Pauline refused to walk back with Strauss to their hotel after the performance, preferring not to be seen in the company of the composer of such a poor work! Strauss, who called it 'a child of sorrow', recounted [1] that 'its way over the German stage was fraught with misfortune. In Vienna itself, owing to the strain imposed by the vocal parts and to the difficulties over the sets, the opera was withdrawn more often than it was performed. It was a serious blunder to entrust this opera, difficult as it was to cast and produce, to medium and even small theatres immediately after the war'. The work was first produced satisfactorily at Dresden in 1927 but even so it remained intermittently in the German opera houses' repertories. It was not

[1] R. Strauss: 'Reminiscences of the First Performances of my Operas'.

produced in New York and London until 1966. Hofmannsthal, in 1921, could not agree with his critics that the libretto was to blame. He added: 'I believe the work *will* live. But I say "I believe"—in the case of *Ariadne* I say "I know".'

Strauss's Vienna appointment began on 1st December 1919, to run until 30th November 1924. He agreed to be committed to Vienna for five months of each year, from 15th December to 15th May. Eventual discord in co-direction with Schalk was guaranteed by the vagueness with which their functions were defined. Schalk was 'Head of the Opera House' and Strauss 'artistic supervisor'. Yet it must have been obvious that, with his fame and prestige, Strauss would be generally regarded as the major partner, however unjust this might be to the long-serving Schalk. Strauss made his official début in January 1920 in an uncut *Lohengrin*, the opera with which Mahler had first conquered Vienna in 1897. But the sacerdotal fanaticism with which Mahler the martinet led the Opera was not to be Strauss's way. He was out for enjoyment, the audience's and his own, and at first he and Schalk worked well together. The singers at their disposal were among the greatest of the century. They included survivors of the Mahler era in Anna von Mildenburg, Marie Gutheil-Schoder, Selma Kurz, Erik Schmedes, Leo Slezak and Richard Mayr, and later stars, among them Maria Jeritza, Maria Ivogün, Lotte Lehmann, Elisabeth Schumann, Maria Olczewska, Lotte Schoene, Luise Helletsgruber, Alfred Piccaver, Karl Aagard-Oestvig, Richard Tauber, Hans Duhan, Alfred Jerger and Josef Manowarda. Singers adored working with Strauss, who was extraordinarily indulgent to them in his own music. He would encourage sopranos to take liberties with the score if he liked the sound of what they did; and to Hans Hotter he said: 'Who told you I wrote my songs for beauty's sake?' He wanted the high notes to sound effortful.

Strauss fulfilled his intention of spring-cleaning the Opera's classical repertoire. He conducted re-studied performances—

several in what amounted to his own productions, so closely did he supervise the stage action—of *Der Freischütz*, *Carmen* (with Jeritza), *Tannhäuser*, *Hänsel und Gretel*, *Hans Heiling*, *Fidelio*, *Don Giovanni* and *Der fliegende Holländer*. At the end of their first season, in May 1920, he and Schalk inaugurated the Vienna 'festival months of master performances'. Strauss conducted his beloved *Così fan tutte* and, of his own works, *Salome* and *Elektra*. He and Schalk restored the operas of Puccini to the Vienna stage; other contemporaries whose 'novelties' were performed were Pfitzner (*Palestrina*), Franz Schreker (*Die Gezeichneten*) Erich Korngold (*Die tote Stadt*), Julius Bittner (*Die Kohlhaymerin*), Franz Schmidt (*Fredigundis*), Zemlinsky (*Der Zwerg*), and Weingartner (*Meister Andrea* and *Die Dorfschule*). In 1922 the co-directors incorporated the beautiful Hofburg Redoutensaal with the State Opera. There they conducted performances of *Le nozze di Figaro*, *Il barbiere di Siviglia*, *Don Pasquale*, *Jean de Paris* and, as a triple bill, Mozart's *Bastien et Bastienne*, Pergolesi's *La serva padrona* and Weber's *Abu Hassan*. Since 1917 Strauss had been a director, with Hofmannsthal and Reinhardt, of the Salzburg Festival Association and worked hard towards re-establishment of the festival, conducting a memorable *Così fan tutte* there in 1922 from which the total acceptance of this masterpiece into the world's operatic repertory may be traced.[1]

It was at this time that Strauss created the legend of his laconic, unobtrusive conducting, sometimes regarded as cold and aloof, although this was not the impression received by those who heard his performances. Like Mahler, he greatly modified his demeanour on the rostrum after the excesses of his youth. Here is Arthur Johnstone of the *Manchester Guardian* describing Strauss conducting Liszt's *Faust Symphony* at Düsseldorf in May 1902:

[1] For a fascinating and detailed account of several of Strauss's interpretations see Leo Wurmser's 'Richard Strauss as an Opera Conductor', *Music & Letters*, January 1964, pp. 4–15.

'A sphinx-like person who, as his abnormally big head sways on the top of his tall and bulky figure, to the accompaniment of fantastic gestures, works up his audience into a sort of phosphorescent fever.' Twenty years later the fantastic gestures had disappeared, as is evident from Romain Rolland's description of him in 1924: 'He is tall, slim, cold, impassive, precise; he makes very few gestures; at rare moments of musical frenzy one discerns the intense nervous vibration which stirs him and which suddenly makes the orchestra flare up: it's like an electric spark applied to gunpowder.' [1]

His obsession, at this period particularly, was his overriding desire to ensure that the audience should hear the words and understand the plot. This underlay the 'Ten Golden Rules for the Album of a Young Conductor', which he wrote in 1922, and his Preface (of 1924) to his opera *Intermezzo*. Norman Del Mar has described the Rules as cynical, facetious and lacking integrity, a rather harsh judgment which leaves out of account the clue to this cynicism provided in the Preface when Strauss castigates the tendency of German orchestras to play too loud, encouraged by 'the many concert-hall conductors who have unfortunately nowadays taken to conducting opera'. Such rules as 'Never look encouragingly at the brass' and 'If you think the brass is not blowing hard enough, tone it down another shade or two' were the outcome of long practical experience and, indeed, only echoed his master Bülow. He advised his 'Young Conductor' to conduct *Salome* and *Elektra* as if they were fairy music by Mendelssohn and advised singers to 'sing *mezza voce* and pronounce your words clearly and the orchestra will automatically accompany you better'.

Strauss's audience in Vienna in 1920 was very different from Mahler's. There is a famous cartoon by Theo Zasche depicting an evening at the opera, with Strauss conducting, Slezak and

[1] R. Myers (ed.): *Richard Strauss and Romain Rolland* (London, 1968), p. 162.

Jeritza singing, Rosé leading the orchestra; some of the audience are standing with their backs to the stage shouting to friends, a man is drinking from a bottle, many are reading papers, couples are embracing, in two boxes the occupants are playing cards, in another they are very drunk. It is an audience of *nouveaux-riches*, of profiteers. Among the true opera-lovers at this time one would hear remarks like: 'There mustn't be a full house for *Elektra*; the real enthusiasts only half fill it.' Yet in the Press and among the *aficionados* the controversies and feuds endemic to the Vienna Opera raged as potently as ever.

In the late autumn of 1921 Strauss made his second visit to the United States as accompanist to the soprano Elisabeth Schumann and as guest conductor of his own works with the New York Philharmonic and Philadelphia Orchestras. Everywhere he was welcomed; he played poker until the early hours; and he took home a large sum of money. His first post-war visit to London was in June 1922. Any misgivings he may have had were allayed by a letter from Elgar: 'I send you a word of warm welcome and an assurance that your return to our country gives the greatest pleasure to myself and to very many of my musical countrymen.' Elgar and Bernard Shaw entertained him to lunch at the United Services Club. From June to September 1923 he was in South America with the Vienna Opera.

In Vienna itself the inevitable clash between Schalk and Strauss had first occurred in 1922. There was growing discontent with Strauss's absences and with his habit of granting leave to leading Vienna singers such as Lehmann to sing his rôles in other opera houses. This caused havoc with the salary system, already complicated by the precarious state of the currency. Schalk had to try to keep the Opera's head above water and not unnaturally felt that his co-director was of little assistance. 'I am here to lose money,' was Strauss's retort when shown the budget. In addition, the Press complained that the Opera had become a Richard Strauss Theatre. During his five years' tenure he conducted thirteen performances of *Rosenkavalier*, sixteen of *Salome* and thirteen of *Ariadne*. *Die Frau ohne Schatten* was given twelve times, *Feuersnot* seven times and the ballet *Josephs- legende* nineteen times after its Vienna première on 18th March 1922. Apart from the last, these figures do not seem excessive. He was also criticized for excluding new works, but on this point he made his views remarkably clear in an article published in the *Neues Wiener Journal* on 22nd June 1922. He argued that new works should only be produced in the smaller theatres, not in Berlin and Vienna where audiences were cosmopolitan and critics all-powerful.

Strauss's downfall was to come in 1924, one of the most event- ful years of his life. It began happily with the marriage of his son Franz to the Jewish Alice Grab on 15th January (a Viennese witti- cism was that at the service Strauss buried his anti-Semitism— '*zu Grab begraben*'). But, in the background, the State bureau- crats in charge of the Austrian theatres were threatening drastic economies. Strauss wrote to Schalk on 4th February to say that without funds his post was meaningless, everyone was dis- satisfied, he had been criticized for going to Rome to conduct *Salome*, and there was talk of the bankruptcy of the Opera, but 'was it ever solvent?' He would make another effort to reach understanding with the officials but he was pessimistic. 'Even if I become the ex-director I'll remain in Vienna: you and I can then play piano four hands or play chess. Poor *Oper*! It is really sad.'

He knew he would stay in Vienna because his house on the Jacquingasse was nearing completion. In anticipation of his sixtieth birthday the Viennese had 'lent' him a plot of land in the Belvedere for several decades. A house, harmonizing with its surroundings, was to be built to Strauss's specifications at the city's expense. Strauss agreed to some extra engagements with the Philharmonic and presented the city with the manuscript score of *Der Rosenkavalier*. As he prepared for the move from his flat in the Mozartstrasse he signed a new contract in April 1924 in which he stipulated that Schalk should be retired after the 1924–5 season. The Austrian Education Minister, Schneider, was hesitant but Strauss was convinced that the authorities would concede this point. All was set, then, for the celebrations of his birthday.

This event was a national occasion in Germany and Austria. Strauss weeks were held in Berlin, Munich, Dresden and Breslau; he was made an honorary citizen of Vienna and Munich; a square in Dresden was named after him. Vienna also honoured him with a week's festival of his operas and orchestral works. He had also planned a gift to the Viennese: his new ballet named after the whipped cream Austrians love, *Schlagobers*, a gay confection set in a confectioner's shop. He had completed it in October 1922 and conducted the first performance on 9th May 1924. It fell flat: the Vienna of the 1924 privations was in too sour a mood for whipped cream. If one seeks social comment in music on the Vienna of this period it is to be found in Ravel's *La Valse*, not in the pages of *Schlagobers*. A vivid account of this Strauss week is contained in the diaries of Romain Rolland, who attended the festival: [1]

11th May . . . Vienna: a big old provincial town. It has no inkling of new trends, of the accelerated rhythm, of the contribution of such people as Stravinsky, Honegger, etc., of this frenzy which we can no longer do without in music. . . . I feel here that I am with distinguished old people half-asleep and habit-bound.

12th May: I find [Strauss in his flat] surrounded by a circle of ladies and boring Society people. Strauss, serious, heavy, affectionate. Very preoccupied by nationalist follies, by our threatened European civilisation. . . . He never has a smile on his face. No sudden bursts of gaiety, of unconscious 'ragamuffinery', as there used to be. . . . The question of money also preoccupies him. . . . His ballet *Schlagobers* has just been slated by the Viennese critics. Strauss appears affected by its

[1] R. Myers (ed.): *Richard Strauss and Romain Rolland*, pp. 162–8.

failure. 'People always expect ideas from me, big things. Haven't I the right, after all, to write what music I please? I cannot bear the tragedy of the present time. I want to create joy. I need it.' He appears to be absolutely indifferent to national questions and to national quarrels.

Strauss overplayed his hand in Vienna, relied too much on his fame to overcome all snags. He forgot that he was at the Opera for only five months of the year, whereas Schalk was there all the time. Schalk dealt with the Ministry officials who administered the theatres, and he won their support. During the summer of 1924 he negotiated a new contract for himself with a clause that in Strauss's absences, he should have sole responsibility for making decisions. Strauss returned to Vienna in September for the first performance on the 20th of Beethoven's *Die Ruinen von Athen*, a 'festive spectacle' also incorporating parts of Beethoven's *Prometheus* ballet music which he and Hofmannsthal had adapted, and on 1st October he conducted the first Vienna performance of *Der Bürger als Edelmann* in the ideal setting of the Redoutensaal. Neither was a success.

Strauss then went to Dresden where his *Intermezzo* was to have its first performance on 4th November with Fritz Busch conducting and Lotte Lehmann in the principal soprano rôle. During the final rehearsals Ludwig Karpath, who was the Austrian Education Ministry's adviser on the national theatres, arrived from Vienna to tell Strauss the details of Schalk's new contract and to gain his agreement to the 'sole responsibility' clause. It was made quite clear that he had to agree. Strauss refused and handed Karpath his resignation, though he was under no illusion but that he had been dismissed. His only public statement was that he was 'neither angry nor bitter', but to Andrian he compared his position with Wagner's departure from Munich. ('Richard must go, the Minister stays.') To Hofmannsthal on 29th January 1925 he explained: 'The annoyance with that —— Schalk was too much, the means for achieving anything worthwhile too little, and the offer of the Minister—who only wanted me as window-dressing and as a willing drudge for when he gets the post of "Director General of the State Opera", said to have been already promised him when he resigns as Minister—unworthy of me.'

11 Helen and Arabella

Strauss's output, large though it was, diminished between 1916 and about 1940, with his five years in Vienna the thinnest period. Partly this may be attributed to his preoccupation with operas, some of which took several years to compose and stage, but there are grounds for belief that he himself was searching for a new means of expression, recognizing that his early fertility had gone and also that he was more self-critical. In his career he wrote 213 songs: his last very fertile year for *Lieder* was 1918 in which he composed twenty-nine. By the end of that year his total was 189; in the following thirty-one years he wrote only twenty-four. Between 1915 and 1925 his only works for orchestra were the ballet *Schlagobers*, publication of the suite from *Le Bourgeois Gentilhomme* and (another ballet) an arrangement for small orchestra of some keyboard pieces by Couperin (1922–3). His principal work at this time was the two-act *Intermezzo*, completed in Buenos Aires on 21st August 1923.

No wonder the world of music regarded him by then as almost a fossil. To the non-specialist audience his name was known because of his early tone-poems and his earlier operas. To all intents and purposes, *Der Rosenkavalier* of 1911 was his last word. An English critic, Cecil Gray, wrote in the 1920s [1] of 'the gradual degeneration and final extinction of his creative powers . . . he has become a man of second-rate talent'. Strauss was still in the dilemma he had foreseen and outlined to Hofmannsthal in

---

[1] C. Gray: *A Survey of Contemporary Music* (London, 1924).

1916. He had no more wish to be affected by the 'frenzy' Rolland mentioned than had Elgar. He knew what he did best, and that did not include writing a *Wozzeck*. Berg did that best.

But Strauss, like Puccini at this same period, was well aware of his need to do something new and different in his own line. In his correspondence with Hofmannsthal he makes continual reference to this, always suggesting something light-hearted. In his way he was as sensitive to the theatre-going public's mood in the 1920s as were the impresarios of the musical-comedy stage in New York and London who provided a decade of *Rose Marie*, *Rio Rita*, *Bitter Sweet* and the like. Even Hofmannsthal reflected something of this mood, probably unconsciously. He would certainly have been horrified if it had been pointed out to him that the Sheikh he introduced into *Die ägyptische Helena* had perhaps strayed from *The Desert Song* and the celluloid world of Rudolph Valentino; and that Arabella's 'Aber der Richtige . . . der wird einmal dastehn, da vor mir' ('But the right man . . . will stand there one day, there before me') is not far removed from Gershwin's 'Some day he'll come along, the man I love'. Significantly, both Strauss and Hofmannsthal admired Fritzi Massary and Richard Tauber. Neither Strauss nor anyone else realized at the time that the greatest operas of the 1920s were being written by Janáček.

Although there is a gap of six years—1918–24—in the operatic collaboration between Strauss and Hofmannsthal, this does not imply a breakdown in their relationship. It reflects the difficulty they had in finding a mutually acceptable subject and also their changed circumstances since the war. Early in 1920, noting Strauss's renewed interest in ballet, Hofmannsthal suggested a *divertissement* and offered a 'light-hearted, operetta-like three-act sketch which closely approaches the world of Lucian' (this was called *Danae* and was to be the basis of a Strauss opera fourteen years later). Neither suggestion was taken up. In 1922 came the collaboration on Beethoven's *Die Ruinen von Athen*.

But in February of that year Hofmannsthal took Strauss an outline for an opera about Helen of Troy. Strauss assented, but progress was slow. A year later Hofmannsthal wrote of his difficulties in finding the right style for a scenario 'of a lighter kind'. He added: 'What you told me recently of the unbridgeable gulf between your music even at its lightest, and the common-or-garden operetta did not need saying at all.' Hofmannsthal had never forgotten hearing Strauss say to Pauline in a Berlin restaurant when discussing Lehár: 'In a few bars of mine there is more music than in a whole Lehár operetta.' Returning from South America in September 1923, Strauss wrote of how he hoped to find *Helena* awaiting him 'preferably with entertaining ballet interludes; a few delightful elf or spirit choruses would also be most welcome'.

'Tell yourself that you mean to handle it as if it were to be merely an operetta,' Hofmannsthal advised him. This, and more in the same vein, perhaps deluded Strauss into the belief that he was getting the Offenbach *Belle Hélène* of the twentieth century, whereas Hofmannsthal's fatal penchant for mythological philosophizing took command, producing an extraordinary plot in which an Egyptian sorceress carries off Helen and Menelaus, after their marriage, to an oasis where a Sheikh and his son fall in love with Helen. Into this, Hofmannsthal worked magic potions, a talking sea-shell, and some obscure symbolism about death and marriage with Faustian overtones. When Strauss told Romain Rolland about it, Rolland commented in his diary: 'Why does Strauss, who so well realizes his inaptitude for great subjects of thought, let himself be caught by them again?' On the other hand, George Marek's assertion [1] that in his letters to Hofmannsthal Strauss showed little conviction is wide of the mark, at any rate at the start. 'Most of it virtually sets itself to music,' he wrote from Garmisch in October 1923 when he had received Act I.

[1] G. Marek: *Richard Strauss: the Life of a Non-Hero* (London, 1967), p. 261.

'It's coming on unbelievably fast and is giving me no end of pleasure.' (He even composed a stage direction again.) A fortnight later: 'Everything so far is wonderful.' Hofmannsthal was delighted: it reminded him, he said, of the cheerful way Strauss had received *Rosenkavalier*. But Act II was a different matter. Strauss kept asking for it and Hofmannsthal kept telling him how good it would be but he could make it better still. It was the familiar pattern, but Hofmannsthal was writing under difficulties. The privations of the time greatly affected him: he told Strauss of 'sleepless nights, eternal headaches and nightmares' and badgered him about the project for a film of *Rosenkavalier* because of his precarious financial state. He asked for the loan of a particular book because 'at the moment I cannot afford to buy any'.

By 31st July 1924 the first draft of Act I was composed. Strauss had some of Act II by now but made little progress. He could not find the style for the Egyptian oasis, and it is significant that when Hofmannsthal had first told him the plot he said after Act I: 'Surely that's the end? What could happen in the second act?' In the last months of 1924 he wrote a work for the one-armed pianist Paul Wittgenstein in fulfilment of a request made some time before.[1] Stimulus came from the recovery of his son Franz, who had contracted typhus in Egypt just after his marriage, and Strauss called the new work *Parergon zur Symphonia Domestica*, basing it on the Child's theme from *Domestica*.

The year 1925 was comparatively uneventful for him. He took no part in the *Rosenkavalier* film, leaving Hofmannsthal to provide the expanded plot and sub-titles and Otto Singer and Karl Alwin to arrange the music, though he composed a new march. He also left to his son the editing for publication of selections from his correspondence with Hofmannsthal.[2] In June

[1] Wittgenstein also commissioned works from Ravel, Prokofiev, Britten, Franz Schmidt and others.
[2] F. Strauss (ed.): *Briefwechsel mit Hugo von Hofmannsthal* (Vienna, 1925).

87

he was still 'stuck' near the start of Act II of *Helena* where the Sheikh enters. He found it difficult to avoid 'degenerating into the so-called realism of *Salome*'. At Hofmannsthal's urgent request he conducted the first performance of the *Rosenkavalier* film in Dresden on 10th January 1926, and in April went to conduct it in London where he also made an electrical recording of some orchestral extracts.[1] In March, Strauss had played Act I of *Helena* to Hofmannsthal who wrote that he was 'more delighted . . . than, I believe, about any of your other composi- tions ever . . . Everything so light and transparent, for all its high, noble seriousness'. In May the full score was finished and Strauss wrote: 'I am off to Greece tomorrow [5th May] to get a few beautiful tunes for Act II—even though my biographer, Herr Specht, considers it old-fashioned that nowadays I have *only* the ambition to "make beautiful music".'

Even so, the opera was not completed for another sixteen months. In the meantime Strauss had re-visited England in April and November 1926 and in December made his peace with the Vienna Opera when he conducted *Elektra*. He was still an active and powerful *éminence grise* in its affairs. For example, in June 1926 he had confided to Hofmannsthal: 'A re-engagement of Weingartner, even as a guest conductor, would be a bad thing. . . . The aim is still: Clemens Krauss as Director with two chief producers: Wallerstein and Turnau.' The Vienna-born con- ductor Krauss, thirty-three years old in 1926, had caught Strauss's eye when he was an assistant conductor at the Vienna Opera from 1922 to 1924. Since 1924 he had been director of Frankfurt Opera, where he had conducted a *Frau ohne Schatten* which Strauss had admired. Strauss was to entice him back to Vienna in 1929 as successor to Schalk. At the age of thirty-six

[1] 'Selected orchestral passages' from the film version of *Der Rosen- kavalier*, Augmented Tivoli Orchestra conducted by R. Strauss, HMV D 1094–7 (seven sides). Recorded 13th April 1926 in Queen's Hall.

Krauss was the youngest director since Mahler, and a year younger than Mahler had been on taking office in 1897.

On 8th October 1927 Strauss completed the full score of *Die ägyptische Helena*, saying that it had 'turned out very beautiful, brilliant yet simple'. The first performance was in Dresden on 6th June 1928, with Elisabeth Rethberg as Helen. Fritz Busch conducted. Leo Wurmser was on the staff of the State Opera and has left an enlightening account of the final rehearsals.[1] Busch had been ill and had missed all the piano rehearsals. Strauss was more interested in the production than in the music (no doubt he was still worried by the sea-shell, which he had described to Hofmannsthal as 'rather like a gramophone'). Pauline sat in the front of the stalls clamouring for real horses in the desert scene and complaining that there was not enough thunder at the end of Act I. Strauss let her have more, saying *sotto voce* to the orchestra: 'Women always want to thunder.' At the first dress rehearsal Busch conducted the first act while Strauss followed the score. He then asked Busch to let him conduct. 'It was like a different opera: one big broad line from beginning to end, the right tempi and rubatos, co-operation with the singers and many of the 4/4 passages beaten in 2.'

The opera flopped, not only in Dresden but in Vienna five days later, when Strauss conducted and Jeritza sang, and in Berlin, Munich, Hamburg and New York (with Jeritza) later the same year. 'Ponderous, dreary, dated, mediocre' were among the critics' adjectives. Some years later, when it was rehearsed at Salzburg, Stefan Zweig sat with Strauss as he listened:

All at once he began to drum inaudibly and impatiently with his fingers upon the arm of the chair. Then he whispered to me: 'Bad, very bad! That spot is blank.' And again, after a few minutes: 'If I could cut that out! O Lord, Lord, that's just hollow, and too long, much too long!' A little later: 'Look, that's good!' He appraised his

[1] L. Wurmser: *Richard Strauss as an Opera Conductor*.

own work as objectively and unconcernedly as if he were hearing the music for the first time and as if it were written by a composer unknown to him.[1]

This objectivity deluded Fritz Busch into the conclusion that Strauss was not 'penetrated and possessed' by his marvellous talents like other great artists but 'simply wears them like a suit of clothes which can be taken off at will'. Busch should have looked at Strauss's eyes, described by Zweig as 'perhaps the most watchful eyes I have ever seen in a composer, not daemonic but somehow clearsighted, the eyes of a man who recognizes his mission down to its very fundamentals'. This clearsightedness was often mistaken for cold detachment, whereas it was the hallmark of Strauss's continual striving to realize himself to the full.

What was to be the last Strauss-Hofmannsthal opera began with a remark in a letter from Strauss on 12th September 1922: 'I feel like doing another *Rosenkavalier* just now!' A year later he dropped the same hint: 'A second *Rosenkavalier*, without its mistakes and *longueurs*! You'll just *have* to write that for me some day: I haven't spoken my last word yet in that genre.' As work on *Helena* ended, Strauss's usual restlessness set in. On 1st October 1927 Hofmannsthal wrote: 'Two years ago I occupied myself with a comedy. . . . It was called *The Cabby as Count* (*Der Fiaker als Graf*). . . . Last night it occurred to me that this comedy might perhaps be done for music, with the text in a light vein.' There was a ballroom scene [2] of 'enchanting possibilities', he said, and a touch of *Rosenkavalier* about it, with 'a most attractive woman as the central figure'.

On 13th November he told Strauss that the action of *Der Fiaker* was too flimsy for an opera, but he had combined 'features of this cabbies' world with elements from another projected comedy' to give him the scenario for a three-act opera, 'indeed

[1] S. Zweig: *The World of Yesterday* (London, 1943).
[2] At the annual Vienna cabbies' festival a carnival queen was chosen. All social barriers were relaxed.

almost an operetta . . . which in gaiety does not fall short of
Fledermaus, is kindred to *Rosenkavalier*, without any self-
repetition'. He had had the inspired idea of incorporating the
plot of his short story *Lucidor*, written in 1909, and a week later
he was still bubbling. 'The characters . . . are cutting their capers
under my very nose . . . the comedy might turn out better than
Rosenkavalier. . . . The two girls (sopranos) could develop into
magnificent (singing) parts. . . . As lovers a high tenor and a
baritone. This latter is the most remarkable character in the piece,
from a semi-alien world (Croatia), half buffo and yet a grand
fellow capable of deep feelings, wild and gentle, almost daemonic.'

On 16th December Hofmannsthal read Strauss the outline of
what he had already titled *Arabella*. Here at long last was a
subject Strauss could understand: no Freudian symbolism, no
Faustian mythology. His reaction was closely and intelligently
critical. He did not want this Croatian grand fellow as the main
character. 'The character which ensured final victory for *Rosenkavalier* is the Marschallin. . . The new piece . . . lacks
a genuinely interesting female character.' Don't worry, Hofmannsthal replied, this Croatian, Mandryka, sets the action going
but the main character is Arabella: 'She is the queen of the big
ball and of the whole piece and, as in a fairy-tale, she marries the
rich stranger in the end.' He sent the libretto of the first act to
Strauss at the end of April 1928.

Strauss had many criticisms to make, chiefly that Arabella was
not yet a part. Hofmannsthal patiently revised it. 'We understand
each other better every year,' Strauss wrote. 'A pity such good,
continuous progress towards perfection must come to an end
some day.' He made detailed suggestions, just as he had for Act
II of *Rosenkavalier*—'it seems to me we've reached the same
point'. By August 1928 they had made many changes, but on
1st November Strauss confessed he did not yet feel enthusiastic
enough to start writing the music. They met in Vienna on 29th
December and talked it over. Strauss liked Acts II and III and

Richard Strauss

Hofmannsthal agreed to re-draft Act I. Progress was slow, both men being ill in the early part of 1929. 'Could a little more lyricism be fitted into *Arabella*?' Strauss pleaded. 'The *aria*, after all, is the soul of opera. . . . Separate numbers with recitatives in between. That's what opera was, is and remains.' On 2nd July Hofmannsthal explained his revisions, which met all Strauss's objections. Strauss was thrilled. Just one thing more, he said; he still wanted the act to end with a long aria for Arabella. Hofmannsthal sent him the text of 'Mein Elemer' on the 10th, and on the 14th Strauss telegraphed: 'First act excellent. Many thanks and congratulations'.

Hofmannsthal never opened the telegram. On 13th July his son Franz had shot himself. The great poet was grief-stricken. For three years he had been suffering from arterio-sclerosis and as he dressed to attend Franz's funeral on 15th July he had a stroke and died a few minutes later. Strauss wrote to his widow next day from Garmisch: 'No musician ever found such a helper and supporter. No one will ever replace him for me or the world of music.' It was nearly thirty years since Hofmannsthal had first written to Strauss. They had collaborated on six major operas and several lesser works. 'I believe,' Hofmannsthal had written, 'that they, not all of them, but nearly all of them, with their inseparable fusion of poetry and music, will continue to live for some considerable time and will give pleasure to several generations.' Despite all their bickering, these two men understood one another. Hofmannsthal's private tribute to Strauss on the composer's sixtieth birthday in 1924 should not be overlooked in any assessment of their strange relationship: 'The only person who always recognized whatever there was, who received it with real joy, received it productively and translated it into higher reality, was you.'

12   Under the Nazis

With his collaborator dead and only one act of the *Arabella* libretto in its final form, Strauss eagerly began to compose the music as a dedicated tribute. By September 1929 Act I was almost sketched but progress became slower as he realized, when problems arose, that he was on his own. He willingly laid it aside when the Czech producer Lothar Wallerstein, at Clemens Krauss's suggestion, asked him to collaborate in preparing a new version of Mozart's *Idomeneo*, then practically unknown. Strauss worked on this through 1930. He rearranged numbers, composed new music for every recitative, added an interlude and a closing ensemble. He conducted the first performance at the Vienna Opera on 16th April 1931.

During the late summer of 1931 Anton Kippenburg, the publisher, called on Strauss and mentioned one of his authors, Stefan Zweig, who at this date was fifty and at the height of his popularity as novelist and biographer. 'Ask him if he has an opera libretto for me,' Strauss said. This led to a meeting in November when Zweig suggested a free adaptation of Ben Jonson's *Epicene, or the Silent Woman* (*Die schweigsame Frau*) on the lines of his *Volpone* adaptation, which Strauss had enjoyed. Zweig described later [1] how delighted he was by Strauss's quick response:

While the nature of the material was being explained to him he was already shaping it dramatically and adjusting it astonishingly to the

[1] S. Zweig: *The World of Yesterday.*

93

limits of his own abilities of which he was uncannily cognizant. . . .
'I am not one to compose long melodies as did Mozart. I can't get
beyond short themes. But what I can do is to utilize such a theme,
paraphrase it and extract everything that is in it, and I don't think
there's anybody today who can match me at that.'

In mid-June of 1932 Zweig delivered the first section of Act I of
Die schweigsame Frau. 'It is delightful,' Strauss told him, 'the
born comic opera . . . more suited to music than either *Figaro* or
The Barber of Seville. . . . I am burning to get started on it in
earnest.' But the Dresden Intendant, Alfred Reucker, and Busch
urged the claims of *Arabella*. Strauss completed it on 12th
October, with a dedication to them.

On 17th January 1933 the complete Zweig libretto was in
Strauss's hands. Thirteen days later the German President,
Hindenburg, appointed Adolf Hitler as Chancellor. Four weeks
later, as a result of the Reichstag Fire, Hitler established one-
party rule, the rule of his National Socialists who, since September 1930, had been the second largest party and had risen to
favour because of general disillusionment, rising unemployment
and their selection of a scapegoat for all Germany's woes—the
Jews. Strauss who, like other artists, had regarded himself as
impervious to all politicians, was slowly to find that the Nazis
could not be disregarded. His conduct was often contradictory,
and his name has been besmirched because of that conduct. All
that follows should, however, be viewed in the context of a
comment passed by the shrewd Hofmannsthal in a letter to
Strauss in December 1926. He was referring to the *rapproche-
ment* with the Vienna Opera, and added: 'I do not think you
care very much about these things—or indeed about almost anything apart from your productive work.' It should also be
remembered that Strauss's wealth made him unpopular. F. W.
Gaisberg, of the Gramophone Company, wrote to Elgar in April
1932 describing Strauss, Lehár, Oscar Straus and Kalman as
having 'usurped the position of wealth and influence formerly

occupied by the great Viennese bankers. . . . They seem to be the only ones in Vienna who have any money and are the envy of the threadbare Viennese.' [1]

Strauss's world was music, mostly his own music, and he was wholly wrapped up in it, composing, conducting, planning. His career began in the old Germany of ducal courts. They had gone, he remained. He had paid them lip-service, a motet for a wedding, a military march for some dreadful parade, and they left him alone. After all, he had defeated the Kaiser over *Salome*, why should these Nazis be any different? He was the man to take them on, for his own sake. War, hunger, currency deflation—these he regarded as personal slights, interfering with his work. He was almost naïve in his belief that nothing could touch him. But did he not see that these men were evil? What about the treatment of the Jews? Strauss was very far from being alone, in Germany and elsewhere, in viewing Hitler's 1933–9 Germany in a light quite different from that in which we, with the benefit of hindsight, see it so clearly.

Why did he not leave, as Thomas Mann did? Why did he not make a gesture of protest, as Toscanini did? The answer is that he was not a deep thinker, like Mann, and he was not cut out for heroics, like Toscanini and Hubermann. In Paris in 1900 he had said to Rolland: 'I am not a hero, I haven't the necessary strength. I prefer to withdraw.' Otto Klemperer said that Strauss remained because in Germany there were fifty-six opera houses and in America two, and the reduction of income involved in such a gesture was not to be contemplated. He was also —this creator of the Marschallin and the Empress—human; and his beloved daughter-in-law was Jewish, his grandchildren therefore half-Jewish, he had worked for over twenty years with the half-Jew Hofmannsthal, his publisher was a Jew, and his new librettist was a Jew. Which of us, except authors like George

[1] J. N. Moore: *Elgar on Record* (London, 1974), p. 167.

Marek and film-makers like Ken Russell who see life in black-and-white with no blurred edges, dare make a moral judgment on Strauss? Or on Shostakovich? Schoenberg said at this period: 'There are more important things today than art.' It was not that Strauss believed that nothing was more important than art: he simply did not recognize the conflict, a symptom of his blinkered mentality as a court composer. He kept his nose in his score and ignored the raised voices in the next room.

The cultural climate of the new régime was soon apparent. On 7th March 1933, when Busch, who was not a Jew, entered the pit to conduct *Il Trovatore* at Dresden he was received with obscene catcalls. He and Reucker were dismissed from their posts. So, in Berlin, were Klemperer and Reinhardt. At a meeting in Berlin some days later, Strauss made it clear that if Busch did not conduct and Reucker produce the *Arabella* première, then it was off. He meant it, and tried to withdraw the work but was held to his contracts. Krauss conducted the first performance, at Dresden, on 1st July, with Viorica Ursuleac as Arabella and Alfred Jerger as Mandryka. Later it was performed in Berlin, Munich and Vienna (21st October, with Lehmann in the title-rôle). It was a success of a kind, but the inevitable (and misleading) comparisons with *Der Rosenkavalier* were to its disadvantage. The wits in Vienna called it *Der Sklerosenkavalier*.

In March 1933, also, Bruno Walter was ordered not to conduct a Berlin Philharmonic concert and was warned that if he did, the hall would be wrecked. Heavy pressure was exerted on Strauss to conduct in Walter's place, not only by the Nazis but by Jewish impresarios. He agreed and gave his fee to the orchestra, who were to have been paid by Walter. He did it, he said, for their sake. In the summer he agreed to conduct *Parsifal* at Bayreuth in place of Toscanini, who had withdrawn because of 'painful events'. Toscanini is said to have commented: 'To Strauss the composer I take off my hat; to Strauss the man I put it on again.' But what must have weighed most heavily with Strauss was that

1933 was the fiftieth anniversary of Wagner's death. Not unnaturally Strauss's actions were interpreted as showing his approval of the régime and this view was strengthened when, on 15th November, Joseph Goebbels, the Nazi Minister of Propaganda, established a state music bureau, the Reichsmusikkammer, and announced, without consulting him, that Strauss was its president.

Some months later Strauss explained this 'mime' to Zweig as 'knowing where my artistic duty lies. Under any régime I would have taken on these pestiferous honorary positions, but neither Kaiser Wilhelm nor Herr Rathenau [1] has ever dictated to me'. A factor not to be ignored was his determination to defeat Nazi resistance to signing the 1934 Berne copyright agreement, so vital to the economic well-being of his fellow-composers.

Strauss's principal creative occupation during late 1932 and early 1933 was a major revision of Act II of *Die ägyptische Helena* to try to make it dramatically intelligible. The libretto was amended by Lothar Wallerstein and the new version was performed under Krauss at the Salzburg Festival on 14th August 1933, with Ursuleac as Helen but with no more success. Strauss had by then lost interest, for he was excited by Zweig's libretto, which he set almost without alteration. *Die schweigsame Frau* was completed in short score by November 1933 and the full score was finished on 20th October 1934, after Strauss had passed his seventieth birthday.

Through the proscribing of non-Aryans, whereby theatres were forbidden to produce works by Jews, Zweig was obviously threatened. The news that Strauss was at work on a libretto by Zweig was announced on the radio and described as 'scandalous'.

[1] Walther Rathenau (1867–1922) was an industrialist who from 1916 directed Germany's war economy and in 1918 founded a new Democratic Party. In the Weimar Republic he was first Minister of Reconstruction (1921) and later Foreign Minister. He was assassinated by anti-Semitic nationalists.

Zweig knew this meant the end of the collaboration, but Strauss was sure the law did not apply to Austrians. He approached Goebbels, who agreed that there were no political accusations against Zweig. That was in May 1934; in August, at Bayreuth, Goebbels again raised the matter and warned Strauss there might be trouble at the première. However, it was referred to Hitler, who was sent the libretto and told Strauss personally that he would allow—and attend—the performance even though it broke the laws. At this point the Nazis seemed unwilling to incense world opinion by acting against Strauss.

But they had no compunction, a few days later, in forbidding him to conduct *Fidelio* at the Salzburg Festival because Walter and Toscanini were taking part. He was already disillusioned with the Reichsmusikkammer, which, without reference to him, was extending its non-Aryan policy to forbid performances of *Carmen* and was prohibiting the use by artists and musicians of 'foreign-sounding names'. Strauss wrote to a friend on 4th October 1934: 'I have no wish to take part in such embarrassing blunders . . . my extensive and serious proposals for reform were rejected by the Minister. Time is too precious for me to participate in such dilettantish rubbish.' Just before Christmas he composed the Hymn commissioned from him for the opening ceremony of the Olympic Games to be held in Berlin in August 1936. To Zweig he wrote of composing it for 'this common lot—I, the outspoken enemy and despiser of all sport!'

Throughout this period Strauss was constantly imploring Zweig, who was in Zürich, to collaborate with him again; he could not believe that providence would deprive him of such a librettist. Why not work secretly, he suggested; he would lock the operas in a drawer. 'In a few years, when our works will be ready, the world will probably look very different' (24th August 1934). 'I will *not* relinquish you just because we now have an anti-Semitic government.' Zweig was more realistic. The most he would do, he said, would be to suggest subjects and to supervise their completion by others. On 17th June 1935 Strauss exploded in exasperation:

Your letter of the 15th drives me to despair! This Jewish obstinacy! It is enough to drive one to anti-Semitism! This racial pride, this feeling of solidarity—even I feel a difference. Do you imagine I have ever been guided in any course of action by the thought that I am Germanic (perhaps, *qui le sait*)? Do you suppose that Mozart was consciously 'Aryan' in his composing? For me there are only two sorts of people: those who have talent and those who haven't, and for me the People only begin to exist when they become the Audience. It's all the same to me if they come from China, Upper Bavaria, New Zealand or Berlin, so long as they have paid full price at the box office.

He then wrote the remark about standing in for Walter and Toscanini and the 'pestiferous' post of Reichsmusikkammer president quoted earlier.

Strauss posted this letter in Dresden, where he was attending rehearsals of *Die schweigsame Frau*. Two days before the première Strauss sent for a proof of the programme and saw that Zweig's name had been omitted. Furious, he demanded its restoration or he would return home. Paul Adolph, the intendant, re-inserted Zweig's credit line. He was later dismissed. The first performance, on 24th June, was a success. Karl Böhm conducted and Maria Cebotari sang the principal part. But Hitler and Goebbels did not attend, as they had promised. Bad weather had prevented their flight, it was said. Three more performances were given; after the fourth, in the second week of July, the opera was banned throughout Germany. Strauss's letter to Zweig had been intercepted by the State police and sent to Hitler on 1st July by a *Gauleiter*. Five days later, on Goebbels's orders, two officials called on Strauss to demand his resignation from the presidency of the Reichsmusikkammer 'on the grounds of ill-health'. A week later Strauss wrote to Hitler to explain the background of his letter to Zweig, that its 'improvised sentences', dashed off 'in a moment of ill-humour', did not 'represent my view of the world nor my true conviction'. He added:

> My whole life belongs to German music and to a tireless effort to elevate German culture. I have never been active politically nor even expressed myself in politics. Therefore I believe that I will find understanding from you, the great architect of German social life. . . . I will devote the few years still granted to me only to the purest and most ideal goals. . . . I beg you, my Führer, most humbly to receive me for a personal discussion.

There was no response to this letter of a frightened old man.

During these perilous days Strauss wrote three secret memoranda, not published until after his death, in which he commented on these affairs. They are worth quotation:

> These are sad times when an artist of my standing has to ask a brat of a Minister what he is permitted to compose, or perform. I belong to a nation of 'servants and waiters' and almost envy the racially persecuted Stefan Zweig. . . . I must confess I do not understand this Jewish solidarity and I regret that the artist in Zweig is unable to rise above political vagaries.

But that was written before he knew the Gestapo had his letter. In a later addition he confessed his total inability to understand the Nazis' Aryan policy. He acknowledged the help and inspiration he had received from Jews, adding that his own most malicious enemies had been Aryans—Perfall, Schalk and Weingartner among them. At the end of that crucial year of 1935 Strauss received a State questionnaire asking whether he was Aryan and requiring the names of two witnesses to his professional ability. He wrote: 'Mozart and Richard Wagner'. He was still Till Eulenspiegel, even if the heavens were beginning to fall.

13 Gregor and Krauss

In 1934 Strauss and Zweig had discussed their next projects. Zweig suggested a comedy by the eighteenth-century Abbé Casti called *Prima la Musica, poi le Parole*. This title, which was the germ of *Capriccio*, intrigued Strauss, but he was keen on an historical subject based on the medieval Peace of Constanz. Zweig, an earnest pacifist, leapt at the idea, and Strauss had by then read Calderón's play *La Redención de Breda*, which deals with Spinola's magnanimity to the defeated Dutch army in 1625. Zweig suggested transferring the action to the Peace of Osnabrück, which ended the Thirty Years' War, and calling the one-act opera *24th October 1648*.

Writing to Strauss on 21st August, Zweig outlined his plot—a besieged fortress where the Commandant refuses to yield to pleas to surrender but, knowing he can no longer hold out, plans to blow it up, himself with it. His wife prepares to die with him. The fuse is lit, but is extinguished when a cannon shot is heard. They prepare to die in open battle, but news of peace comes. The enemy Commandant arrives and the two adversaries embrace, vowing to work for a new world.

A further indication to Strauss that he could no longer pretend that politics and art were separate worlds was given in December 1934, when Furtwängler was forced to resign from the Berlin Philharmonic and had his passport confiscated because he defended Hindemith against the condemnation of *Mathis der Maler* by the Nazis. Strauss was in Amsterdam to conduct *Arabella*. Goebbels announced that he had received a telegram

from Strauss congratulating him on his actions against Furtwängler. It was a forgery. Strauss did not send it, and it would
have been wholly untypical of him to have done so. So he cannot
have been unprepared for the intensification of pressure against
his collaboration with Zweig, who suggested other librettists,
among them Josef Gregor, a Viennese theatrical archivist and
historian. Gregor called on Strauss in April 1935 with a draft
libretto based—at Zweig's prompting—on Hofmannsthal's
Semiramis project which Strauss had always coveted. But Strauss
sent him packing. On 2nd June 1935 Strauss met Zweig at
Bregenz in Austria, when it emerged that he was still devoted to
the *1648* opera. Zweig said Gregor was the man for it and Strauss,
grudgingly, saw him on 7th July. Gregor, who was obsequiously
anxious for the distinction of becoming Hofmannsthal's successor, took six sketch-libretti from which Strauss selected three, the
1648 theme, an opera on the Daphne legend and another not
positively identified (probably *Danae*).

In August 1935 Strauss was in Vichy to preside at the festival
of the International Society of Composers. At the memorial
concert for Dukas, who was of Jewish origin, he conducted
L'Apprenti sorcier. The German Ambassador to France withdrew
from the festival. This gesture by Strauss would be noted in
Berlin. It is noticeable that between 1935 and 1939 Strauss
accepted as many conducting engagements outside Germany as
he could. From the mid-1920s also, he went for 'a cure' each
summer at such spas as Carlsbad, Kissingen, Bad Nauheim,
Baden-Baden and Baden-bei-Zürich.

Strauss showed no pleasure in the partnership with Gregor.
He was still unconvinced by Zweig's attitude and he treated
Gregor in a manner that suggests he was enjoying being 'top
dog' after all the years of tact and cajolery with Hofmannsthal.
His reception of Gregor's libretto for *1648* was expressed thus:
'I don't think I can ever find music for it. These are not real
people. . . . The dialogue of the two commandants . . . is how two

schoolmasters would hold a conversation on a given subject:
"30 Years' War".'

Zweig supervised the work—which in October 1935 was
retitled *Friedenstag* (*Day of Peace*)—and revised the scene
between the commandants. Strauss thanked him warmly, adding:
'I have now been busying myself for a few weeks with composing it, but it won't turn into the sort of music I must expect
from myself. The material is after all a bit too everyday—
soldiers, war, hunger, medieval heroism, people all dying
together—it doesn't really suit me.' But he continued, with
Gregor living at Garmisch. The opera was completed on 16th
June 1936, but no plans were made to perform it.

Gregor also worked quickly on the second of the libretti in
which Strauss had shown interest and by October 1935 had
completed a draft of *Daphne*. Strauss wrote to Zweig: 'No doubt
our dear friend is very gifted, but what is lacking is strength and
ideas . . . as also, which is most disturbing, any distinctive
theatrical atmosphere. . . . Words upon words—schoolmaster
banalities.' He began composition in the summer of 1936,
interrupting it for a visit to London in November to conduct the
Dresden State Opera's performance of *Ariadne auf Naxos* at
Covent Garden on the 6th. On the previous evening he was
presented by Sir Hugh Allen with the Gold Medal of the Royal
Philharmonic Society before a performance of *Also sprach
Zarathustra* conducted by Boult.

Strauss pondered for the best part of a year over the finale of
Daphne. Gregor had planned the work as a double bill with
Friedenstag, each to end with a cantata-like chorus, but Strauss
did not care for this in *Daphne*. He thought it absurd if people
sang to Daphne after her metamorphosis into a tree; so did
Clemens Krauss, who solved the problem for him. Strauss wrote
to Gregor on 12th May 1937: 'Now, in the moonlight, but fully
visible, the miracle of transformation is slowly worked upon her
—*only with the orchestra alone!* . . . Right at the end, when the

tree stands there complete, she should sing without words—only as a voice of nature—eight more bars of the Laurel-motif!'

Friedenstag was dedicated to Clemens Krauss and his wife Viorica Ursuleac, and Krauss put pressure on Strauss (much to Gregor's annoyance) to allow it to be given separately, preceded by Beethoven's *Prometheus* ballet, at the Munich festival on 24th July 1938—Strauss's first operatic première in his native city. The cast included Ursuleac, Hans Hotter and Ludwig Weber. Strauss was now favourable to the Munich State Opera, for Krauss had become director in 1937, with Rudolf Hartmann as producer and Ludwig Sievert as stage designer. This famous trio made a speciality of Strauss's operas, with such singers as Ursuleac, Adèle Kern and Julius Patzak. The two works were first presented as a double bill in Dresden on 15th October 1938 when the dedicatee of *Daphne*, Karl Böhm, conducted its first performance. Daphne was sung by Margaret Teschemacher, Apollo by Torsten Ralf and Leukippos by Martin Kremer. A few more double performances were given, one of them at Vienna in June 1939 as part of the comprehensive celebrations of Strauss's seventy-fifth birthday not only in the Austrian capital under Krauss but in Munich, Berlin and, of course, Dresden. Since then *Daphne* has made its way separately. It was Pauline's favourite among her husband's operas.

During 1936 Willi Schuh, the critic and Straussian authority, sent from Zürich a three-year-old copy of the magazine *Corona* in which had been printed Hofmannsthal's scenario *Danae, oder die Vernunftheirat* (*Danae*, or *The Marriage of Convenience*). Hofmannsthal had sent this to Strauss in April 1920, but perhaps because he was so involved in Vienna, Strauss put it in a drawer where it lay until 1933 when he let *Corona* have it. But now he was thrilled and asked Gregor if he had read it. Gregor replied that he had prepared a draft of his own on this mythological subject, but Strauss brusquely said he wanted the Hofmannsthal sketch re-worked. He began to compose the opera as a means of isolating the various problems, most of which, as the correspondence shows,[1] centred on Jupiter and Midas. The opera's title was at first *King Midas* but was changed at Viorica Ursuleac's suggestion to *Die Liebe der Danae* (*The Love of Danae*).

The third act proved especially intractable until Krauss made valuable suggestions, although this brought Strauss and Gregor near to a final breach and caused Gregor to stay away from the première of *Daphne*. But Strauss had the ending he wanted and saw the chances it offered to him. 'I can continue the farewell mood of Jupiter to the end,' he wrote to Gregor in 1939. 'In the last scene . . . you need not restrict yourself for space. If it contains genuine wisdom and beautiful poetry. . . I will cope! And in a posthumous work everything is allowed!' He completed it on 28th June 1940, convinced he would never hear it. *Danae*, he told Gregor, must not be staged until at least two years after the end of hostilities—'that is to say . . . after my death. So that's how long you'll have to be patient'.

Nevertheless he was already at work on another opera. He had always been deeply concerned with the relationship between music and words and in 1933 had remarked to Krauss that he would like to write 'an opera about opera . . . I really ought to write something of this sort, no lyricism, no arias, but dry wit, intelligent dialogue—a theatrical fugue'. That was why he was drawn to Zweig's suggestion of the Casti comedy *Prima la Musica; poi le Parole*, which Salieri had set and which describes the composition of a scena by composer and librettist for their patron. Zweig wanted to re-shape it and in June 1935, when he had decided to withdraw, he passed to Gregor his idea that the setting should be a feudal castle where strolling players put on an entertainment under the direction of a caricature of Max Reinhardt—a similar situation to the *Ariadne* prologue. Strauss rejected the Gregor libretto—he was furious it was not by Zweig

[1] R. Tenschert (ed.): *Briefwechsel mit Joseph Gregor* (Salzburg 1955).

and it was because of this that he wrote the fatal letter which the Nazis seized—but revived it in March 1939. Another draft was rejected as 'nothing like what I had in mind'. Eventually Strauss invited Krauss to write it.

By now the principal character had emerged as a woman, the Countess, Strauss's last great soprano stage rôle, and the setting was a French château just before the Revolution. There poet and composer, both in love with her, collaborate in a sonnet. She cannot decide between them, as one cannot decide between words and music. Strauss and Krauss worked well and fast together, each making suggestions in a long and interesting correspondence [1] early in 1940. The introduction and first scene were composed by July and eight months later the opera was finished in sketch. At the end of July 1941 Strauss reported that the full score would be ready that week (it was finished on 3rd August) and that he was 'concerned with making the instrumentation of the last scene especially beautiful for our dear friend [Ursuleac]'. The title, *Capriccio*, and the sub-title 'A conversation piece for music', were suggested by Krauss.

Krauss was at this time supreme in German music-making. A great conductor, he was no less great an opportunist. He made no secret of his support for the Nazis,[2] and undoubtedly this eased Strauss's position because Krauss's devotion to his music ensured its continued performance in Germany and Austria even though the composer was in disfavour. With so many of his colleagues in exile or in hiding, Krauss held several of the highest conductorships and in 1942 became director of the Salzburg Festival. To celebrate this he implored Strauss to let him give the première of *Die Liebe der Danae*, but to no avail. Strauss suggested that *Capriccio* should be staged there: 'Never forget that our *Capriccio* is no piece for the broad public, any

---

[1] *Briefwechsel mit Clemens Krauss* (Munich 1964).
[2] But there is proof beyond doubt that he helped very many victims of Nazi persecution to escape.

more than it should be played in a big house.' But Krauss had won Goebbels's approval for a Strauss Festival in Munich in October 1942 and it was there, on the 28th, that *Capriccio* was first performed and enthusiastically received. Ursuleac sang Countess Madeleine, Horst Taubmann was Flamand and Hans Hotter was Olivier.

Late in 1941 Strauss and his family had moved to Vienna to reoccupy their Belvedere Schlösschen which they had vacated at the start of the war. In Garmisch their position had become precarious because both Strauss and Pauline made no attempt to disguise their contempt for the Nazi authorities, who retaliated by making life difficult for them in material ways and by ensuring ostracism of Alice Strauss, their Jewish daughter-in-law, and her children. So when Baldur von Schirach became governor of Vienna and announced that he would make it once again the cultural centre of Europe, Strauss offered his help if he and his whole family could return to their home. The 'deal' was that Alice and the children would be left alone if Strauss made no public anti-Nazi remarks. (Even so, Pauline is said to have told Schirach at a reception that, when the war was lost, she and Richard would always give him refuge at Garmisch, 'but as for the rest of that gang . . .'). In gratitude for this arrangement, Strauss allowed the Sextet which opens *Capriccio* to be played six months before the stage performance, at a gathering in Schirach's house on 7th May 1942.

Strauss's return coincided with the centenary of the Vienna Philharmonic Orchestra. He had hoped to give them a symphonic poem about the Danube with a choral finale, but, as he explained to the orchestra in a letter on their birthday, 18th February 1942, 'emotion is not as easily turned into music as in the days of the great old masters. . . . I should like to put my words of praise today into one short sentence: "Only he who has *conducted* the Vienna Philharmonic players knows what they are!" But that will remain our very own secret!' The work was never finished, and in gratitude for their congratulations on his eighty-fifth birthday in 1949 he sent the orchestra a page of the sketches inscribed 'A few drops from the dried-up source of the Danube'.

Perhaps it was the atmosphere of Vienna, perhaps it was the knowledge that in *Capriccio* he had written the work he had long had in mind, perhaps it was that in old age his thoughts went back to his youth and shut out the appalling present—whatever the cause, the fact remains that from 1942 dates Strauss's instrumental 'Indian summer', not in my opinion an emergence from decline but an astonishing 'last period' filled with creative flair. Like his own Don Quixote, he had renounced his battles, abandoned his grandiose visions and come home to simpler harmonies. The first manifestation of this new phase was the Second Horn Concerto, hardly credible as the work of a man of seventy-eight, so young is it in heart. He knew it was good but remarked characteristically that it had kept him occupied because 'one can't play skat *all* the time'. Although he and Pauline had recurrent illnesses in the first quarter of 1943, he began work on a sonatina for wind instruments which he sub-titled 'from an invalid's workshop'. During the summer he returned to Garmisch, and in November he completed *An den Baum Daphne*, a setting for unaccompanied chorus of the discarded choral finale of the opera. (Strauss thus salved his conscience about his summary 'sacking' of Gregor.)

On the night of 2nd October 1943 bombs destroyed the Munich National Theatre. 'I am beside myself,' Strauss wrote to his sister Johanna. To Willi Schuh he elaborated what the building meant to him:

. . . consecrated by the first *Tristan* and *Meistersinger* performances; in which seventy-three years ago I heard *Freischütz* for the first time, where my good father sat for forty-nine years in the orchestra as first horn. . . . This is the greatest catastrophe of my life, for which there can be no consolation.

At last the impact of the war penetrated even the rampart of indifference behind which Strauss had tried to entrench himself in cocooned isolation. Shortly after the Munich bombing, Nazi officials visited Garmisch to order Strauss to take evacuees into his large home. He refused, adding: 'I didn't want war. No one had to die on my account.' The remark was reported, and Strauss was saved only through the intervention of Dr Hans Frank, a Nazi leader who later butchered thousands of Poles but apparently liked music. Not entirely saved, however, for Hitler's deputy, Martin Bormann, spoke to Hitler about the affair and on 14th January 1944 transmitted Hitler's order that the Garmisch porter's lodge was to be commandeered and that 'leading party personalities who have hitherto had personal contacts with Dr Richard Strauss are to cease to do so in any way'. Strauss was also forbidden to go to Switzerland for his annual 'cure'.

He moved back to Vienna. There, at least, he was still regarded highly, and in spite of the Nazi hierarchy's other edicts they did not forbid, though they did nothing to encourage, celebration of his eightieth birthday. The music could be honoured, but not its composer. Strauss weeks were held in Dresden and Vienna, where the old man conducted *Symphonia Domestica* and Böhm conducted *Ariadne*. Strauss also recorded on tape almost all his orchestral works, conducting the Vienna Philharmonic, but only that of the *Domestica* survived an air raid. One other major celebration remained. After the success of *Capriccio*, Krauss had at last persuaded Strauss to let him produce *Die Liebe der Danae* and the première was fixed for the Salzburg Festival of 1944. But after the Allied invasion of Europe, Goebbels banned all festivals. For a time it seemed as if Salzburg was excepted, but on 19th July Goebbels cancelled it specifically, though the local *Gauleiter* was still prepared to allow the *Danae* première to go ahead. Ultimately only a dress rehearsal was allowed on 16th August.

Strauss arrived in Salzburg on the 9th, knowing this would

probably be his last première. He attended Krauss's rehearsals, saying little but listening intently. After the orchestra had played the Interlude before the last scene, of which he was especially proud, he went to the rail of the pit, raised his hands in thanks and said: 'Perhaps we'll meet again in a better world.' Rudolf Hartmann, the producer, described what followed: 'He was unable to say any more. . . . I led him gently from the auditorium. A little while later, leaning on my arm, he walked back through Salzburg in bright sunlight. He pointed out the route he wanted to take: "Let's go that way, past my beloved Mozart!"'

To all intents and purposes that historic, strange and emotional first performance was the end of Strauss's operatic career. When Krauss tried to arrange a *Danae* production after the war Strauss adamantly refused. 'Perhaps in five or ten years the new Vienna Opera can open with it,' he wrote. 'Mercury can then personally deliver my greetings telegram.' When Krauss urged collaboration on a successor to *Capriccio* the refusal was graceful and witty but equally firm: 'Do you really believe that . . . anything better or even as good can follow? Isn't this D flat major the best conclusion to my life's work in the theatre? After all, it's only possible to leave *one* will!'

Stefan Zweig shot himself in exile in Brazil in February 1942, leaving a note hoping that his friends might see the dawn—'being too impatient, I go before them'. Romain Rolland died in December 1944. On 1st September 1944 Goebbels closed all German opera houses and theatres. 'My life's work is in ruins,' Strauss wrote to Hartmann; 'it would have been best if the great geniuses of Olympus had called me to them on the 17th August [the day after the *Danae* première].'

Around him his beloved Germany lay devastated. On 12th February 1945 Dresden was totally destroyed and with it the theatre where his most famous operas had been born. 'I am in despair,' he wrote to Gregor. 'The Goethehaus, the world's greatest sanctuary, destroyed! My lovely Dresden—Weimar—Munich, all gone!' In March, the Vienna State Opera House was destroyed. Sixteen months earlier, when Munich's opera house was bombed, Strauss had sketched a few bars which he inscribed 'Mourning for Munich'. He left them on one side, for they reminded him about a waltz he had written early in 1939 for a film about Munich which had been banned by Hitler. He looked it out and added a minor-key section headed 'In Memoriam'. This new version was finished on 24th February 1945. Now he returned to the 'mourning' sketch. Between 13th March and 12th April he composed *Metamorphosen*, a study for twenty-three solo strings, the title referring not to any musical process but to Goethe's use of the term in his old age: Strauss had distracted himself in the 1944–5 winter by re-reading all Goethe. *Meta-*

morphosen is an elegy, profoundly moving and inspired, for the destruction of the German culture which had nurtured Strauss.

At the end of April the Third Reich perished in the flames of Berlin. The Americans had occupied Munich and their soldiers went to the villa at Garmisch. Its owner was no more pleased to see them than he had been to see the Nazi officials. 'I am the composer of *Rosenkavalier*,' he informed them. 'Leave me alone.' At this time he wrote his 'artistic testament' in a letter to Karl Böhm. This was a plan for the revival of opera in Germany and Austria, reverting to his Vienna idea of two or even three theatres, one devoted to established masterpieces—an 'opera museum', the equivalent of the Prado and the Louvre—and the other(s) to lighter works and new works. He sent Böhm a suggested repertoire for each theatre. For the opera museum he selected all Wagner from *Rienzi* to *Götterdämmerung*, five by Gluck, five by Mozart, Bizet's *Carmen*, Beethoven's *Fidelio*, three by Weber, two by Berlioz (*Benvenuto Cellini* and *Les Troyens*), three by Verdi (*Aida, Simone Boccanegra* and *Falstaff*) and nine of his own. For the second house the list is longer. It includes operas by Chabrier, Smetana, Gounod, Korngold, Pfitzner, Auber, Lortzing, Tchaikovsky, Johann Strauss and seven by Richard Strauss, only four by Verdi, with *Otello* specifically excluded, and none by Puccini and Rossini.

Strauss listened to the broadcast announcement of Germany's surrender and to a subsequent performance of the *Eroica* Symphony, a theme from which he had quoted in *Metamorphosen*. 'And *yet* Beethoven was a German,' he said. Still he worked, quoting to friends a saying by the French sculptor Maillol: 'Je ne travaille pas, je m'amuse.' He completed a second Sonatina for sixteen wind instruments, inscribing it 'to the spirit of the immortal Mozart at the end of a life full of thankfulness'.

Life was hard for Strauss and Pauline at Garmisch. Neither was well, Pauline in particular having become something of an invalid. They had had their golden wedding on 10th September

1944. Shall we ever understand this extraordinary marriage between the easy-going, laconic man of genius and the petite, tactless and fearless virago, house-proud to the point of its being an obsession, flash-tempered, bossy, snobbish? Nobody else seems to have liked her much. Alma Mahler found her conversation intellectually beneath contempt. Mahler regarded the Strauss marriage as 'verging on masochism' and Pauline's public displays of temper and temperament as vulgar and embarrassing. Rolland called her 'a terrible wife' and 'a woman in a sick state of nerves'. For all that they dreaded her, opera producers found that her presence at rehearsals often led to good results on the stage because of her suggestions. If one's breath is taken away by her remark at a Paris rehearsal of *Salome* in 1907 that 'it's time we Germans came back to France with bayonets', this is recognizably the same woman who also put no guard on her tongue when speaking about 'the Nazi gang'. The story is told of Strauss on tour in the 1930s reading out 'another lovely letter from Pauline', full of references to him as 'ass, fool, idiot' and stronger terms. 'What is so lovely about that?' his companions asked. 'Ah, you don't understand, the lovely part is between the lines.' If her antipathy to some of her husband's works seemed to verge on dottiness at times, she was also a shrewd and perceptive critic.

Strauss, however, in 1945 continued to 'amuse himself' at his desk with what he called 'wrist exercises'. One of the American soldiers who were invited over the Garmisch threshold was John de Lancy, principal oboist of the Philadelphia Orchestra. He asked Strauss for an oboe work, and what was to become a full-dress concerto was completed in short score on 14th September 1945. A month later Strauss and Pauline yielded to friends' advice and went to Switzerland. All his funds and royalties were 'frozen' in Germany and, because he had held official office under the Nazis, it was expected that Strauss would have to appear before a 'denazification' tribunal. He completed the concerto at

Baden-bei-Zürich at the end of October. A sign of his financial state was that he copied out the full scores of some of his early tone-poems so that these manuscripts could be sold.[1] In January 1946 *Metamorphosen* was given its first performance by the Zürich Collegium Musicum, conducted by Paul Sacher, though Strauss conducted some of the rehearsals. A month later the Oboe Concerto was performed by Marcel Saillet and the Tonhalle Orchestra. (Before the work was published, two years later, Strauss revised and extended the coda of the finale.) [2]

In May 1947 Strauss's friend and publisher, Dr Ernest Roth, suggested, at the instigation of Beecham, that London should hold a Strauss Festival and invite the composer to attend. There was still some doubt in England about Strauss's rôle under Hitler, and it was hoped that renewed personal contact would dispel it. Strauss agreed, and made his first flight at the age of eighty-three on 4th October. Pauline refused to accompany him.

His visit caused the expected stir. To the Press he was laconic and uncommunicative—(asked about his plans for the future, he replied: 'Well, to die')—but he delighted in the Royal Philharmonic Society's reception and dinner in his honour and in visits to art galleries. He attended the rehearsals and performances of Beecham's two concerts with the Royal Philharmonic Orchestra at the Theatre Royal, Drury Lane. The first, on 5th October, was the Suite from *Le Bourgeois Gentilhomme*, the Closing Scene from *Feuersnot*, *Don Quixote*, and the new fantasia from *Die Frau ohne Schatten*. This last work was conducted by one of Beecham's horn-players, who was at the start of his conducting career, Norman Del Mar. During the rehearsal Strauss went to the conductor's desk, 'glumly regarded the score for a few moments, muttered "All my own fault", and went

---

[1] At this time, too, he arranged the *Josephslegende* fragment.

[2] The recording made by Leon Goossens in 1947, and issued in January 1948, includes the original (1946) finale. (Columbia DX 1444–1446, 78 r.p.m.)

away'.[1] The soloist in *Don Quixote* was Paul Tortelier, whom Richard Capell described in the *Daily Telegraph* next day as 'a marvellously gifted young French cellist'. This was his English début.[2] For the second concert on 12th October the programme was *Macbeth*, an entr'acte from *Intermezzo*, *Ein Heldenleben*, and the Closing Scene from *Ariadne*, with Maria Cebotari as Ariadne.

On 19th October Strauss himself conducted the Philharmonia Orchestra at the Albert Hall in *Don Juan*, the *Burleske* (soloist Alfred Blumen), the *Rosenkavalier* Waltzes and the *Symphonia Domestica*. Before going on to the platform he said to Roth: 'So the old horse ambles out of the stables once more.' It was at a rehearsal for one of these concerts that he made one of his most frequently quoted self-analyses. 'No,' he told the orchestra, 'I know what I want, and I know what I meant when I wrote this. After all, I may not be a first-rate composer, but I *am* a first-class second-rate composer.' He also attended the first of two B.B.C. Third Programme performances of *Elektra*, in which on 24th and 26th October Beecham conducted the B.B.C. Chorus and the Royal Philharmonic Orchestra at the Maida Vale studio. Strauss warmly embraced his English champion at the end.[3] What was to be his last public appearance in England was at the Albert Hall on 29th October when he conducted *Till Eulenspiegel* at a B.B.C. Symphony Orchestra concert, the remainder of which was conducted by Sir Adrian Boult. He flew back to Switzerland two days later and Roth told the Press that he took with him all

[1] N. Del Mar: *Richard Strauss: a critical commentary on his life and works*, Vol. I, p. xi.

[2] He was not quite so young as this suggests, being thirty-three. Ten years earlier he had first played the work under Strauss's direction and Pauline had told him it was the first time she had ever enjoyed it— another of her extraordinary comments on her husband's music.

[3] Although Leo Wurmser in his article on Strauss as an opera conductor, op. cit., wrote that 'what went on in the difficult and complicated scenes was nobody's business'.

the earnings of his four-week stay. In addition, by the recent treaty with Austria, he recovered royalties due since 16th September 1946. After tax, the sum taken back was slightly under £1,000.[1]

In November came signs of a bladder infection, but this did not prevent Strauss from setting to work at once on some sketches for a Duett-Concertino for clarinet and bassoon, with strings and harp, which he completed on 16th December. This had been in his mind since October 1946, as we know from a letter of that date to Hugo Burghauser, former principal bassoonist of the Vienna Philharmonic, who had emigrated to America: 'I am busy with an idea for a double concerto for clarinet and bassoon, thinking especially of your beautiful tone.' This work was performed for the first time on 4th April 1948 by soloists and orchestra of Radio Lugano.

Lugano and Pontresina had been 'home' for the exiles during 1947. Strauss was happy anywhere provided he had work to do, but Pauline was bored and missed her friends. She treated hotel after hotel to her tantrums and complaints, and hotel after hotel asked the distinguished guests to leave. In 1948 they settled at the Palace Hotel, Montreux, and it was there that Strauss composed his last work. Towards the end of 1946 he had read Eichendorff's poem *Im Abendrot* (*In the Sunset*) about an old couple who at the end of a long and eventful life look tiredly at the sunset and ask 'Is that perhaps death?' This so exactly fitted the Strausses' situation that he began to set it and was so emotionally stirred that he decided on accompaniment for large orchestra. He completed it on 6th May 1948. A little while before that, an admirer sent him a volume of poems by Hesse. He selected four to make a cycle of five with *Im Abendrot* but completed only three. They were *Frühling* (*Spring*) on 18th July, *Beim Schlafengehen* (*Falling Asleep*) on 4th August, and *Septem-*

---

[1] *Daily Telegraph*, 30th October 1947.

Strauss in London, 1903

Strauss aged thirty-nine

With his wife, Pauline, in 1914

Part of the autograph MS. of the quartet 'Eine Störrische zu trösten' from *Ariadne auf Naxos*, 1912

A signed photograph of
Strauss in 1925

Conducting the *Alpine Symphony* in Vienna, 1942

With Hugo von Hofmannsthal
t Garmisch, 1911

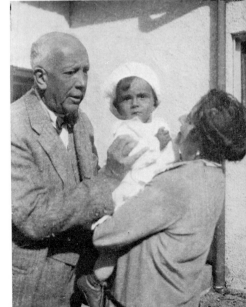

With Pauline and their elder
grandchild Richard, 1929

Arriving at Northolt Airport, 4th October 1947, after his first flight at the age of eighty-three

In Berlin, 1942, with Heinz Tietjen (right), Intendant of the Staatsoper, and Herbert von Karajan, the conductor

With Clemens Krauss in London, 1947

Rehearsing the Philharmonia Orchestra in London, 1947

ber on 20th September. Among the friends to whom they were dedicated was Maria Jeritza.

In June 1948 the Denazification Board cleared Strauss's name from complicity in the evils of the Third Reich. He was free to return home, but in December, after a year of increasing discomfort, he underwent a severe bladder operation in Lausanne. 'I ask myself why I am being called back into an existence in which I have outlived myself,' he wrote to a friend. But he made sketches for a choral work with a fugue, a setting of Hesse's *Besinnung*, and he studied Beethoven quartets and his beloved *Tristan*. On 10th May 1949 he and Pauline returned to Garmisch. He was not well enough to go to Paris for the French celebration of his eighty-fifth birthday but wrote to Gustave Samazeuilh: 'The fact that the broadcast of *Friedenstag* coincides with the Foreign Ministers' Conference is a sign of fate, and I would like to see it as a happy premonition that my vision as an artist in 1938 . . . could now radiate over all the earth from the enlightened city that is Paris.' [1]

On 10th June, the night before his birthday, Strauss miraculously found the strength to travel to Munich to the dress rehearsal of *Der Rosenkavalier*. What is more, he asked to be allowed to conduct the finales of Acts II and III. This episode was filmed and included in an historic documentary, *A Life for Music*, together with later film of his conducting the Presentation of the Silver Rose. The Bavarian authorities had asked which of his works he would most like to see, and surprisingly he chose *Der Bürger als Edelmann*. On 13th June he saw a new production of it at the Gärtnerplatz Theater and was delighted. 'It's a pity Hofmannsthal couldn't have seen it too,' he said. A month later, on 13th July, he returned to Munich to conduct the radio orchestra in the Moonlight Music from *Capriccio*. He never conducted again.

[1] G. Samazeuilh: 'Richard Strauss as I knew him' (*Tempo*, Summer 1964, pp. 14–17).

His health now began to fail rapidly. He had written no music since leaving Switzerland but he was mentally active with plans for the reconstruction of the Munich National Opera. During August he had several minor heart attacks. On the 29th the Munich producer, Rudolf Hartmann, went to see him and subsequently wrote a moving account of his visit:

I hear the deep rather hoarse voice speaking about his ever-recurring anxiety for the continuance of the European Theatre. . . . After a while he goes on quietly, in a different tone of voice: 'Grüss' mir die Welt' ('Greet all the world for me'). He stops, asks 'Where does that come from?' I think of the similar words from *Walküre* and say so, but he shakes his head: 'No, no, it's not that, this occurs somewhere else'. . . .[1] He stays silent for a long time. I see that his face is showing signs of fatigue and that it is time to go. . . . He once more grasps my right hand in both of his and holds me back: 'Perhaps we'll see each other again; if not, you know everything.' A last vehement grip, his hands release me, and I quickly leave the room.'[2]

The great master of bringing down the curtain was in superb form on his own death-bed. He said to his daughter-in-law Alice, 'Dying is just as I composed it in *Tod und Verklärung*.' In the afternoon of 8th September 1949 he died while sleeping. At his cremation in Munich three days later, the singers he had conducted three months earlier again sang the Trio from *Rosenkavalier*. Less than a year later, on 13th May 1950, Pauline died, nine days before the first performance of the *Four Last Songs*, sung by Kirsten Flagstad and conducted by Furtwängler, in London, the city which in 1922 and again in 1947 had drawn Richard Strauss back into the international fellowship of music where he belongs. 'Grüss' mir die Welt.'

[1] It is Isolde's farewell to Brangäne in Act I of *Tristan*.
[2] R. Hartmann: 'Letzte Besuch bei Richard Strauss' (*Schweizerische Musikzeitung*, Jg. 90, Vol. 8/9).

15 Early works

The 'received opinion' of Strauss's career is of radiant dawn, a glorious noonday, a sleepy afternoon and a glowing sunset. The sleepy afternoon has tended to dominate critical assessment of him, even though its contents are much less well known and therefore perhaps superficially judged. Slings and arrows have been aimed at his achievements from one source or another for the past fifty years, but all attempts seriously to diminish his stature have failed. He has been castigated for what he was not, which is wasteful, negative criticism. He was not a Mahlerian figure, agonizing over mankind's destiny; he was not a spiritual philosopher; he was not a fully-paid-up member of the *avant-garde* of successive generations; he was not a mystic nor was he a demon. Stravinsky, whose antipathy did not prevent his acknowledging Strauss's greatness, said of him: 'He is not a composer, he is a connoisseur.' But so was Stravinsky! Most composers are eclectics. Provided they have a leavening of genius, it is a fruitful condition.

Strauss was an entertainer, a story-teller, an illustrator, a sensualist. He regarded music as a holy art, Mozart's art, and it is a silly evasion of the problems he presents to misrepresent him as some sort of composing-machine for ever churning it out from Garmisch. The impression is often conveyed that he was lacka-daisical and complacent in his approach to composition. In fact, he was meticulous in his complete concentration on the task in hand, whatever it was. He would make any sacrifice for music, which obsessed him to the point where it seemed to represent the only reality, hence his egoism and his apparent insensitivity to the sufferings of the twentieth century. But is not this insensitivity a major flaw in his art? Does it not show him to lack real depth and passion? Only if one judges the extent of music's depth by its involvement with subjects such as threnodies for Hiroshima and memorials for Lidice. Strauss knew himself— and perhaps knew the art of music—better than to trespass in such fields. It is significant that he loved *Così fan tutte* above all other operas—where Mozart probed the human heart through artificial trivialities. Strauss confined himself to the Marschallin's sense of the passing of time, to Till's eternal cocking of snooks at authority, to the Countess's dilemma over words and music, to Mandryka's unsophisticated goodness of heart, to his own identification with the great German artistic tradition symbolized by the Munich and Dresden opera houses. Cold, dead-pan exterior may be a mask to disguise banked-up fires, and in Strauss's case it was also a form of self-protection. The disguise was abetted by Pauline, who ensured that every material comfort should ease the process of composition. Her violent behaviour at home deflected Strauss from concern with the outer world (and was also possibly her own outlet for emotional frustration). There is no more symbolic reflection of the Strausses' relationship than the day of Hofmannsthal's death, when Pauline 'diverted' Strauss from the full shock of the news by a series of explosive rages over domestic trivialities such as mud on the carpet or a mistake by the cook. This was the only antidote Pauline knew; useless for Strauss to try to explain that his grief must find some outlet, and not only in continuing to work on *Arabella*. So he took the libretto and called on Elisabeth Schumann, intending to read it to her and Karl Alwin. But she had a small house party and persuaded Strauss to read it to a select few while she entertained the other guests. Later she was told how Strauss 'had suddenly stopped during the reading and burst into a flood of tears. He had wept long and unrestrainedly, tears forced from the very depths of his soul'.[1]

Equally revealing is Lotte Lehmann's admission (in radio interviews) that when staying at Garmisch she was slightly disappointed by Strauss, because his talk was always of fees and royalties and the house seemed to be dominated by Pauline. 'As a rule,' Lehmann said, 'he appeared utterly aloof and impersonal, so cold in his reaction to people that they would withdraw instantly and give up any misguided attempt at friendliness.' But, she added, when it came to rehearsing, he was supreme, he came alive.

Strauss's early works are not widely known today. They explain how, before he was twenty, he could be regarded by Bülow with special interest, for they show no subversive signs of 'progressive' music. These works present an accomplished musician in the Classical-Romantic tradition, well versed in Mendelssohn, Schumann, Beethoven, Weber and Brahms. He had learned his lessons assiduously, for, charming though these works are in many respects, they lack real originality. A bar here and there foretells the mature Strauss; and the obvious discomfort he felt within the rigid confines of sonata-form development points to the enthusiasm with which he later recognized his salvation in the symphonic-poem. But the overall impression is of a Mendelssohn disciple, genial and bland, probing hardly at all beneath a polished surface. Pianists who wish to vary their recitals of Romantic keyboard music should look up the *Five Pieces*, Op. 3, the B minor sonata, Op. 5 and the *Stimmungsbilder*, Op. 9. In the last-named the fifth movement, *Heidenbild* (*On the heath*), is a strangely atmospheric piece, the bare fifths in the bass forming an imaginative background to two contrasted thematic figures.

[1] A. Mathis: 'Elisabeth Schumann', *Opera*, Vol. 25, No. 1, January 1974, pp. 27–8.

Richard Strauss

The Violin Concerto, Op. 8,[1] combines neatly tailored virtuosity with a rapturous melodic flow, particularly in the slow movement, and earns the gratitude of listeners, if not of performers, by excluding that curse of the concerto, a cadenza. Cellists ought not to overlook the Cello Sonata, Op. 6, haunted by the spirit of Beethoven and dedicated to and first played by Hanuš Wihan, later to be dedicatee of Dvořák's Concerto. Here the clumsy structural handling may have been the result of a strong urge towards emotional expression. No wonder Joachim praised Strauss for the opening theme, typical already of Strauss's ability to begin a work with a bold gesture:

Ex.1

p con espress.

Although this momentum is not maintained, the first movement has several surges of heroic endeavour before Strauss reverts to the mood of Mendelssohn's *Songs Without Words* for the lyrical Andante. In the finale he quotes from Mendelssohn's C minor Piano Trio, Op. 66—Strauss was never reluctant to acknowledge his sources—before saluting Wagner with a cadence from Act II of *Parsifal*, which he had heard at Bayreuth while composing the sonata. Despite these obvious models, the finale is impressive in its confident assurance even if it is over-reliant on repetition of sequences.

In some passages of the Cello Sonata may be discerned the Strauss of the tone-poems. His gentler, slippers-by-the-fire aspect, when he became charmer as well as explorer, is shown in the two delightful works for 13 wind instruments, the one-

[1] The opus numbers of Strauss's early works are a misleading guide to dates of composition and publication.

movement *Serenade in E flat*, Op. 7, and the later *Suite in B flat*, Op. 4. Of these the short, well-constructed *Serenade* is the more immediately beguiling, but the four-movement *Suite*, while Brahmsian in spirit and form, is full of Straussian prophecies, notably of his skill in developing short themes. The duet for horn and clarinet in the Allegretto (first) movement is an inspiration; and no one, hearing the oboe solos in the second and fourth movements, need any longer be surprised by the effectiveness of the oboe in *Don Juan*. Yet the best movement is the Gavotte, a pointer to the wit of *Le Bourgeois Gentilhomme*.

Now that the early symphonies of Dvořák have been re-habilitated and interest has been re-extended to the symphonies of Raff, Gade and Goldmark, it is surprising that so effective an example of the German Romantic symphony as Strauss's Symphony No. 2 in F minor, Op. 12, should remain neglected, even though it lasts 45 minutes. It establishes beyond doubt that Strauss at twenty was a master of the orchestra. The work is in cyclic form, each movement sharing a theme in fourths first heard on trumpets and horns. The two middle movements, a scherzo and a romantic *Andante cantabile*, are the best. Theodore Bloomfield [1] has pointed out an interesting resemblance between a canon for trumpets and horns in three pairs a quaver apart in the slow movement and the canon for brass in the first movement of Bartók's *Concerto for Orchestra*, perhaps an atavistic reversion by the Hungarian to his youthful enthusiasm for Strauss. The major error in the symphony is the finale, where themes from the previous movements are recalled in a gauche manner, no doubt the occasion for Brahms's remark about 'thematic irrelevancies'.

The Piano Quartet in C minor, Op. 13, is a massive act of homage to Brahms, from whom several of the themes are shamelessly plagiarized. Yet it is a step forward from the Symphony because it shows Strauss in control of his design—the develop-

---

[1] T. Bloomfield: 'Richard Strauss's Symphony in F minor', *Music and Musicians*, March 1974, pp. 24–8.

ments flow easily, the transitions are less contrived—and its emotional content is stormier. As Arthur Johnstone wrote in 1904, it 'might rank as the mature work of anyone but Strauss'. It was composed in 1883–4. Four years later, in the Violin Sonata, Op. 18, Strauss advanced as far again. This was the last of his classically designed works and his last piece of orthodox chamber music. It is superb. He was already at work on *Don Juan*, and the opening theme and several others have a comparable verve and sweep as if they had been conceived in orchestral terms. The climax of the first movement is almost operatic in its broad proportions, as is much of the impassioned rhetoric of the finale. But Strauss makes the finale structurally interesting by following a sombre introduction with a brilliant episode and by interposing scherzo-like passages among the fervent displays of melody, almost on a scale appropriate to a concerto. The central *Andante cantabile* (*Improvisation*) was written last but shows no sign of hard labour. Its elegant grace has ensured it a separate existence. It pays tribute to Strauss's models: the piano part in the dramatic middle section is so like that of Schubert's *Erlkönig* that the allusion must be deliberate. The return to the main melody is made by way of Chopinesque nocturne references and, in the coda, Strauss links his theme with that of the *adagio* of Beethoven's *Pathétique* pianoforte sonata. *Tristan* is quoted in the finale. For Strauss, musical quotation was a legitimate and potent source of inspiration. No composer except Shostakovitch has employed it more effectively, with such point and wit.

High though the Violin Sonata stands among Strauss's early works, two stand higher. The Horn Concerto No. 1 in E flat, Op. 11, is aptly enough his first wholly satisfying composition, since he grew up with the sound of his father's horn as a daily counterpoint to childhood's first impressions. In barely sixteen minutes the work achieves an almost Mozartian grace and humour. Its three movements are played without a break, strict sonata-form is abandoned, and the conversion of the opening flourish into the capricious rondo theme of the finale anticipates other Straussian uses of this method by three or four years. Thematic connections are subtle throughout the concerto and give it a convincing unity. The melodies are memorable, the orchestration is entrancing.

Yet it is the *Burleske* in D minor, for pianoforte and orchestra, which may be described as Strauss's first masterpiece. He never gave it an opus number and seems only to have realized its merits in his last years. It is hard to know which is the more surprising, Bülow's calling it unplayable or its infrequent inclusion in concert programmes today. It is not yet *echt*-Strauss: there are still the influences of Brahms and Schumann. But here are the first authentic glimpses of the urchin humour of *Till Eulenspiegel*, the stirrings of Don Juan's ardour, the wit, fantasy, sparkle and inventiveness of the creator of a gallery of stage characters. Here above all is the fantastic conjuror of the orchestra, juggling with pianist and orchestra as if they were featherweights and producing a rabbit out of the hat for them at the start in the shape of this splendid theme for four timpani:

Ex. 2

which is answered by the orchestra, interrupted by the pianoforte in a burst of merriment, and provokes all that follows thematically. It is not all banter: a lazy waltz episode (an augmentation of the orchestral presentation of the first subject) forms a beautiful middle section which is recapitulated in the coda. The nineteen-minute work brims over with ideas, all fertile and concise. It needs a virtuoso performance combining aristocratic reserve with epigrammatic quicksilver.

16   The tone-poems

Strauss's fame in the concert-hall rests securely on five of the ten large-scale orchestral works, symphonic poems in one form or another, which he composed between 1886 and 1915. Their composition coincided with the height of the barren controversy about the relative values of 'absolute' music and music which described something, 'programme music'. Barren, because no music can be entirely 'absolute'; equally, can music really describe anything, or does the listener, taking the composer's hint, do most of the work? Would the last scene of *Die Walküre* suggest fire if we did not know what was happening on the stage? Can music sound like fountains, rivers or fireworks? Like Falstaff or moonlight? Realistic 'effects' are one thing, character-studies quite another. Yet such is the suggestive power of music that we 'see' Falstaff as vividly in Elgar's music as in Shake-speare's words—when we know that it is 'about' Falstaff.

Mahler's view was that no music from Beethoven onward was without an inner programme. But, he added, music was worth nothing if the listener had to be told what experience was being re-lived. Strauss's views were equally ambivalent. In 1888 he wrote to Bülow: 'From the F minor Symphony onwards I have found myself in a gradually increasing contradiction between the musical-poetic content which I wish to convey and the ternary sonata-form inherited from the classical composers.... I consider it a legitimate artistic method to create an appropriate new form for each new subject.' In 1905 he expressed these views to Rolland: 'To me the poetic programme is no more than the basis of form and the origin of the purely musical development of my feelings—not, as you believe, a *musical description* of certain events of life.' By 1929 he was saying: 'Programme music is a derogatory word in the mouths of those who have no ideas of their own.' He was pulling some nincompoop's leg when he said he wanted to describe things so accurately in music that the listener could tell whether a glass of beer was Pilsener or Kulmbacher. No music will survive unless it has independent life as music: no 'programme' will keep bad music alive. Most of Strauss's programme music can be enjoyed for its purely musical quality. How many listeners, when they have once followed the detailed programme, pay much attention to it again? Very few, I suggest. The music transcends it.

Strauss's first tone-poem was *Aus Italien*, Op. 16, a 'Symphonic fantasy' which is really a four-movement symphony on the lines of Mendelssohn's *Italian Symphony*, showing several signs of influence by Berlioz and Tchaikovsky, with a leavening of Brahms. Yet the real Strauss is beginning to come through, and it is surprising that conductors have not shown more interest in recent years in such a picturesque, melodious and delightfully orchestrated work. The Lisztian first movement, romantic and rhapsodic, is the best and most promising, and in the second ('Ruins of Rome') there is the characteristic sound of Strauss's divided strings which gave such a strong hint to Elgar for *In the South*. The abandonment of sonata-form in pursuit of whatever the 'poetic idea' dictates certainly led in the third movement ('On the beach at Sorrento') to Strauss's first piece of magical tone-painting, with shimmering cascades on violins and flutes suggesting sunlight on the sea, and a broad flowing melody prophetic of the operatic *cantilena* in which he was to excel. It is customary to gibe at Strauss because the 'Neapolitan folk-song' of his finale is Denza's popular song *Funiculi, funicula*. But it is not a very terrible mistake for him to have made; the catchy tune sounds thoroughly Neapolitan and is treated with wit and restraint. The charge of vulgarity is often levelled against Strauss, but there is no vulgarity if his music is well played and conducted with a respect for the score. This finale is a case in point: it should sound exuberant and bright, not blatant and brash.

A passage in this finale may cause listeners to think of the fight episode in Tchaikovsky's *Romeo and Juliet* (1870). The same reminiscence occurs in *Macbeth*, which really precedes *Don Juan*, although its opus number, 23, and first performance followed it because of extensive revision. Here for the first time Strauss devised a single-movement form based on, but diverging from, Liszt's pattern. It is a sonata-form movement, unified by a

Ex.3

motto-theme referring to Macbeth's royal state and with a long, elaborate development section containing two episodes, the first a dialogue between Macbeth and his wife, the second a ceremonial interlude describing Duncan's processional arrival at the castle. It is rich, sombre and well-constructed, interesting to Straussians because of its hints of later masterpieces, but it has understandably been eclipsed by its successors. One has only to hear the exciting, lusty, marvellously scored and imaginatively original opening to *Don Juan*, Op. 20 (see Ex. 3), to perceive that real inspiration has taken the place of meritorious workmanship, for out of this composite first statement individual features are to be extended and developed.

The structure of *Don Juan* is the same as that of *Macbeth*, the two independent episodes being a love-scene and a carnival; not that any detailed programme matters, for the music vividly represents 'youth's fiery pulses'. The love-scene is dominated by an oboe solo which is the first of many Strauss themes conveying a mingling of hope and regret, of spring and autumn. Strauss's maturity is signalled by the masterly way in which he continues the work after this spell-binding interlude: the music stirs uneasily back to life and to the emergence of a great new theme on four horns, worthy of a hero of any kind of battle, of love or war:

Ex.4
4 Horns

f molto espress. e marc.

ff

Strauss makes this magnificent idea the climax of his recapitulation, when it returns a third higher on the horns, to be repeated with even more thrilling effect by unison strings and wind. After this glorious display of orchestral colour, Strauss, with the dramatic instinct for contrast of the born stage composer, swiftly and daringly ends the work with Juan's death—a single dissonant trumpet note—and his last gasps for breath (descending trills). There is not a note too many, not a miscalculated effect, in the whole wonderful score. Rehearsing it, Strauss once told an orchestra: 'I would ask those of you who are married to play as if you were engaged and then all will be well.'

His next tone-poem, *Tod und Verklärung*, Op. 24, aimed higher and was the first for which Strauss provided a detailed 'plot': of an idealist on his death-bed who, amid physical pain, recalls his childhood, the loves of his youth, and his unfulfilled striving towards his ideals. After death, his soul voyages 'to find gloriously achieved in everlasting space those things which could not be fulfilled here below'. As in *Don Juan*, Strauss's mastery is shown in the skilful deployment of short germinal motifs allied to superb orchestration. The depiction of the sick-room, the dying man's writhings and his memories of childhood and youth is graphic and moving. Strauss again bends his classical training in sonata-form to his own uses: a slow introduction, an allegro section, a love-scene and a finale in which all the themes are woven into a symphonic epilogue. This final 'transfiguration' episode has been much criticized for failing to achieve 'sublimity'. By respecting the directions in the score, the best Strauss conductors achieve a convincing nobility in these final pages which are the forerunner of several of his best operatic finales, using harmonic modulations of ravishing beauty controlled with a sure and steady sense of climactic rise and fall. To achieve the desired effect Strauss had to invent a memorable melody, as he had in *Don Juan*, and the so-called Ideology theme of *Tod und Verklärung*, with its aspiring octave leap, is *echt-Strauss*, a tune he was to quote several times.

Five years were to elapse before the first performance of Strauss's next tone-poem, *Till Eulenspiegels lustige Streiche*, Op. 28. He had in the meantime written an opera, *Guntram*. Its poor reception by the philistine Munich public perhaps accounts for the cocking of snooks at authority which gives a sharp and contemptuous, even spiteful, edge to the impudent humour of *Till*. (Strauss's recorded interpretation is more barbed than anyone's.) His choice of rondo form for this virtuosic display of musical humour was not the least of the happy touches which abound. Although Strauss later outlined the events illustrated—Till causing havoc in the market place; Till in love, arguing with academics, mocking religion, being hanged—the music is self-sufficient and is illuminated by an unchallengeable certainty of orchestral effects, governed by a light touch which German music had not known for half a century. It is hardly necessary to go into detail about such a well-loved and firmly established favourite, except to underline the aptness of the orchestration. This keeps the work pristine and is epitomized by the unforgettable horn-theme representing Till:

Ex.5

which is doubly effective for coming after the gentle 'once-upon-a-time' opening. Equally memorable is the use to which the D clarinet is put, its shrill, cheeky sound being entirely apt for this subject. Yet if Strauss's instrumental expertise in *Till* is employed with a sophistication which entitled him to be regarded as the playboy of the symphony orchestra, his skill in composition is no less awe-inspiring. His trump-card, especially in his operas, was the metamorphosis of themes. The 'once-upon-a-time' opening assumes insolent mockery:

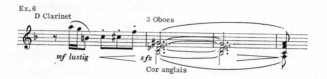

as easily as the principal Till motif (marked x in Ex. 5) is transformed into romance:

These themes undergo several other changes, for Strauss's ingenuity seems limitless. The wit that was evident in the *Burleske* finds its apogee in *Till*, as Strauss the great actor-manager plays all the rôles in his repertoire. Few moments in his music are more magical than the swift change from the huge and savage orchestral trill with which Till finally derides the professors to the carefree ditty representing his saucy departure from their company.

Till was to be the last of Strauss's short tone-poems; henceforward they were to last at least thirty-five minutes and to require a huge orchestra. The first of the 'mammoths' was *Also sprach Zarathustra*, his homage to Nietzsche. This association of music with the poetry and philosophy of that much-discussed author was a brilliant opportunist stroke in 1896, but it means little today. Yet the work grows in popularity with audiences only a fraction of whom are likely to have read a word by or about Nietzsche and even though critics still deride its 'bombast' and 'vulgarity'. It is best enjoyed as a virtuoso example of sumptuous orchestral sound. Its 'sunrise' opening, thematically simple yet massively impressive, was brilliantly commandeered by Stanley Kubrick for a film about space—an acute piece of musical criticism because the passage concerned is film music written before such a commodity was required. Although nothing in the work is as memorable as this in invention, Strauss retains interest by his total mastery of the episodic form in which the tone poem is cast, welding it into a convincing unity. His sense of humour must have been responsible for the Dance of the Superman being a Viennese waltz—the first occurrence in his music of this dance-form, which assumed for him the same kind of significance as the *Ländler* and the march had for Mahler. Norman Del Mar rightly refers to the distinctive flavour of *Also sprach Zarathustra*, its transcendental quality exemplified by the beautiful coda, a nocturne in B major. It will always remain a target for the anti-Straussians, for there is obvious disproportion between the musical achievement and the highfalutin aim of the Nietzschean tribute. But there is something to be admired by all but the most bigoted in Strauss's daring in this work, whether it is the once-novel and still startling polytonal effects or the staggering ease with which he manipulates orchestral tone-colour.

He returned to humans in his next major orchestral work, *Don Quixote*, 'fantastic variations on a theme of knightly character', as he accurately sub-titled it. This too is daring in design: a long contrapuntal introduction, ten variations and an epilogue, an episodic scheme tending towards disjointedness. The use of solo cello and solo viola as the Don and Sancho Panza gives it a concerto element which must be underplayed if it is to succeed completely. As in *Till*, the episodes of Don Quixote's knight errantry are skilfully chosen for musical delineation and contrast.

It is wonderful how Strauss conveys the 'fantastic' element, the insane-sanity of Don Quixote, the borderline between laughter and tears, the poignancy and pathos of the Don's death. The variations are, in effect, musical character-sketches as pithy and picaresque as the nearly contemporary *Enigma Variations* of Elgar.

Don Quixote is the product of affection and admiration for the literary original. It drew from Strauss some of his happiest melodic inventions, notably the Dulcinea theme (an even love-lier oboe lady than Don Juan's *innamorata*) (see Ex. 8) and a dazzling display of thematic transformations of the various Don Quixote motifs. The famous pictorial episodes—the sheep, the windmills, the flying horse (with a pedal D to show that it never leaves the ground)—are so vividly done that at first they diverted attention from the work's pervasive poetry of which they are an integral and musical part. Even today some hearers are outraged by the score of *Don Quixote*: it is their grudging way of acknowledging that it is a masterpiece.

So is its companion-piece, *Ein Heldenleben*. Useless for apologists blushingly to try to overlook this tone-poem's pro-grammatic basis: it is mainly autobiographical and none the worse for it. The heroine is Pauline, drawn in all her moods, from shrew to coquette, in one of the greatest violin solos in the orchestral repertoire. The adversaries (music critics) were identi-fied by Strauss as specific targets. The hero's 'works of peace' are a collage of quotations from his own works. *Heldenleben* is not only a glorious example of a rich orchestral palette used with consummate skill: it is a witty work, never wittier than in the waspish treatment of the critics.

The construction is again masterly. Strauss constantly takes the listener by surprise, like a good novelist who prepares unexpected twists in his plot. The six sections are thematically closely linked and a fine performance should leave no doubt of the homogeneity of the work. A curious 'flavour', as distinctive

Ex. 8

as that of *Zarathustra*, is imparted to the harmonic scheme by
the flattened notes which occur first in the seventh bar of the
hero's expansive principal theme:

Ex. 9

Throughout the forty minutes the tone-poem lasts one senses Strauss's enjoyment of a sense of risk, of treading a knife-edge between grandeur and grandiloquence. How shocking, his critics say, how exhibitionist, to be the hero of one's own work. He is not alone in this: it was a badge of the Romantic Era. Mahler was the hero of his second symphony, Elgar the hero of the *Enigma Variations* and other works, culminating in his choral ode *The Music Makers* in self-quotation on a *Heldenleben* scale and with comparably potent effect.

An astonishing emotional gamut is run in *Heldenleben*, from heroic endeavour to tender erotic passion, from the exuberance of battle to the contentment of pastoral retirement. The Battle Scene was described when it was new as 'an atrocity', but its exhilarating course, involving contrapuntal wizardry on an enormous scale, holds few terrors today. Two of the surprises mentioned above occur within a few pages as the Battle ends. Just as it seems that a normal recapitulation of the hero's themes is under way, Strauss produces a superb new theme ready to provide the basis of the final coda and, as this theme builds to a climax, the moment of crisis is reached with the horns' thrilling statement of the *Don Juan* theme (see Ex. 4). This sets in motion the once-controversial but marvellously contrived assemblage of quotations from other tone-poems, the opera *Guntram* and songs, which paradoxically forms one of the strikingly original passages in *Heldenleben*.[1] This section underlines the emotional links with *Don Quixote*, for it concludes with a turbulent dissonant passage in which the hero is again tormented by the critics' barbs. He seems to succumb but finds escape in a version of the shepherds' pastoral theme from Variation II of *Don Quixote* while the drums throb like an over-taxed heart just as they did in Variation X when Don Quixote rides home from battle. A great conductor of *Heldenleben* will draw from the concluding section not only beautiful sounds for strings and horns but a nobility comparable with the Knight's vigil in Variation V. And just as the nocturnal peace of that courtyard is ruffled by disturbing memories, so the hero's idyll is suddenly shattered by a nightmare which only Pauline's soothing violin caress can dispel. This hero is no superman, just a Kapellmeister.

With *Till*, *Don Quixote* and *Ein Heldenleben* Strauss achieved a supremacy as an orchestrator which is still one of the marvels of music. He used a huge orchestra, as Mahler did, but although harmonically his music sounds 'fatter' than Mahler's, it is often scored with similar restraint and delicacy. Both knew the value of contrast and the advantages to be gained from keeping something in hand for the true climactic moment of each work. Both, too, for different reasons suffered in their lifetime and afterwards from the constant accusations of 'tastelessness'—that imprecise and subjective term. What was said about *Heldenleben* was mild compared with the abuse hurled at Strauss's next orchestral work, the *Symphonia Domestica*, one of his most endearing works.

After one of the first English performances, Ernest Newman wrote that 'the orchestral colour is grossly overdone; the polyphony is often coarse and sprawling; the realistic effects in the score are so pitiably foolish that one listens to them with regret that a composer of genius should ever have fallen so low'. One reads this with regret that a powerful critic should have shown so

[1] See Appendix E for a full list.

little perception. Yet Norman Del Mar confesses [1] to 'appalling
doubts', finds the programme 'intolerable' and 'on that very
account' finds the music 'markedly less great than in any of the
previous major works since his maturity'. I do not agree. The
music, while detailedly programmatic, is strong and inventive
enough to stand without the prop of a story. Far from being
overdone, the orchestral colours are limned with a humour and
deftness analogous to those of Mahler's Fourth Symphony:
allowing for the temperamental differences between the composers, these two works represent their creators, masters of
grandiose effects, in relaxed and childlike mood, though they
highlight the problems each had in ensuring uneasy co-existence
between sophistication and naïveté.

Although *Domestica* is in one continuous movement, the four
sections of a symphony may be discerned—an introduction
(instead of a regular first movement) on the *Don Quixote* model,
followed by scherzo, adagio and fugal finale. The opening is
lightly scored, the first theme (Strauss himself) being a collection
of short motifs each marked by a change of mood: easy-going
(cellos), dreamy (oboe), morose (clarinets), fiery (strings) and
merry (trumpet). Pauline's motifs follow, tender, hot-tempered
and waspish. The first three notes of her theme are the direct
inversion of her husband's. Theme III, the child, is introduced
by solo oboe d'amore, an inspired choice of instrument. In the
scherzo ('the child at play, his parents' happiness') the child's
theme is treated like a folk-song, with beautiful writing for
woodwind and violas. The parents' themes (notably the wife's on
solo violin) flit in and out; and in this section, as in others, one
can detect future Strauss works and procedures in embryo. This
is particularly obvious in the beautiful lullaby (after the notorious
bath) where Strauss alludes to a Mendelssohn *Song Without
Words* (Op. 19, No. 6) and orchestrates it like the Marschallin's

[1] N. Del Mar: *Richard Strauss*, Vol. I (London, 1962), pp. 196–9.

soliloquy in Act I of *Der Rosenkavalier*. Superb writing for flute and oboe distinguishes the beautiful reverie which ends this section.

The Adagio has two episodes, the first depicting Strauss at work, inspiration gradually becoming intense. When the wife's themes return, an explicit love scene is followed by the most imaginative part of the work in which the couple's dreams are suggested, their themes being combined, inverted and fragmented ('coarse polyphony' but magical). With the return of day, the household wakes, noisy, bustling, quarrelsome, just the occasion for a double fugue. In the long and exuberant closing section all the themes are treated with surpassing orchestral virtuosity, the horns being called upon to perform heroic feats in final glorification of the child's theme.

The English critic who referred to *Ein Heldenleben* and *Symphonia Domestica* as 'barrage balloons' and deplored the growing enthusiasm for them [1] represents a kind of puritanism which Strauss's music engenders in certain temperaments. Most of us, though, are hedonists who revel in the fine melodies, wonderful orchestration and considerable humour of these works. We can also find pleasure in his penultimate large-scale orchestral work, *Eine Alpensinfonie*. Scored for an orchestra of over 150, this work describes twenty-four hours in the mountains. The twenty-two sections include sunrise, the ascent, a waterfall, flower-meadows, a glacier, the summit, a storm and sunset. The pictorialism is extremely graphic, with Mahlerian cowbells and some approximation to Mahlerian nature-worship, and certain passages are deeply impressive, not only as majestic sound, but in their Brucknerian evocation of the grandeur and remoteness of the Alps which Strauss could see from Garmisch. But the work has been generally underrated. It is far more than the sum of its remarkable effects; repeated hearings reveal its fascination and

[1] *The Listener*, 16 May 1974, p. 643.

strength as music pure and simple. This is no eccentric piece of self-indulgence: it is a well-knit, often very moving orchestral creation with a pantheistic spiritual exaltation not found again in Strauss's output until *Daphne*. It is marred by the length of the storm, which is too real to be poetic—Strauss's one serious miscalculation in an extraordinary achievement.

Strauss did not help the work by his remark about wishing to compose 'as a cow gives milk' which his enemies seized upon with malicious delight. No doubt he felt justifiable pride in what Samuel Langford, writing in 1923, called the 'long and gorgeous weft of sound' and the effortless mastery of orchestral counterpoint. Yet there is a deeper undertone, a solemnity, which perhaps may be associated with the years of its composition, 1911–15. It is a long farewell to the sumptuousness of the post-Wagnerian orchestra, and its final sunset before the return of night is peculiarly apposite and affecting. Even Strauss must have known that the world after the war would be a leaner, less extravagant place. So he brought down the curtain on his chief orchestral works not with a character-study of a rogue or a hero but with a celebration of elemental and unchanging Nature. In this respect, the work may surely be regarded as Strauss's homage to Mahler. He was working on it when he received the news of his friend's death and he wrote in his notebook words which link him and this music with Mahler: 'Purification through one's own strength, emancipation through work, adoration of eternal glorious nature.'

Some regard *Eine Alpensinfonie* as symptomatic of the onset of Strauss's long decline. That is not my view. It was the end of the beginning. Henceforward Strauss was obsessed by the theatre, having given the world a series of works which will remain indispensable for as long as symphony orchestras continue to exist. But conductors must believe in them. Dispassion or clinical analysis will not do.

17 The operas (1)

GUNTRAM, FEUERSNOT, SALOME, ELEKTRA

Strauss's fifteen operas represent a major attempt by a major composer to extend the boundaries of the form. They reflect his belief in the continuing expansion of repertory opera. This faith was nurtured at Meiningen where, as a young man, he saw drama produced under ideal circumstances. He became and remained stage-struck; and when, as an old disillusioned man in 1945, he wrote his 'artistic testament', it was in the form of proposals for the re-establishment of repertory opera. The view that Strauss stood still after 1912, stuck in the mud and yearly becoming more of an anachronism, is not only superficial but misguided. Earlier chapters have shown with what assiduity Strauss searched for subjects which would extend him further within his capacity.

His first opera, *Guntram*, has never established itself despite the cuts and revisions Strauss made to his 'child of sorrow' in 1940. In a sense he had to write it to purge himself of Wagnerianism—'all of *Guntram* is a prelude', he said in old age. It belongs to a world influenced by *Parsifal* and *Tannhäuser*, as the title suggests, but as well as looking back it gives several hints of impending Straussian works, and the broad soaring melodies given to Guntram and the heroine Freihild in Act III have a radiance familiar to us from the later operas. In an ideal operatic world, when Strauss's vision of true repertory-opera has materialized, there will be little justification for continued neglect of a work which, for all its miscalculations and *longueurs*, contains so much good, striking and amazingly mature music.

But there is already much less reason for overlooking his second opera, *Feuersnot*, the first of the trio of one-act operas written between 1900 and 1908. This 'poem for singing'—*Singgedicht*—was composed after the great tone-poems and is in the witty and satirical vein of *Till* and *Don Quixote*. Its bawdy plot, scandalous at the time, would hardly flicker an eyebrow today. There is a link with Wagner, of course, through *Die Meistersinger*—both operas are set at midsummer—and there are several Wagner quotations in the score. Dramatically it creaks a bit, and the satire has lost some point, but its musical virtues are so strong that a good producer should easily overcome these handicaps.

The importance of *Feuersnot* is that it is, as Strauss himself emphasized just before he died, the first of the works in which he was to develop his own operatic style, 'dealing with a quasi-personal subject'. After the thick orchestration of *Guntram* the score of *Feuersnot* is brilliantly light and varied, with the warmth and colour of *Rosenkavalier* and the transparency of *Ariadne*. The children's choruses are delightful (if a good children's chorus can be found to sing them) as is the cunning use of Munich folk-songs; and the childlike exuberance of the score, its unsophisticated yet highly polished geniality and humour, remain unequalled among the later works. It is a good deal more than merely a transitional work, for it is too assured in manner to be regarded as anything but mature. If anything, it attempts too much. Kunrad's oration to the populace, a temptation to Wagnerian moralizing, is treated as the occasion for an early display of Strauss's pot-pourri style and is highly successful. It includes a love-theme from earlier in the work transformed into this waltz, the ancestor of Baron Ochs's favourite tune (see Ex. 10).

As has been seen in *Also sprach Zarathustra*, the waltz was of cardinal importance to Strauss. It marks him out as a child of his time in company with Mahler, selecting the elements of his music from many disparate and 'impure' ingredients and blending them into a distinctive style. Both composers were quick to

seize on features of popular music to forge their styles. *Feuersnot* is a clear pointer to the Strauss of *Der Rosenkavalier* and a useful essay in the one-act form in which Strauss always excelled and was about to produce two masterpieces.

A weakness of both *Guntram* and *Feuersnot* is that neither contains a really rewarding principal rôle, the sort of rôles that generations of sopranos, baritones or tenors will want to sing come hell or high water in order to present their credentials. In his next two operas Strauss was to provide such rôles, and he continued to do so with enviable prodigality. *Salome* is the first of his immortal individual vocal creations. In Wilde's play he found both a central character whom he could portray operatically as vividly as he had depicted Don Quixote orchestrally and a theme which enabled him to dabble in the fashionable orientalism of the time. Other Eastern operas, he said, 'lacked the colour and the sunlight of the East'. He would provide them. In fact he provided, with astonishing technical resource, the Palestinian night, bathed in moonlight, sultry and fragrant.

Salome is a study in obsession. Gabriel Fauré described it in

1907 as 'a symphonic poem with vocal parts added', an accurate assessment when one contemplates the immense and immensely inventive details of the orchestral score. Using over 100 instrumentalists, Strauss achieves fantastic effects of tone-colour to mirror not only every action on the stage but the thoughts of each character in the drama. Time has not dimmed the startling effects he obtains by means of trills dominated by the E flat clarinet, the exotic percussion, and a whole armoury of sensational string sounds, notably the eerie sound which breaks the silence as Salome leans over the cistern in the execution episode and which is created by four double basses 'pinching' the string with thumb and forefinger and striking it sharply with the bow.

Yet the operatic nature of *Salome* should not be underestimated. Its nightmare intensity, the relentless build-up of horror as Salome's insane sexual desire for Jokanaan's death blots out all other feelings, is achieved by vocal characterization and insight to match the orchestral legerdemain. Perhaps Ernest Newman was right in his belief that the opera grew from the Closing Scene, modelled on Isolde's *Liebestod*, for this is the most fluently organic section of the score, erotic, seductive and genuinely tragic, words and music more closely interlocked than in some earlier parts of the opera. This perverted *Liebestod* includes some of Strauss's most daring harmonic adventures in dual tonality, with cellos in A major clashing with the F sharp major of the violins, the latter being a favourite key for Strauss when expressing consummation of every kind. This startling moment is exceeded by the epoch-making dissonance with which Strauss takes Salome, in C sharp major, to the depth of degradation as she exults 'I have kissed your mouth, Jokanaan' (see Ex. 11).

Arduous and taxing rôle though it is, Salome attracts sopranos both by reason of its vocal fertility and its opportunities for a striking psychological portrayal. It can be filled by a heroic Wagnerian soprano or by a lighter voice. There is an inherent contradiction in the conception of this sixteen-year-old princess

Ex. 11

singing with the force and maturity of Isolde. Few singers could encompass satisfactorily both the childlike and the sensual elements in the part. Strauss recognized one who could in Elisabeth Schumann and offered to conduct for her and to damp down the orchestra. She did not sing Salome, but for Maria Rajdl at Dresden in 1930, also a light soprano, Strauss reduced the orchestration. Strauss became disturbed, too, by the tendency of singers to overact the rôle, especially in the Dance of the Seven Veils, where cavortings and capers aroused his ire. 'Salome, being a chaste virgin and an oriental princess, must be played with the simplest and most restrained of gestures,' he wrote. His interpretation of the score was markedly 'deadpan'. He had written all the emotional expression into it and it needs no extra gloss.

If Salome is the first of Strauss's great female rôles, Herod is the finest tenor part he was ever to write. 'It is not a voice, it is a disease' was Bülow's opinion of tenors, and basses and baritones are generally better served. But while Jokanaan is more impressive in wrath than in prayer, Herod is a magnificent study in pathological weakness, perversity, feigned dignity and outraged revulsion. In Herodias, too, Strauss created a detached character, enigmatic and chilling. What is perhaps most impressive about *Salome* is its meticulously calculated construction, so typical of Strauss. The music seethes, writhes, glitters, insinuates, yet there is not a stray note. Detachment and control are Strauss's strongest dramatic virtues. Whatever went on in his heart—and in *Salome* he was putting hysteria on to the stage—the brain that guided the hand in the study at Garmisch remained cool. The neat handwriting on all the manuscripts tells its own story.

If, by writing *Salome*, Strauss saw the opportunity to cut into Puccini's box-office profits, it is still understandable that he should have been daunted by the idea of following it with a subject so similar in almost every respect, *Elektra*, the first of his collaborations with Hofmannsthal. Here again was an opera in one act about a demented woman in the grip of an obsession, this time that of revenge. The marvel is that though it is composed almost to the same formula as *Salome*, the resulting music is so different. *Salome* begins with a clarinet *glissando* followed by Narraboth's apostrophe to Salome's beauty, and his discussion with the Young Page which succinctly sets the scene for the audience before Salome appears; *Elektra* opens with a similar instrumental *Leitmotiv*, followed by the discussion between the serving-maids which describes the whole vile atmosphere of Klytemnestra's palace and Elektra's part in it, preparing us for Elektra's first monologue. The opening motif represents Agamemnon, the avenging of whose death has obsessed his daughter Elektra for years (this is another of Strauss's memorable short phrases, similar to the *Naturthema* in *Also sprach Zarathustra*). Both operas are constructed in sections like the episodes of a symphonic poem, with the orchestra taking almost a protagonist's rôle at an emotional climax; both have a brief and effective moment of light relief in *Till*-like vein, the Jews' theological bickering in *Salome* and the male servants in *Elektra*; both build inexorably towards the heroine's vocal orgasm as she achieves her objective; and in both operas the heroine's consummation is associated with a dance, voluptuous in Salome's case and an epileptic paroxysm in Elektra's.

Yet the opulent glittering score of *Salome* is the more consciously beautiful, even elegant, notwithstanding its marvellous flavour of depravity. *Elektra* is a heavier, thicker score, the colour of blood, with every effect as carefully calculated as in *Salome*. It is a score of amazing richness, the strings divided into several sections, balanced against forty-one wind instruments, including five clarinets (E flat, B flat and A), a heckelphone, two basset-horns and Wagner tubas. This huge array is used with surpassing skill to convey terror, cruelty, frustration, all the darkest secrets of human nature. It produces gigantic dissonance and superb diatonic splendour. In his use of bitonality and of polytonality (especially in combinations of minor triads) Strauss stretched his harmonic vocabulary as far as it was ever to go, to the frontier of atonality, in order to project the nightmare aspects of the drama, thereby giving hints to Schoenberg for *Erwartung*, as can be heard in the extraordinary passage in Klytemnestra's aria when she describes the nameless nocturnal horror which devours her. Music at this date had never probed so deep into human psychology and found the right sounds to match. Yet it is not all blood and thunder, not all exhibitionist violence. There is lyricism, some of it among the truest-hearted Strauss composed: Elektra's tender recollection of her childhood, for example:

Ex. 12

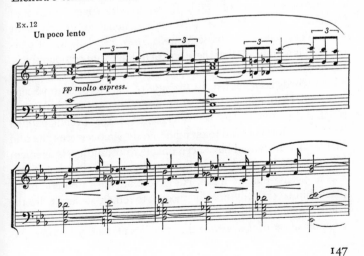

which comes all the more impressively after the great motif in octaves which Ernest Newman unforgettably described as 'rising threateningly from the depths to the heights of the orchestra like a great clenched fist'. Again, in Elektra's quasi-Lesbian declaration of love for her sister Chrysothemis, the fervent and conventional E flat episode heightens the sudden return to frenzy when Chrysothemis shirks involvement in matricide.

Greatest of all is the Recognition Scene, where Elektra and her brother Orestes are reunited, and Strauss rises to one of the supreme moments in classical drama with a colossal orchestral climax gently subsiding into Elektra's transcendental solo, accompanied by an orchestra in which the strings are much subdivided to produce a bewitching luminous sound, and the soprano sustains a soft high B flat as she sings 'erhabenes Gesicht, O bleib' bei mir' ('Noble countenance, O stay with me'). These and other passages give *Elektra* its balance of contrasts. It is significant that these lyrical passages are comparatively short. Strauss's lyricism was dependent on dramatic situations to which words contributed. In the case of the Recognition Scene he asked Hofmannsthal for some extra lines to enable him to sustain the mood. He was incapable of the broad-spanned lyrical invention needed for symphonic slow movements; he told Mahler that he would have been unable to compose a movement like the Adagio of Mahler's Fourth Symphony. In essence, his was a 'jigsaw-puzzle' mind. His invention was often commonplace, but so skilfully does he piece it together, so subtle are the transformations and so psychologically apposite is the constant re-application of *Leitmotive* that this jigsaw ability becomes his principal hallmark. (For a fully detailed analysis of this procedure, the interested reader is referred to Mr Del Mar's volumes and their copious music examples.) Strauss once confessed that he 'always spoilt' his music by the use of too much counterpoint, for his mind worked naturally in complex and contrapuntal terms. This was said in a self-doubting moment, but his creative spirit rightly led him into self-indulgence of his gifts, where his strength lay.

Hofmannsthal's libretto gave Strauss, for the first time, three major rôles for women's voices, two sopranos and a mezzo. In their next opera, *Der Rosenkavalier*, this combination was to encompass the varied moods of love; in *Elektra* it explores psychological obsessions. Elektra herself, Strauss's Brünnhilde, is a classic case of father-fixation. She exists by thinking of 'the deed' she is to do—the murder of her mother and her stepfather Aegisthus—and for which she has buried an axe in readiness. Yet when Orestes comes, he does the deed and she forgets to give him the axe. Her ghastly final dance is an orgy of frustration. Chrysothemis personifies lack of maternal fulfilment. The aria in which she expresses her longing for a normal married life is touching if the character is portrayed as a tragic, wasted, neurotic woman. In Klytemnestra we see the vengeance that guilt can wreak on the body and mind by psychosomatic means. Strauss drew these three wretched hysterical women in sharply defined vocal characterization; the rôles are extremely testing but eminently singable. *Salome* and *Elektra* are 'shockers'—they make the Italian *verismo* composers seem like something from Children's Corner—but if they sound crude and vulgar the fault lies with singers and conductors, not with Strauss's meticulous scores. When he spoke of *Salome* as 'fairy music by Mendelssohn' and of *Elektra* as like Lortzing, he was of course exaggerating, but he was giving interpreters the strongest possible clue to his intentions. *Elektra* is particularly vulnerable to a too loud and unvaried assault by a badly conducted orchestra; the invariable result is devaluation of the music, which is thereby often exposed as no fiercer than Brahms.

Elektra ends with a chord of C major, as if to emphasize that, despite having peered down the harmonic abyss, Strauss had no intention of pursuing a revolutionary course. It is sometimes said that thereby he drew back from reality and took refuge in rococo artificiality. If Strauss had wished to continue along the atonal path, he could easily have done so: few composers have been so formidably equipped technically. But he was a realist. He knew there was room for only one *Salome* and one *Elektra* in his music. He had pioneered that path, let others follow it wherever it might lead. He wanted to do something different and he wanted it to be comedy.

DER ROSENKAVALIER, ARIADNE AUF NAXOS

Strauss was always alert and responsive to the mood of the day, holding a mirror to contemporary life. In *Salome* he reflected the *fin-de-siècle* fashion for decadence and *art nouveau* in the manner of Wilde and Aubrey Beardsley; in *Elektra* there are Freudian overtones, even if they are accidental; and in *Der Rosenkavalier* he wrote the opera *par excellence* which enshrines pre-1914 Europe, its opulence and gaiety, the sense of time running out, the cynicism, the beauty, the abundance of melody, and the refusal to face reality. (Conversion to belief in a *Zeitgeist* is practically ensured by contemplation of the year 1910, with Mahler composing his Tenth Symphony, Elgar his Second and Strauss *Der Rosenkavalier*.) In composing his greatest opera Strauss created a unique and unmistakable atmosphere, a Vienna, city of everyone's dreams, inhabited by four marvellous characters who rank in the operatic portrait-gallery with the *dramatis personae* of *Le nozze di Figaro* and *Die Meistersinger*. Yet, ironically, the work is a Bavarian parody of Vienna, even to the waltzes, which time has turned into 'the real thing'.

It seems sometimes that everything Strauss wrote before 1909 was sketchwork for *Rosenkavalier* and everything he wrote after it took it as a point of reference. It is his quintessence and understandably his most popular work. It has everything that the public loves most: a good plot, sentiment, a mixture of elegant wit and broad farce, waltzes, soaring melodies, a hovering between laughter and tears, and a period setting. (One of Hofmannsthal's many masterstrokes was to place the work in mid-eighteenth century Vienna, an era closely parallel to that of the early twentieth century, when society was on the edge of the precipice; Strauss added a musical masterstroke by underpinning the whole structure with a glorious anachronism, the waltz.) It is also on the grand scale, offering opportunities for beautiful sets and costumes, and the libretto is one of the half-dozen best in existence, truly a 'comedy for music' but with an independent life as a remarkable piece of dramatic characterization.

With *Rosenkavalier* Strauss moved away for ever from the neo-Wagnerian saturation of *Elektra* and began the refining process which was directed towards equating words and music in his brand of music-drama. True, a large orchestra is still used, but the predominant feature of the score is the clarity and refinement of the orchestral writing, with the full forces reserved for passages where their effect will be greatest. Strauss's craftsmanship in *Rosenkavalier* is of a superior order, not only in intricate and subtle deployment of short and memorable motifs but in the illustrative quality of the scoring, every detail touched in—a poignant oboe, a romantic horn, a splash of trumpet tone, a rhythmic allusion.[1] Not a movement on the stage, not the lift of an eyebrow nor a meaning glance but is reflected in the orchestra. The erotic horn-calls in the Prelude tell of the

---

[1] It should be added that it remains exceedingly difficult to play well. When Karl Böhm conducted the 199th Dresden performance he called nineteen orchestral rehearsals, and one of the senior players told him afterwards: 'It was not one too many. It hasn't got any easier.'

consuming physical nature of Oktavian's relationship with the Marschallin; the flute describes the hairdresser's fingers in the Levée; the candles at the inn in Act III are lit to woodwind trills.

But the orchestral virtuosity goes deeper than mere illustration. The justly famous passage of the Presentation of the Rose, one of the great moments in opera, represented for Hofmannsthal the kernel of the plot, the moment when two young people meet and are instantly attracted before they know anything of each other's imperfections, a moment of dreamlike, idealistic romance. Strauss sets it marvellously, evoking all the rapture and wonder of the scene, and he produces an unforgettable sound to fix this moment: shifting harmonies for three flutes, three solo violins, two harps and celesta.

Yet by these very harmonies the worldly Strauss also conveys the disillusionment to follow, the brittleness of lovers' vows. *Rosenkavalier* is full of such subtleties. Perhaps the most surprising of them, though the most Straussian in its daring use of thematic transformation, concerns the other climactic passage, the wonderful Act III Trio in which the soprano voices soar and blend and diverge as the Marschallin, Oktavian and Sophie express their private thoughts at this crucial juncture in their lives. The melodic basis is:

Ex. 13

This has first been heard earlier in the act as the comic waltz to which Oktavian, disguised as a girl, sings 'Nein, nein, I trink kein Wein' when Ochs tries to make her drunk as a prelude to seduction.

Strauss gloried in the challenge of writing for three sopranos, and he created rôles which are as indispensable to women singers as Brünnhilde, Isolde, Leonora and Violetta. The part of Oktavian, the Rosenkavalier, is a *travesti* rôle, descended from Cherubino, demanding lustrous tone and a gift for comedy from its singer. Perhaps its most arduous requirement is in making the contrast between the impetuous young lover of an older married woman in Act I and the lover of naïve and inexperienced Sophie in Acts II and III. It is fascinating to hear the style Strauss adopted for Elektra's taunting of Aegisthus transformed into Oktavian's mockery of Baron Ochs auf Lerchenau. Sophie, too, is a difficult rôle, needing a high lyric soprano who can in a sophisticated manner float the ecstatic phrases of the Presentation scene:

and can also suggest without archness an innocence comparable to that required for the last movement of Mahler's Fourth Symphony.

In the bass and baritone rôles of Ochs and Faninal, Strauss's music penetrates to the lewd country-cousin boorishness of the former and the *nouveau-riche* snobbery of the latter. Nevertheless the finest rôle in the opera, the creation which lifts it on to a higher emotional level, is that of the Feldmarschallin. Though she never appears in Act II and only in a comparatively short episode of Act III, she is the dominant figure. In Strauss's gallery of women the Marschallin (musical cousin of Mozart's Countess) is the most hauntingly and closely observed, a part written by a composer who understood every inflexion of the soprano voice and who also understood women.

Through the Marschallin, Strauss imparted to *Rosenkavalier* the poignancy which is a vital ingredient of the finest comedy—'one eye wet, the other dry', as he himself expressed it. There is much to be learned about his skill as a composer of operas from the way he builds the Marschallin's character during the superb first act, so that by its end the audience is at her feet. He does this by means of three subdued monologues which are the parallels of the finest variations in *Don Quixote*. For the first half of the act there is nothing about her specially to engage our sympathy: a thirty-two year old wife, bored by her older husband and engaged in the latest of a succession of amorous diversions, holding her morning levée like a Lady Bountiful and becoming irritated because her hairdresser has made her look older. It is only when the levée is over and Ochs and his retinue have left that the woman's deeper feelings begin to emerge—the first time that she is alone. The orchestration, which during the levée [1] has been Strauss the picture-book illustrator at his most graphic—monkeys, parrots, dogs, orphans, all are delineated—is now

[1] This levée scene is an almost exact replica of the fourth drawing in Hogarth's 'Marriage à la Mode'.

reduced to the intimacy of chamber-music to accompany the Marschallin's musings. Strauss completely changes the mood of the opera by themes like these:

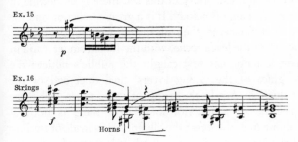

Oktavian returns ready to resume the love-making of the first scene but finds the Marschallin changed and in a mood he cannot understand. It is wonderful how Strauss's music conveys this emotional change, with Oktavian's impulsive ardour quelled by a new theme in which all the Marschallin's sense of the evanescence of life is expressed:

In Act III, when she acknowledges that she has yielded Oktavian to Sophie, this theme is recalled with memorable effectiveness. It heralds, in Act I, the tensest music of the opera as Oktavian's youthful pleadings are answered by the Marschallin's philosophizing: 'Bis in mein Herzhinein. . . .' 'In the depths of my heart I sense that one should keep nothing . . . everything dissolves like mist and dreams.' There is no soaring cantilena here, just radiant arioso-like melody culminating in the famous description of Time and of how she sometimes creeps from her room in the night and stops all the clocks. Her simple religious faith permeates the next duet when she explains to Oktavian that she knows he will one day leave her for a younger woman.

If nothing else in the opera, except the final Trio, attains the level of musico-dramatic unity in this act, there is no decline in vitality or outpouring of melody. It is a great confection and for some tastes it is too sweet (the fault of the taste, not the music). The virtuosity of the levée scene, with the Italian singer's aria in which many a tenor has first caught the public's notice; the Mozartian grace of the young lovers' final duet and of the 'breakfast duet' in Act I; the string of waltz tunes—all these suggest pastiche of a superior kind.[1] Yet there is nothing 'pseudo' about *Rosenkavalier*; the Silver Rose is made of sterling silver and the icing on the cake is hard. It is a very long opera (Ochs's part being second only to Susanna's in *Figaro* in length), and there are *longueurs*, intensified in a poor or poorly sung production. It shares some of the faults, as well as the virtues, of *Die Meistersinger*: the spinning-out of the plot until it threatens to snap, and the cardinal flaw that the discomfiture of Ochs and Beckmesser is not really funny. (Here, also, much depends on how Ochs is acted. Strauss emphasized that he was 'a member of the gentry' if 'at heart a cad'. He modelled him on Falstaff.)

The period element in the opera is simply a dramatic convenience, for it transcends period and becomes timeless, like medieval Nuremberg in *Die Meistersinger* and eighteenth-century Seville in *Figaro*, because the characters are contemporary with every age. *Rosenkavalier* may be bracketed with them without offence to the spirits of Mozart and Wagner because it is an opera of inexhaustible fascination, enabling successive singers, conductors, producers and listeners to find something new in it at each revival, to vary the nuances and stress the accents. Though there is much in the rest of Strauss that has

---

[1] The waltz Ochs sings at the end of Act II is identical, even to key, with Josef Strauss's *Dynamiden*, Op. 173—whether by accident or design is not known.

been underrated and compared disadvantageously with his
greatest success, the unalterable fact remains that he will be
known first and foremost as the composer of *Der Rosenkavalier*
—and justly so.

Earlier chapters have traced the stormy genesis of *Ariadne auf
Naxos*, a crucial work not only in the Strauss-Hofmannsthal
collaboration (for it shows them pulling different ways yet
arriving at the same destination) but in Strauss's musical development. The original Molière-play–Strauss-opera version is
feasible only where and when the Utopian situation exists of
first-rate theatrical and operatic companies working in close
partnership.[1] The second version, ill-starred at first, has now
won a steady place in the repertoire and is particularly effective
in a small opera house like Glyndebourne where exquisite production and singing are *de rigueur*.

No production, however, can disguise the dichotomy of
Hofmannsthal's concern for the deep seriousness of his treatment of the Ariadne legend, with its basic theme of fidelity, and
Strauss's delight in the *commedia dell'arte* characters, particularly
Zerbinetta, who fed his growing appetite for his own lighter,
Till side. The combination of *opera seria* and *opera buffa*, on the
lines of Monteverdi's *L'incoronazione di Poppea*, enabled Strauss
to show off his versatility and to employ a small orchestra
(thirty-six players), as he had done in the Marschallin's monologue in *Der Rosenkavalier*. Even more brilliantly effective is the
Prologue added in 1916 which, in its use of *secco* recitative,
parlando dialogue and bursts of melody, is the stylistic forerunner of *Intermezzo*, *Arabella* and *Capriccio*. Here, too, Strauss
showed himself a 'modern', a pioneer, by putting on to the
operatic stage the realism—albeit within a 'period' frame—of
backstage tantrums and panics, of a composer undergoing the

[1] It has twice been revived in Britain since the Second World War,
very successfully by Beecham at the Edinburgh Festival of 1950 (nine
performances) and less well at Glyndebourne in 1962.

pangs of inspiration amid the need to make cuts and alterations, of a tyrannical Maecenas, a philistine impresario, and that general air of makeshift which is indispensable to the world of the theatre—you can almost smell the greasepaint and the size, and it is all done by sophistication mixed with the bran-tub.

By making the Composer an Oktavian-like figure, Strauss created yet another rewarding and appealing soprano rôle which, short though it is, attracts the finest Straussian exponents. Because Strauss understood these Prologue characters, knew their counterparts in life (none cleverer than he at placating jealous sopranos), his music for them veers from his humorous witty vein (Zerbinetta's backchat) to his soaringly lyrical, as when the Composer composes, when he and Zerbinetta discover that they are soulmates, and finally in the Composer's ecstatic outpouring to the holy art of music:

Ex. 18

These moments of rapture for a soprano voice—deriving from his *Lieder*—were rapidly becoming Strauss's stock-in-trade, but though it is easy to say that with each example he was repeating himself, in fact they are all subtly varied to suit the character portrayed. This can easily be seen in *Ariadne* by comparing the Composer's arias with those given to Ariadne herself, which are equally lyrical yet sound as if they were conceived instrumentally in the manner of the final scenes of *Elektra* and *Salome*, whereas the Composer's spring from the text. Strauss certainly understood Ariadne, and in the main part of the opera she achieves musically the importance Hofmannsthal intended. Even so, a listener's memories of *Ariadne auf Naxos* are probably principally of the Nymphs' Rhinemaidenish trio and of Zerbinetta's showpiece aria (mercifully much reduced and eased from its first, rather tiresome version) rather than of the long Bacchus-Ariadne love-duet which ends the work. Fine though this is, it makes a conventionally rhetorical ending to a delightful if self-consciously 'specialist' entertainment, and one regrets the elimination of the original finale in which Zerbinetta and her followers bring down the curtain on a note of mockery and artificiality.

There is good music in the final duet. William Mann perhaps goes too far in calling it 'a lengthy failure'. Admittedly one has heard performances which justify this stricture, but also ones which, if only temporarily, sweep away one's conviction that this is Strauss below his best, attempting to re-create the Recognition Scene of *Elektra* but without the real impetus to do so. The genuine note of exaltation is either missing or contrived. Perhaps he felt that Hofmannsthal's text never fully succeeds in conveying the lofty content of the poet's intentions; or perhaps the root of the trouble is that he was always more inspired if there was an element of scepticism in the text. Part of the reason why the end of *Rosenkavalier* is so moving is the worldliness of the unanswered questions: will Oktavian and Sophie be happy, has the Marschallin really renounced him? Strauss was a master of this cynical mood. He tried to inject it into the end of *Ariadne* by giving the closing passages of the love-duet echoes of the *Rosenkavalier* Trio and by prefacing Zerbinetta's brief final entry by the celesta, but we do not experience a comparable *frisson*.

For Ariadne, especially when writing in D flat, the key he loved best for passionate exposition, Strauss could nearly do the trick; the stumbling-block is Bacchus, a tenor. Strauss could write well for character-tenors—Herod, Aegisthus, Valzacchi—but the tenor as hero was not his element, even less so when Hofmannsthal had drawn such a wooden, not to say stupid, Bacchus. There is also the visual factor. 'Young, magical, dreamy' is the stage description of this god when he arrives—after a big build-up from Echo, Naiad and Dryad—tactlessly mistaking Ariadne for Circe, with whom he had spent the previous day. Few tenors with the voice for Bacchus have the looks, too, and in that respect the rôle is more convincing on a recording.

The student of Strauss will find continual delight in the quotations buried in the score—references to *Tristan*, to a Schubert song and to Mendelssohn, among others—and in the felicity of the scoring. An interesting inclusion is the harmonium, already used in *Feuersnot, Salome* and *Rosenkavalier* but here given an important function in the *opera seria* sections to supply something of the warm and full sonority of which Strauss had deprived himself by his chamber format. He used it, in his own words, 'simultaneously with, and as a substitute for, whole groups of instruments, such as fifth and sixth horns, trombones, bassoons, flutes, oboes, clarinets, etc.'. In the *buffo* episodes the pianoforte is used as the continuo instrument, entirely happily.

These instrumental forces, excluding the harmonium, are also those required for the music for *Der Bürger als Edelmann*, now usually known under its French title *Le Bourgeois Gentilhomme*. This is more familiar to audiences as a concert suite of nine movements. Indubitably this is the best of Strauss the connoisseur. In his vein of highest-quality pastiche there is nothing to touch it. By comparison the *buffo* music of *Ariadne* is less sparkling. The wit is Haydnesque, the elegance and charm are Mozartian, the whole is Straussian. There is the inevitable waltz, one of the most delicious he wrote, and the melody which the Composer writes on stage in the Prologue to the second version of *Ariadne*—'Du Venus Sohn'—is first heard as the oboe melody of the Sicilienne, as captivating in its lilting grace as are the Minuet and Courante. The Dinner Music is the acme of Straussian parody, Jourdain's menu being carefully devised by Hofmannsthal to give his partner every chance for apt allusions. The waiters enter to a distorted version of Meyerbeer's Coronation March from *Le Prophète*; Rhine salmon evokes the Rhine motif from Wagner's *Ring*; the saddle of mutton evidently came from the flock of sheep Don Quixote encountered, and while it is eaten a solo cello suggests that the Don is not far away; a dish of larks and thrushes provides the opportunity to recall the birds in Act I of *Rosenkavalier*; and the surprise in the *omelette surprise* is provided by the kitchen boy who jumps out of the huge dish and dances—not such a surprise—a Viennese waltz.

In *Music Ho!* Constant Lambert called Stravinsky the 'time-traveller'. The term may be applied to many composers, not least to Strauss. It was the age of time-travelling in music—Ravel to Mozart and Couperin; Webern, Schoenberg, Elgar and others to Bach and Handel; Vaughan Williams to Tallis; Debussy to the Javanese; Stravinsky to Pergolesi. Strauss time-travelled to Lully, Couperin, Mozart, to the waltz, to the age of Schumann. He borrowed their styles and made them his own so convincingly that they are valuable in their own right, not as imitations. *Le Bourgeois Gentilhomme* stands with Stravinsky's *The Rake's Progress* and Prokofiev's *Classical Symphony* as a supreme example of its genre.

DIE FRAU OHNE SCHATTEN, INTERMEZZO

Die Frau ohne Schatten (*The Woman without a Shadow*) is likely to remain the most problematical and tantalizing of Strauss's operas. Some consider it to be his greatest, but although it contains passages which rank as the greatest music he wrote, its satisfactoriness as an opera is questionable, because of the labyrinthine complexity of Hofmannsthal's plot and libretto. It is a hymn to the sanctity of marriage, and deals with the vital need for sexual satisfaction between the partners, allied to the importance of children and the problems arising from childlessness. But these elementals are camouflaged amid such a forest of obscure and pretentious symbolism, prolonged to Wagner proportions, that the majority of the audience leaves the theatre baffled by the meaning of it all and even perhaps sniggeringly contemptuous of such scenes as unborn children pleading to be brought into existence while fishes materialize from the air and land in a frying-pan; dream lovers appearing in visions; and *Zauberflöte*-like trials by fire and water. The analogy with Mozart's last opera is further emphasized by the contrasted strata in which the action occurs: the fairy-tale world of Emperor and Empress dominated by the magician Kaikobad and the drab human world of the dyer Barak and his barren wife.

Hofmannsthal enjoyed implying that Strauss was much his intellectual inferior, and his admirers blame Strauss for failing fully to comprehend the genius of the poet's ideas. Strauss was certainly, if not an intellectual, a man of intellect in his own right when one considers his deep knowledge of Goethe and of classical literature, his love of paintings and his encyclopedic knowledge of a vast range of music, but he was never pretentious. His practicality and his Bavarian bourgeois common sense protected him from the bogus. He appreciated the inner meaning of *Die Frau ohne Schatten* but, as the letters quoted in Chapter 9 show, he feared it would not come through in the opera-house in dramatic terms. He sensed that the characters were symbols, not true human beings, and he felt ill at ease with abstract ideas. It remains a near-miracle, therefore, that he was able to breathe so much operatic life into them.

Operas survive obscure libretti if their music is strong enough, and Strauss saved *Die Frau* by a Herculean display of prowess. Norman Del Mar's application of the term 'mental lethargy' to post-1913 Strauss, and many other writers' too glib assumption that Strauss ceased to progress after *Elektra*, are alike confounded and contradicted by the wonderful score of *Die Frau ohne Schatten*. In every way it is an astonishing advance, technical and emotional, on all that he had hitherto written. As *Also sprach Zarathustra* has a special quality of sound among the tone-poems, so has *Die Frau* among the operas. Writing for a large and exotic orchestra, Strauss achieved a major advance in his striving towards a correct balance and blend between voices and instruments. The translucent quality of the scoring, and the emphasis on a *concertante* instrumental style, suggest the influence of Mahler's *Das Lied von der Erde* (indeed the spirit of Mahler broods over the whole work, for the grandiose finale owes much to the finale of the Eighth Symphony and fails for most of the same reasons).

Act I in particular is a *locus classicus* for students of Strauss's orchestration. It is the best act in the opera, for one senses Strauss's initial enthusiasm for the subject and his interest in creating the characters. Its episodic lay-out allowed him to revert to the symphonic-poem style of *Salome*. He worked best when short-winded, or when vignettes were required rather than landscapes, and it is noteworthy that for all its large and opulent scale *Die Frau* might have been called 'fantastic variations on a theme of magical character', with the eight orchestral interludes playing a significant part in conveying by exclusively instru-mental means the ideas which Hofmannsthal failed to elucidate. Here, in the first scene, are the ingredients which guaranteed

Straussian success: creation of a sinister atmosphere, depiction of hunting, of a falcon (a superb and unforgettable theme, first heard on piccolo, oboes and E flat clarinet), the limning of a beautiful woman (the Empress, bewitchingly introduced and

Ex. 19

2 Flutes & Oboe

Solo Viola

Solo Cello

2 Cellos (muted)

Solo Double Bass

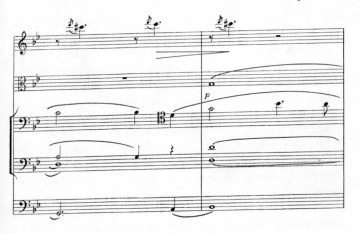

accompanied by solo viola, solo violin, flageolets on the second
harp, and piquant woodwind), and a sunrise.

More unexpected is Strauss's success in writing convincingly
lyrical heroic and passionate music for the tenor who sings the

165

Emperor. Yet fine as his Act I aria is, even finer is that in Act II, Scene 2, a long monologue in the Emperor's hunting-lodge. This is preceded by a masterly orchestral introduction in which the falcon's desolate cry on the woodwind is superimposed on two of the Emperor's principal themes played with melancholy and sombre beauty by a solo cello and elaborated by solo cellos, solo viola and solo double-bass in a notable anticipation of Strauss's late-period writing for strings (see Ex. 19 above).

Equally successful, when one recalls the relatively ineffective Jokanaan in *Salome*, is Strauss's treatment of the good-hearted character of Barak the dyer, one of his most rewarding bass-baritone rôles. The explanation may be sought in the auto-biographical nature of the characterization, since Strauss would easily identify himself with an even-tempered, hard-working, simple man like Barak, whereas he would never have laid claim to the pious godliness of a prophet. Barak's wife is also a vivid character, being yet another manifestation of Pauline. A further chapter of the *Symphonia Domestica* is the very beautiful orchestral interlude in the first scene between Barak and his wife which epitomizes Barak's compassionate nature and his love for her. The passage is a simple melodizing round the tonic key of D major for full strings with conventional woodwind and brass, and its impassioned warmth suggests a combination of Strauss, Elgar and the Wagner of *Tristan*. It is among the loveliest episodes in any Strauss opera.

This particular passage is harmonically simple. Yet there are several occasions where the harmonies are as rootless and as near to atonal as any in *Elektra*. The extraordinary scene of the Empress's dream, for example, ends with an orchestral interlude in which the strangeness of the harmonies is responsible for summing up the nightmarish quality of the preceding scene. Another amazing orchestral passage is the description in Act I of the journey of the Empress and the Nurse to earth in which the discordant treatment of the themes is intensified by the transference of the falcon's cry to tubas, a crude but undeniably effective device. In this passage Strauss employs his large array of percussion, including Chinese gongs, castanets, whips and xylophone (possibly giving a hint to Puccini for *Turandot*, which in several curious ways resembles *Die Frau ohne Schatten*, and not only in the obvious similarities of an Oriental setting and overtones of erotic sadism). Another feature of the score is a glass harmonica, used with perfect judgment in the final scene where some apposite but unusual sound was needed to depict the Empress's acquisition of a shadow.

The last act is the least successful, although it opens impressively with a magnificent duet for Barak and his wife, Barak's 'Mir anvertraut' being one of the best tunes in the opera, and contains a great aria for the Empress in which the woodwind's accompanying phrases anticipate *Daphne*. But as the plot thickens—no cliché in this case—so does Strauss's power of invention as he struggles to clear a path through the increasingly tortuous complexities of Hofmannsthal's thought-processes. In the last scene, their trials over, the two couples are reunited, soon-to-be-born (presumably) children sing, the Empress's shadow becomes a golden arch, and the whole extraordinary culmination calls for music of transcendental sublimity. Strauss failed to provide it; although he pulls out every stop in the orchestra to provide a feast of colourful sound, he can no more avoid banality than Mahler did when he strove to universalize religion and eternal womanhood in his Eighth Symphony. In terms of such high-flown operatic endeavour, only Mozart in *Die Zauberflöte*, Beethoven in *Fidelio* and Vaughan Williams in *The Pilgrim's Progress* have matched the sublime mood of their final scene. So Strauss's failure may be accounted glorious.

The difficulties of *Die Frau ohne Schatten* lie not only in its symbolism. It is the Strauss-Hofmannsthal 'opera-spectacular' requiring the production skills found more often in Drury Lane musicals of 1935 vintage than in opera houses. Transformation scenes, materializations, scenic effects—only *Das Rheingold* gives the stagehands and electricians a comparably perilous and exacting evening. It is no wonder that Strauss was dissatisfied with most of the productions he saw, for the skills applicable to pantomime were not to be found in Dresden, Munich and Vienna. Also, it is an opera for a cast of great singers under a great conductor. So are all Strauss's operas: nothing but the best will ever do for them, for he was the supreme craftsman turning out very high-class goods. His demands in *Die Frau* are almost superhuman, and he was fortunate that the work was launched by such legendary artists as Lotte Lehmann, Maria Jeritza, Lucie Weidt, Richard Mayr and Karl Aagard-Oestvig. Only when such a cast can be assembled, with a glittering production to support them, can *Die Frau ohne Schatten* be performed with anything approaching justice to its many inspirations of genius, and this usually means that it remains a festival opera.

This is not undesirable. Like *Parsifal*, it needs to be approached in a devoted frame of mind, after due preparation. In such circumstances, as in Karl Böhm's marvellous 1974 performances at Salzburg, its effect can be overwhelming, for the marvels of the orchestral web, the superb writing for superb voices, and the dazzling stage spectacle can induce temporary suspension of any effort to disentangle Hofmannsthal's farrago while one surrenders to the all-important factor, music, and in the process understands the plot. And for nine-tenths of its course *Die Frau ohne Schatten* is music of spellbinding quality.

Yet it is scarcely surprising that, after writing outstanding music for *Josephslegende* and *Die Frau ohne Schatten* against the grain of his nature, Strauss should have turned for relief to a subject in which he knew he excelled—domestic realism. He was not, and knew he was not, a composer like Mahler and Bruckner who attempted to give their work a Beethovenian universality. Hofmannsthal believed himself to be that kind of poet and tried to take Strauss with him to scale metaphysical heights. In three successive works, *Ariadne auf Naxos*, *Josephslegende* and *Die Frau ohne Schatten*, Strauss was required to compose finales which, to borrow Ernest Newman's phrase, would 'give the cosmos its A'. Each time he failed. His way of reaching the hearts of men and women was through the physical attraction of an Oktavian and a Sophie or the worldly renunciation of a Marschallin, not by attempting to follow Hofmannsthal into such philosophical disquisitions as (apropos of the final duet of *Ariadne*): 'Transformation is the life of life itself, the real mystery of Nature as creative force.' It annoyed Hofmannsthal that Strauss was more interested in Zerbinetta than in Ariadne, but Strauss knew that the audience would be more interested in her too. Probably only in *Elektra* and *Arabella* were Strauss and Hofmannsthal composing the same opera.

The finale of *Die Frau ohne Schatten* was composed during 1916 simultaneously with the new Prologue to *Ariadne*; it is obvious which task Strauss enjoyed the more. In creating the Composer and providing the delicate back-stage love-skirmish with Zerbinetta, he was in his element. Moreover, in his avowed desire to intensify natural diction and speed of dialogue in opera, the *Sprechgesang* style he had adopted in the *Ariadne* Prologue fitted his needs perfectly. His alternation of *recitativo secco* and *recitativo accompagnato* was assured and polished, an advance on his treatment of the part of the Nurse in *Die Frau ohne Schatten* in which he attempted 'to inject new life into the style and pace of the old *recitativo secco* by means of an orchestral accompaniment using mainly solo instruments and filling in the background with light strokes'. The Nurse, however, is an enigmatic and unsympathetic part. Now, after his success with the Composer, he was ready to start the domestic 'slice of life' on which he had long set his sights. He originally called it *Marriage Intermezzo*, but later shortened this to *Intermezzo*.

It is well known that *Intermezzo* was based on an episode in the Strausses' life arising from a misunderstanding in a Berlin bar in

1903, when an Italian tenor and an impresario were approached by one Mitzi Mücke for two tickets for the opera. They introduced her to their companion, the company's conductor Josef Stransky (who was later to succeed Mahler in New York). The Italian repeatedly mispronounced his name as Strausky. Stransky forgot the tickets, and the persistent Mitzi looked up what she thought was his name and address in the telephone directory. But she found Hofkapellmeister *Strauss* and sent this note to Joachimsthalerstrasse: 'Dear Sweetheart. Do send me the tickets. Your faithful Mitzi.' This arrived while Strauss was in England and was opened by Pauline, who flew into a rage, assumed that a long-standing affair had been disclosed, and began divorce proceedings. The astonished Strauss was summoned home by his friend Friedrich Rösch, who eventually sorted the matter out and persuaded Pauline of her husband's innocence.

This, with the addition of a mild flirtation Pauline once had, is almost exactly the plot of *Intermezzo*. Most of the dialogue is taken from life: those who knew Richard and Pauline testified to its accuracy. The stage depiction of Pauline is, to quote Lotte Lehmann, 'a monument to her', in her tantrums, snobbishness, chattering, house-proud fussiness and tyrannical attitude to servants. It shows that, maddening though she was, she was also perpetually attractive to Strauss. For a candid biography of Pauline as her husband saw and knew her, one need look no further than *Intermezzo*. Strauss made no secret of the origin of the opera. He thinly disguised himself as Robert Storch, Pauline became Christine, Stransky became Stroh and Mitzi Mücke became Mieze Meier. One of the most brilliant scenes shows his favourite card game of skat. The first singer of Storch at Dresden in 1924, Joseph Correck, wore a mask to make himself look like Strauss, and Strauss and Pauline coached both Correck and Lehmann in making their performances as authentic as possible.

For some extraordinary reason, and especially in Britain, the plot of *Intermezzo* has been regarded as embarrassingly tasteless. (This question of 'taste', always a dubious criterion for forming artistic judgments, seems particularly to trouble English critics of Strauss. One still finds *Salome* described as offensive; and I have known people who, having enjoyed *Rosenkavalier*, are overcome by guilt and purge themselves with a course of Bach fugues.) Even fifty years after *Intermezzo* was first performed, one found (in the 'permissive' era) such judgments as 'When we know that they [the characters] are taken from real life and that excruciating disagreeable episodes of the Strausses' household are being paraded before our embarrassed eyes, even the most hardy audiences must be taken aback. . . . The question arises whether such a scene from his home life . . . should be witnessed on any operatic stage.' [1] Somehow I think that audiences are unlikely to be squeamish at the revelation that married couples row, bicker, falsely accuse each other, and then make up. It is questionable, if Strauss and Pauline did not mind, whether *Intermezzo* was tasteless in their lifetime; it certainly is not now that they have been dead for years. All that matters is whether it is a successful opera.

In fact it is one of Strauss's most successful and sophisticated works, except to those who find its subject-matter not so much tasteless as trivial and inflated. The libretto, by Strauss, if self-indulgent is also skilfully effective. The cinematic short scenes, if not ahead of their time, were a marked advance on what had gone before (and may be compared with those in *Wozzeck*, which was composed at exactly the same time). Both Schoenberg, in *Von heute auf morgen*, and Hindemith, in *Neues vom Tage*, owed something to *Intermezzo*. Whether Strauss succeeded in making the words audible is more debatable, for even if conductors observe his very detailed dynamic markings, the incessant

[1] T. Bloomfield: 'Opera domestica' *Music and Musicians*, Vol. 22, No. 262, June 1974, pp. 34–40.

Richard Strauss

garrulousness of the orchestra in the first scenes is more than a match for Christine's ceaseless chatter on-stage. Even so, the scoring for an orchestra of just over fifty players is outstandingly deft. Strauss used only three horns; the writing for the strings is soloistic; and there is effective and restrained use of the pianoforte. Only in the interludes is the orchestration sonorous and polyphonic in complexity. The most remarkable vocal achievement is the convincing and unforced way in which spoken dialogue and recitative are alternated.

In *Intermezzo* Strauss's inventive imagination was working on a level comparable with the best of *Le Bourgeois Gentilhomme*. It may be, as William Mann avers, that some themes are 'nondescript', but they have a way of lingering in the mind none the less; and the waltzes in the Grundlsee scene are as melodically enticing as those in *Rosenkavalier*, if necessarily less opulent. Those who enjoy the favourite Straussian game of quotation-spotting will find plenty to amuse them in *Intermezzo*: some *Heldenleben* (when Christine mentions a critic), and snatches of Gounod's *Faust*, Verdi's *Otello*, Mozart's *Figaro*, Wagner's *Tristan* and *Parsifal* and Schumann's First Symphony. There is the usual astonishing display of sheer dexterity, the motifs fitting as in a jigsaw and being used with much subtlety. Those for whom musical 'progress' is synonymous with dissonance will find nothing in *Intermezzo*, but it is the first of several works in Strauss's allegedly 'tired' period when his genius was progressing towards the concluding glories of *Capriccio* and the last instrumental works.

Eleven orchestral interludes link the scenes in the two acts. These are designed—and exactly timed by this master theatrical practitioner—to cover scene-changes, but they are an integral part of the opera's psychological unity. Again I must disagree with those who believe that they inflate 'trivial' material out of all proportion—the same criticism that is made with equal injustice about *Symphonia Domestica*. *Intermezzo* is not a trivial work. Hofmannsthal, though repelled by the whole idea, admitted when he heard it that he was surprised by its seriousness. Like the artist he was, he recognized Strauss's skill in concocting such a satisfying mixture of the brittle, the sentimental, the witty, the grotesque and the potentially tragic—for the threat of divorce and the belief of one partner in the other's adultery are not in themselves comic, though legitimate matter for comedy. Strauss admitted that the real-life events took him 'almost to the point of insanity' and wrote to Hofmannsthal in 1927 that 'harmless and insignificant as the incidents which prompted this piece may be, they nevertheless result, when all is said and done, in the most difficult psychological conflicts that can disturb the heart'.[1] This underlying truth-to-life is developed in the interludes—his genuine distress is reflected in the scene in the Prater; the gorgeous fifth interlude in A flat, richly affectionate and tender, is ample testimony to the real meaning of the Richard-and-Pauline marriage, however it may have appeared to others.

Intermezzo is not a 'great' opera in the sense that we apply that adjective to *Tristan* or *Elektra*, but it is a masterpiece of its genre, a highly entertaining evening, and a remarkable early example of what is now known as 'music theatre'. It has no need to rely on the Strauss-Pauline association for its effectiveness: its intrinsic value needs no such meretricious 'publicity'. It has even been shown by a great actress-singer that Christine need not be portrayed as a shrew or harridan, but as a rather beguiling creature. In other words, the work is capable of more than one interpretation. But unless it is performed in a highly stylish manner, it will usually seem twenty minutes too long; and although half the fun is lost if it is not sung in translation, it sounds best in German.

---

[1] It remains puzzling why even the fiery Pauline should have rushed to begin divorce after nine years of marriage, for Strauss was not a philanderer and no extra-marital affairs have ever been authenticated, though rumours persist of a liaison with Elisabeth Schumann in 1921.

Richard Strauss

DIE ÄGYPTISCHE HELENA, ARABELLA

It is no coincidence that of the two operas which Strauss completed in the 1920s—*Intermezzo* and *Die ägyptische Helena*—the former, to his own libretto on a subject he wanted to tackle, is in every way more successful. It was not Strauss who was in decline at this period, but Hofmannsthal (the war had left him psychologically depressed, and he had arterio-sclerosis.)

As earlier chapters have related, the poet was trying hard to accommodate Strauss's post-war desire for a light subject. It is a thousand pities that *Die ägyptische Helena* was not cast in the one-act form Strauss handled so well, so that the satirical mood of Act I could have been sustained to the final curtain. In it are the ingredients of a good spoof mythological opera, anticipating by more than a decade the stage success of *Amphitryon 38*. The soprano sorceress, Aithra, with her odd appurtenance an Omniscient Sea-Shell through which she learns what is happening elsewhere in the world, is a delightful creation. Her colony of elves, mocking and deluding Menelaus, are also a good dramatic device and drew good music from Strauss. The snags arise in Act II where Hofmannsthal wades up to his neck in the symbolism of mistaken identities caused by an overdose, in all respects, of magic potions and introduces a sheikh and his son, Da-ud, who both fall in love with Helen. Hofmannsthal's favourite themes of love-at-first-sight, recognition and the binding influence of children are all worked into this act.

Strauss was deeply conscious of the dichotomy between the two acts and knew it was bound to be reflected in the music. He took a long time to get into the mood for Sheikh Altair, and after Hofmannsthal's death he persuaded Lothar Wallerstein to revise part of the action in Act II for Krauss's Salzburg Festival production in 1933 in an attempt to elucidate it.

Of all Strauss's operas, *Helena* has been the least successful and remains the least known. It has been harshly criticized, but the music does not deserve most of these strictures. It is Strauss's *bel canto* opera, written for the great singers with whom he had been working in Vienna. Act I in particular is full of vocal plums which deserve to be better known. All the music given to Aithra is attractive and brilliant. Helen herself, immortalizing elements of Maria Jeritza and Elisabeth Schumann, is a fully realized creation, warm, unpredictable and sensuous; her duet with Aithra is an example of Strauss's skill in blending two types of soprano. Menelaus is a *Heldentenor* rôle of considerably greater interest than Bacchus in *Ariadne*; indeed, Strauss projects Helen and Menelaus as believable human characters far more successfully than he does Bacchus and Ariadne, even when the words they sing are equally portentous. Their duets in both acts are melodically inspired. I cannot agree that Strauss's invention in this opera is tired and tame; time and again he pulls his librettist's chestnuts out of the fire with a burst of fecund imaginative zeal, such as this glowing theme which dominates the beautiful scene of Helen's awakening:

Ex. 20

Throughout, the orchestration is rich and apposite without becoming fulsome, reflecting a leaner harmonic style of sometimes diamond-like hardness. Helen's great outburst in Act II, 'Zweite Brautnacht', is another superb example of Straussian cantilena for a great soprano, and her scene with Da-ud has a tenderness which says much for Strauss's sheer determination to win some kind of dividend from the characters with which Hofmannsthal had landed him. There is still a future for this opera, if the right producer and the finest singers can be engaged for it. It is not a repertory piece; it is a twentieth-century vocal equivalent of a Bellini opera, strictly reserved for the best.

It would have been sad if the famous collaboration had ended with so seriously flawed an opera as *Die ägyptische Helena*. But in *Arabella* the two men again found a subject with which each was equally at ease. Strauss had kept asking for a second *Rosenkavalier*, had kept hinting at his Offenbach tendencies. His contempt for Lehár perhaps masked envy of that composer's success with subjects for which he himself yearned. He was temperamentally attuned to the characters of *Arabella*, odd bunch that they are. Here, at last, after the mythological and mystical fairy-tales, was a love-story involving fairly ordinary human beings in Vienna, misunderstandings, renunciations and reconciliation. Here was a heroine compounded of elements of the Marschallin and Sophie, in love with one of the oddest 'heroes' in opera but a hero who had to be a baritone. Mandryka, the wealthy, unsophisticated Croatian landowner, is the major difficulty in casting *Arabella*, for he must not only be a fine singer but of impressive physical size.

Hofmannsthal, too, regained his fluency in writing this unimposing libretto. It is direct, affecting, free from pretentiousness. He acquiesced much more gracefully in Strauss's requests for changes, all of them directed to making the work theatrically effective. In spite of his dislike of its subject, Hofmannsthal had been impressed by *Intermezzo* when he saw it, and in *Arabella* he gave Strauss similar opportunities for *parlando* dialogue and for further exercise of his gift for naturalism. There is bound to be a permanent question-mark over the finished result, since there would have been many more changes had Hofmannsthal lived. To that extent, *Arabella* is an incomplete work, falling short of what it might have achieved but still achieving much. A second *Rosenkavalier*? It was intended to appeal to the same kind of audience for much the same reasons, and there are obvious superficial resemblances. But the label adversely affected the acceptance of the opera by the public for at least twenty years, until a series of performances with such singers as Lisa della

Casa, Dietrich Fischer-Dieskau and George London revealed its individual virtues.

In *Arabella* Strauss's orchestra makes some of the most erotic and euphonious sounds to be heard in any of his stage-works. The scoring has none of the ornate splendour of *Rosenkavalier*, little of its glittering rococo decoration and underlining of every movement on stage. It abounds in lyrical thirds and sixths, but it is, for all its fulsome tendencies, a slimmer, more transparent score than *Rosenkavalier*, showing the economic mastery which came with experience. The flavour of Slavonic folk-music in Mandryka's part is both subtle and piquant. This folk element in the Vienna context is another pointer to the close connection of the work with operetta—a genre in which Strauss obviously had a deep interest. Parts of *Die ägyptische Helena* have a similar tendency; and in the second act of *Arabella*, dramatically broken-backed as it is, Strauss aimed for a *Fledermaus*-like variety, with waltzes, with the coloratura polka song by the cabmen's mascot Milli, and with Mandryka's drunken insistence on Moët-Chandon for the whole company. Not to mention that the plot hinges on the fact that Arabella's sister Zdenka has been brought up as a boy and that the exposure of this masquerade brings a happy ending.

But while Strauss could pose as an operetta composer with the minor characters, such as Arabella's feckless parents, he could not maintain it with his heroine, and it is the music he wrote for Arabella and Mandryka that gives this enchanting opera its claim on our affection. Arabella's first aria, in which she examines her attitude to men and proclaims her certainty that she will know the right one—*der Richtige*—when he arrives, is on a similar level of inspiration to the Marschallin's soliloquy and evoked music of comparable grave beauty:

Ex. 21
Moderato

Her long aria closing Act I is equally fine, and is notable for its use of a solo viola in the accompaniment to highlight significant emotional points. The Act II love-duet with Mandryka is Strauss at his most warm-hearted, responding with horns, strings and radiant writing for the voices to every prompting of some of Hofmannsthal's best lines. With this adorable music Strauss ensures that the audience care deeply about Arabella's future, and he composed a memorable and unusual finale, with his heroine descending a staircase offering to Mandryka a glass of water, in emulation of the Croatian village custom of which he has told her, whereby the village girls offer their chosen bridegrooms a glass of fresh water as a symbol of chastity. Sentimental, yes; dramatically effective, too; and a touching 'curtain' to the last Strauss-Hofmannsthal opera. *Arabella* is not profound, but it is splendid entertainment, of more than ephemeral value because of the musical craftsmanship with which it is put together and because it contains two singing rôles of exceptional attractiveness.

Neville Cardus, writing in the 1930s, cited *Arabella* as proof that 'Strauss was still the best composer of a Strauss opera'. It was a witty remark, but wise too. Strauss was seventy in 1934. There is no sign of artistic sclerosis in this score. It looks back rather than forward, but that is irrelevant to its artistic merit. It is fresh, inventive and tender. The elegiac note is entirely missing; clearly he still had more to say. He would have to say it without Hofmannsthal. 'He had a simply astounding flair for the sort of material which, in given circumstances, corresponded to my needs,' Strauss said in 1935. It was a noble tribute, but only partly true, as the careful reservation of 'given circumstances' implies. He wanted to believe it himself, but the zest with which he tackled his first non-Hofmannsthal opera since *Intermezzo* belied him.

18 The operas (2)

DIE SCHWEIGSAME FRAU, FRIEDENSTAG

The extravagant praise Strauss lavished on Zweig's libretto for *Die schweigsame Frau* is understandable only in the context of Hofmannsthal's death. That Strauss sincerely mourned his partner is not in doubt; but neither is his sigh of relief at release from some of the rigours of working with him. By a fluke, Zweig, in picking on Jonson's *The Silent Woman* and moving the action forward to the eighteenth century, had found the subject which Strauss had been trying for years to coax from Hofmannsthal, a comedy which would enable him again to indulge the farcical aspects of *Rosenkavalier* (having re-explored the lyrical aspects in *Arabella*) and to compose in the successful *parlando* style of the Prologue to *Ariadne*. Moreover, the contrived artificialities of Jonson's plot lent themselves to Strauss's innate Bavarian gift for parody and pastiche—and, of course, the subject provided yet another libretto about marriage. Pauline, one feels, is always waiting in the wings.

So in the London of *Die schweigsame Frau* we meet again a company of actors and singers (a chance for anachronistic quotations from Verdi and Strauss himself). The principal soprano, Aminta, is another manifestation of Zerbinetta, a tender heart behind the trills. The plot to trick the rich old sea-dog, Sir Morosus, who abominates noise, into a mock marriage with a silent woman who will turn into a virago and thus teach him how much happier he is by staying single, is another chance to capitalize on the kind of music which illustrated the discomfiture of Baron Ochs. The third act opens with an orchestral fugato, just as in *Rosenkavalier*, and the curtain rises, as in the earlier opera, on a scene of intense activity, with workmen knocking nails into the wall and Aminta, like Oktavian, supervising and instructing.

Strauss's gradual reversion to a 'numbers' opera, detectable in *Die ägyptische Helena* and *Arabella*, took full effect in *Die schweigsame Frau*, which is pastiche Italian *opera buffa* leavened by Strauss's passionate admiration for Verdi's *Falstaff*. A potpourri Rossinian overture; plentiful spoken dialogue; a canzona sung by the Figaro-like Barber, Schneidebart; septet, sextet, nonet; a music-lesson (of a Straussified quotation from Monteverdi's *L'Incoronazione di Poppea*)—there is no question of the kind of comparison Strauss is inviting. He scores for a large orchestra (ninety-five players) but rarely uses it at full strength.

The opera is certainly merry and bright, with not a link of Wagnerian chain-mail left. In the Act I duet for Aminta and Henry; in the ensemble after the 'wedding'; in the poetic curtain to Act II when Morosus, off-stage, falls asleep on a low D flat while Aminta, on-stage with her husband Henry, sings a top D flat; and in the 'reconciliation' scene of Act III, Strauss achieves a blend of Mozartian grace, Rossinian sparkle and the style of his own *Lieder* which rises above mere pastiche. Yet the work fails to deserve a place among the endearing comic operas because too much of the melodic invention is Strauss below his best, not because he was taking it easy but because he was trying too hard. If he had maintained the quality of the examples I have just cited, the contrived twists of the plot would not matter. The last scene of all, a quiet epilogue in which Morosus sings contentedly such Straussian aphorisms as 'How beautiful life is . . . when one is no fool and knows how to live', fails to stir an audience to its depths because the music is predictable, not memorable. (But Strauss thought it 'most successful'.)

Also, Strauss's besetting sin of going on too long, of extract-
ing more than enough from every situation, shows as a worse
fault in comedy than in some of the weightier works. Karl Böhm,
the first conductor of the opera, has since shown that it can be
judiciously cut without major damage; and if the stage production has plenty of pace and freedom, then *Die schweigsame Frau*
can make a delightful evening. It will never replace its models,
but it contains too much that is good and brilliant to vanish
completely from the stage. In it Strauss marked time, looking
over his shoulder at the past, before he turned to the creation of
his four last operatic masterpieces.

His next opera, the eighty-minute one-act *Friedenstag*, is his
most austere. It is also the final answer by Richard Strauss the
artist to critics of his attitude to the politics of his time. *Friedenstag* is an anti-war opera, and the monolithic emotional strength
of the music is testimony to its utter sincerity. In several ways it
is unique among Strauss's mature operas: in its atmosphere of
bleak hopelessness, in the important rôle given to the chorus, in
the total absence of self-consciously 'beautiful' episodes, and in
the predominance of male voices. Gregor's libretto never
achieves the unstilted realism Strauss sought, but it is serviceable,
despite its major flaw: that the proclamation of peace comes all
too pat, robbing the work of a central dramatic climax.

Although Strauss expressed doubts about his suitability for
this subject—'too wearisome a task'—the result was one of his
most original works, beautifully constructed in order to exploit
every possibility of contrast—the Piedmontese youth's Italian
folk-song following the gloomy and despairing opening
choruses, with their funeral-march ground-bass, and preceding
the extraordinary, gaunt music of the starving townspeople's
wailing cries of 'Hunger' and 'Bread'. Equally remarkable is the
stingingly satirical music in which the Commandant recalls the
battle of Magdeburg and inquires from a gunner and rifleman if
they will share his decision to stay in the fortress when he blows

it up. The deliberate use here of a popular style is extremely effective. This scene, for all its ambivalence—are we meant to sympathize or despise?—is a richer musical experience than the subsequent familiar Strauss cantilena of the long aria for the Commandant's wife Maria. It is a noble aria, but its insistence on the sun as the symbol of hope immediately raises the spectre of *Fidelio* which haunts the whole score.

The loyal and loving wife; the besieged townspeople, in effect prisoners; the noble and resolute Commandant; the bugle-call at a climacteric; and the final cantata-like hymn to peace and friendship—can there be any doubt that Strauss had *Fidelio* in mind and was trying to convey its message not in any vain spirit of rivalry but because he believed that a twentieth-century musician should make the same plea? Strauss could not and does not attain the sublimity of Beethoven—his C major finale is rhetoric, not oratory—but if, because *Fidelio* exists, *Friedenstag* is consigned to oblivion, musical injustice will have been done. For though the similarities between the two works are striking, it is the differences which we should study and cherish.

Few passages in Strauss are more impressive than the scene in which the fortress awaits renewed assault but, instead of cannon-shells there comes the sound of bells, silent for years, pealing the news of peace, and this strong theme thrusts upwards repeatedly on the cellos:

Ex. 22

When the enemy (Holsteiner) troops arrive they do so to a brazen military march, brutal and banal, a Mahlerian touch which was obviously intended as further condemnation by Strauss of militaristic tendencies. The bass to the march is the Lutheran choral *Ein' feste Burg*, for Strauss included the cruelties committed in the name of religions, ecclesiastical and ideological, in his general protest:

Ex. 23

If Strauss had produced music of this intensity for the final section of the work, there would be no need for reservations in discussing this impressive opera. Yet despite the lameness of much of the final paean, there are ferocity and gritty harmonic strength in the writing for the chorus and in the orchestral coda that keeps the emotional temperature high.

DAPHNE, DIE LIEBE DER DANAE

For his next two operas Strauss returned to the world of mythology which Hofmannsthal had considered the most fruitful. It is ironically amusing to find him, during the compilation of the libretto for *Daphne*, prodding and goading Gregor in much the same direction as his dead collaborator had led him. Notwithstanding the troublesome gestation of this one-act opera, the result was the most consistently lyrical and beautiful of all his stage works. It was as if the broad and flashing humour of *Die schweigsame Frau* and the sombre starkness of *Friedenstag* had resolved themselves into this serene but fervent style. One has only to consider that between his seventieth birthday in 1934 and the end of 1937 Strauss wrote three such different operas as his *opera buffa*, his political testament and his celebration of pastoral love and Hellenism, each with a contrasted harmonic and melodic vocabulary, to realize the wrongheadedness of the view that he was either an extinct volcano or, at best, a garrulous old man composing from memory. *Daphne* by itself is sufficient proof that his genius was burning strongly with a new and thermal glow.

Within the framework of the familiar classical legend of humankind identified with the deities and with nature, Strauss received the kind of verbal stimulus which released the best music in him. As he told Zweig when criticizing Gregor's first draft, 'instead of remaining that boring virgin, Daphne should fall in love with them both, the god [Apollo] and the man [Leukippos]'. The love interest was one strong stimulus; others were the descriptive elements, the storm, the birds, butterflies and trees, nightfall, moonlight, the sexual act, ritual dances, death—all might have been designed for a Strauss festival.

The instrumental prelude is a microcosm of the whole seraphic work, a succession of inspired melodic fragments for woodwind, first the oboe, followed by basset-horn, clarinet, flute, cor anglais. The principal theme:

Ex. 24

comes to the ear like an ethereal echo from the *Heldenleben* coda, and the prelude as a whole is a foretaste of the mellow yet refined instrumental style of Strauss's last years. The Oboe Concerto, the Duett-Concertino and similar works are side-shoots from Daphne's laurel. It is this cohesive and organic mastery which gives *Daphne* its high place in Strauss's output; it is at once a consummation and a new beginning. Let those who wish examine the libretto's symbolism and analyse Gregor's adaptation of a favourite myth: the music disarms criticism by its flow of pellucid vocal melody set against an orchestral background of delicacy, strength and kaleidoscopic detail.

In the title-rôle Strauss created his finest part for soprano voice since the great rôles in *Rosenkavalier*. The Composer, Zerbinetta, the Empress, Helen, Aminta and Arabella all have wonderful opportunities, but none can compare with the loveliness of Daphne. The brilliance of Zerbinetta, the innocence of Sophie, the radiance of Arabella are combined into a rôle to which Strauss additionally imparts an air of innocent unreality in keeping with the elusive nature of Daphne's character. With neither a superfluous bar nor a momentary suggestion of monotony, Strauss gives his soprano a seemingly endless stream of melismatic song. It is a long rôle but rewarding in every way. Her first aria, in which she identifies herself with nature and apostrophizes her laurel tree, contains the first hints of the marvellous final transformation scene. The strings are divided into several parts, a solo violin twining with the voice while solo woodwind and strings create a mosaic of the pastoral themes associated with Daphne. This silvery sound is unequalled in any other Strauss opera.

Strauss took immense care with instrumental and vocal timbres in *Daphne*. The part of Daphne's Erda-like mother Gaea is given to a contralto capable of a low E flat who is accompanied by the dark colours of the orchestra. Peneios, Daphne's father, is a bass but her lovers, Leukippos and Apollo, are both tenors. This was obviously a deliberate risk on Strauss's part to ensure that high vocal tones should predominate—and his experiences with his Vienna singers in the 1920s seemed to have given him more confidence in tenors as a breed. So well did he understand voices that there can be no confusion between the boyish Leukippos and the heroic Apollo. These are well-delineated rôles, but all are subservient to the central superb creation, Daphne herself, in whom Strauss found yet another example of his favourite theme of metamorphosis: nymph into woman into tree, the whole opera designed in a great curve, from darkness to light and back to darkness, the *Leitmotiv* woven into a symphonic structure even more subtly than in *Salome* and *Elektra*.

Like *Salome* and *Elektra*, the opera has its big set-pieces: the Dionysiac feast, the superb duet for Apollo and Daphne before their night of love, the lament for Leukippos and the final F sharp major transformation scene, a miracle of orchestral poly-phony leading to Daphne's wordless *vocalise* as the music sinks back into the quietness from which it grew. There are tenderness, eroticism, grandeur and mystery in this opera, but gone is the swaggering, eight-horn hero of another age, gone is the playboy of the orchestra, showing off with arrogant virtuosity. All is pure music, suffused with the Apollonian warmth of the sunlight which Strauss always needed if he was to work his best. In *Daphne* he combined successfully at last the chamber-music intimacy of the best of *Ariadne* with the poetic eloquence of the best of *Die Frau ohne Schatten*, and he used a large orchestra with as sure a stylistic touch as he had displayed since *Don Quixote*. Krauss thought the work was too short and wanted Strauss to expand it. Such a course would have been disastrous. *Daphne* shares with *Till Eulenspiegel* the rare distinction among Strauss scores of being perfectly proportioned. For that reason, apart from its intrinsic beauty, it has a special and exclusive place in the hearts of many Strauss enthusiasts.

So, for the comparative few who know it, has *Die Liebe der Danae*, the 'cheerful mythology in three acts' in which Strauss returned to the draft of the 'light, witty' comic opera on a subject which Hofmannsthal had written for him in 1920. The completed opera (1940) may be said to have had five librettists—Hofmannsthal, Zweig, Gregor, Krauss and Strauss himself—and the number of fingers in the pie shows in the dramatic weaknesses and inconsistencies which no producer, however skilful, can disguise.

Strauss had a strong affection for *Danae*. Pointing heavenwards after the 1944 rehearsal he said: 'When I arrive there I hope I'll be forgiven if I take this with me.' He knew there were uneven passages—which he blamed on the text—but some of it, he thought, was as good as anything he had written. When it was performed at Salzburg in 1952 and in London in 1953, the tendency of criticism was to call it 'the mixture as before', and so, like his other *bel canto* opera, *Die ägyptische Helena*, it has since been almost totally neglected. It is time that *Danae* was revived, for it would be found that it is an attractive and stageworthy opera containing many of the same lyrical qualities which are rightly admired in *Capriccio*.

The thesis is that love is more important than riches. Again, it is an opera about marriage. Strauss's remark to Bahr in 1916 that he was planning a cycle of five operas about his wife was to some extent fulfilled since, after *Intermezzo*, marriage is also the subject of *Die ägyptische Helena*, *Die schweigsame Frau*, *Arabella*, and *Die Liebe der Danae*. Hofmannsthal combined the stories of Danae, to whom Jupiter came in the form of golden rain, with that of King Midas, who turned everything he touched to gold. Gregor introduced Jupiter himself as a main character, thus setting himself intractable problems. Those who wish to study the genesis of the libretto will find an excellent account in Mr Del Mar's Volume III, pp. 121–31. What concerns us here is that, notwithstanding its defects, the text gave Strauss what he wanted for an opera which nearly rivals *Die Frau ohne Schatten* in its complexities as a stage-picture. It is perhaps no coincidence that he escaped from the realities of the outbreak of war in 1914 and 1939 into the composition of operas in which fairy-tale and metamorphosis play so big a part.

'Note-spinning' is the pejorative term often applied to Strauss (by himself, among others). But there is no harm in note-spinning if what is spun makes a good pattern and has a firmly woven texture. There is endless fascination to be discovered in Strauss's re-exploration of himself in his last great period, in the consistently more subtle approach to his material, in the re-working of all his familiar harmonic devices, in the mining of new and valuable matter from an old but by no means worked-out seam. In *Die Liebe der Danae*, the old hand has lost none of its cunning but has gained a good deal in economical practice. The autumnal melodic beauty which distinguishes *Daphne* is also marked in *Danae*, notably in the handling of the orchestra. Depicting golden rain must obviously have seemed child's-play to Strauss, but he does it beautifully with harps, piano, flutes and muted strings. Elsewhere the orchestra is used either with entrancing delicacy or as a gorgeously rich and sonorous, but never mushy or sickly, backcloth. The symphonic interlude in Act III known as Jupiter's Renunciation ranks with the Barak interlude in *Die Frau ohne Schatten* for sheer nobility and pathos, and the orchestra is left, as in *Daphne*, to provide the emotional climax at the end of the opera.

But this is a singers' opera. Jupiter is a marvellous part, giving the baritone a Verdian range of expressiveness, from majestic wrath in Act I *via* the paternal Wotan-like nobility of Act II to the final duet with Danae which Strauss modelled on Hans Sachs —and these Wagnerian references are clues to the richness of much of the vocal writing. There are also excellent lighter scenes for Jupiter and the tenor, Midas, and for Jupiter and his four ex-mistresses to whom, in differing disguises, he has previously come as seducer.

Danae is one of the most attractive of the soprano rôles

created for Viorica Ursuleac, exploiting soft high *pianissimo* notes and considerable tenderness of expression in addition to the usual broad-spanned and powerful cantilena. Her big opportunities come in Act III—which was effectively created by Strauss and Clemens Krauss in order to give the singers and the composer an opportunity for a more human and elegiac mood— with an impressive solo aria and the closing duet, but she has earlier had memorable duets with her maid Xanthe in Act I and with Midas in Act I and in Act III when, like Helen and Menelaus, they are in the desert.

'My last acknowledgment to Greece, and the final meeting of German music with the Grecian spirit,' Strauss said in 1944, not knowing that the future would bring Henze's *The Bassarids* to continue his tradition. He knew how much depended in *Danae* on brilliant staging—which is only to repeat that his operas can never be done on the cheap or by any but the best singers. The more I listen to *Die Liebe der Danae*, the more beautiful and successful it seems to me to be. I cannot agree with Mr Del Mar that it 'does not rate a very high place' in Strauss's output. Anyone can see that the opera follows the usual Strauss formula for success, but that hardly matters if it succeeds. From the pungent chorus for the creditors with which it opens to its serene and warming closing chords, *Die Liebe der Danae* is music to delight the ear and uplift the spirit.

CAPRICCIO

In his last opera, *Capriccio*, Strauss set out to please himself and ended by pleasing everybody more, perhaps, than by any of his operas except *Rosenkavalier*. The popular success of a work which its composer at first believed—until he saw it on the stage —should be reserved for connoisseurs is an encouraging commentary on the advance in the public's taste for opera, and an enlightening commentary on the vagaries of creativeness, for the

opera—designated a 'conversation piece'—might easily be
thought to be too undramatic and donnish to have much general
appeal.

Ostensibly the work is a debate about the relative importance
of words and music in opera, and this rather academic subject—
which fascinated Strauss all his life—is given dramatic meaning
by the device of introducing a poet (Olivier) and a composer
(Flamand) who are both in love with the young Countess
Madeleine. (The parallel with *Meistersinger* is obvious.) The
scene is a château near Paris in 1770. Artists are gathered
there for an entertainment in honour of her birthday. The
impresario La Roche outlines his plans for this festivity, which
are derided by Flamand and Olivier. To reconcile them he
suggests they should collaborate in an opera. Various subjects
are dismissed and Madeleine's brother suggests that they should
set the events they have just been experiencing. (This, in fact,
was Strauss's idea.[1]) All leave for Paris, and Madeleine learns
that both poet and composer will visit her next day to learn
which of them she chooses—and, symbolically, how the opera
is to end. Earlier Olivier has read a sonnet he has written about
her, and Flamand has improvised a tune for it. Now, in the
moonlight, she sings this to herself and finds she cannot separate
words and music. The question is unanswered, but the audience
are seeing and hearing the opera she has commanded—*moto
perpetuo*.

It could have proved disastrous, but Clemens Krauss provided Strauss with a libretto which is better than any of those in
which Hofmannsthal attempted to mate abstract theories and
their symbolized characterizations. Next to *Rosenkavalier*, Strauss
never had a better libretto. But the miraculous feat was that it
provided him with his best opportunity for years to compose

[1] La Roche had asked for an opera about real people instead of
mythological heroes, just as Strauss had pleaded with Hofmannsthal
for a contemporary subject.

what he did best—autobiography. For this opera is really about Richard Strauss's way of writing operas; one feels that its seed had been in him, fertilizing slowly with the long years of experience, since his stage-struck youth at the Meiningen court. Elements of pastiche, quotations, allusive asides, nostalgic tenderness, a beautiful aristocratic soprano rôle (one-third *Figaro*-Countess, one-third *Rosenkavalier*-Marschallin, one-third *Lieder*-singer), an impresario with characteristics of both Reinhardt and Hofmannsthal, the theatrical ambience of the Prologue to *Ariadne*—one can almost picture the glee with which the seventy-six year old wizard of Garmisch shut himself into his study, shut out the distractions of a European war, and lost himself in setting a text which demanded all the lyricism and wit of *Daphne* and *Die Liebe der Danae* but catered for them so much better.

The opera is designed in the arch-like structure which Strauss handled so well—an instrumental introduction and a long final monologue enclosing a series of 'numbers', including three dances (a chance for some Couperin pastiche), a mock Italian love-duet (a chance to emulate a *Rosenkavalier* 'hit'), a fugal Laughing and Quarrelling Octet in which the ensemble-writing sparkles and bubbles as it never quite did in *Die schweigsame Frau*. In all these he can flaunt his time-travelling mastery of styles with spontaneous ease, and he recaptures the wit and grace of *Le Bourgeois Gentilhomme* and the relaxed sophistication of the *Ariadne* Prologue. As for quotations, he has a field-day: references, all prompted by the historical allusions in the text, to Gluck's *Iphigénie en Aulide*, to Rameau's *Les Indes galantes*, to *Tristan*, to Rossini's *L'Italiana in Algeri* and to several of his own works including *Danae*, *Don Quixote*, *Ariadne* and *Daphne*. (Originally Krauss intended that the opera planned by Flamand and Olivier should be *Daphne*, to be performed as part two of a double bill, but fortunately Strauss had the better idea of making *Capriccio* itself the opera, like a mirror device.) The most significant self-quotation, though, is of the pianoforte interlude from his 1920 song-cycle *Krämerspiegel*, a beautiful melody which becomes the basis in *Capriccio* of the lovely Moonlight Music:

Ex. 25

That was a great invention of twenty years before, but Strauss's melodic genius was burning strongly in 1941. The superb Sextet for strings which opens the opera (and by a brilliant stroke, when the curtain rises, is found to be the music to which the Countess and her guests are listening) is a lyrical effusion as inspired as that which opens *Daphne*, but where that was the essence of pastoral peace, this seems to be an epitome of the domestic delights of chamber-music. The felicity of the scoring throughout the opera is flawless; not a note too many, not a sound misjudged, not a word which cannot be clearly heard, yet with no loss of richness, warmth and harmonic dexterity. The setting of the Love Sonnet—again, a *Meistersinger* parallel, for this is a 'Prize Song'—is exquisite, cool rather than impassioned, but as fine a tenor aria as Strauss wrote, accompanied by harpsichord and very quiet strings.

Thirty years earlier Strauss had told Hofmannsthal: 'It is at the conclusion that the musician can achieve his best and supreme effects.' He had not always lived up to this, perhaps operatically only in *Rosenkavalier*, *Arabella*, *Daphne* and *Die Liebe der Danae*. Most of all in *Capriccio*, and how marvellously he leads to it. The subsidiary characters leave for Paris, each making a subtly delineated farewell. There follows the short scene for the eight male servants who discuss what has been happening, in a charmingly light, scherzo-like ensemble. As the salon darkens and the major-domo begins to prepare for supper, he hears a voice—this is Monsieur Taupe, the prompter, who has slept throughout the rehearsal in the theatre. He, too, needs to go back to Paris. With these two scenes Strauss provides the contrast for his skilfully contrived finale.

As the major-domo leads the prompter away, horns sound distant Cs and the gorgeous interlude begins, with the *Krämerspiegel* melody as its theme. It is moonlight and the Countess appears, dressed for supper. So begins Strauss's operatic *Abschied*, his greatest soprano monologue. She sings the sonnet, looks into the mirror for the answer she seeks, but finds none. The major-domo announces supper. A horn sounds twice and gentle chords bring down the curtain. Sheer magic, but the wonder is that so deliberately contrived a piece of nostalgia should be so effective. For as Madeleine looks in the mirror, we are meant to remember the Marschallin. Even the silver-rose bitter-sweet chords are there. It is very moving.

Capriccio is Strauss's most enchanting opera, it is also the nearest he came to unflawed perfection in a work of art. It is an anthology or a synthesis of all that he did best, and it is as if he has put his creative process into a crucible, refining away coarseness, bombast and excess of vitality. Like that other great Op. 85, Elgar's Cello Concerto, it is a testament of all the strongest elements in its creator's make-up, yet, also like the concerto, it succeeds in spite of a certain weariness in the invention which becomes a positive advantage. For example, the *Leitmotive* which represent the four characters symbolic of the argument between words and music, Flamand and Olivier, the Count and the Countess, are fairly nondescript and scrappy, but Strauss, by sleight-of-hand worthy of a champion skat-player, shuffles them into a continuously interesting texture. When they emerge in the full glory of his autumnal orchestra during the instrumental interludes in Madeleine's final aria, we realize that he has shed all traces of Wagnerian use of *Leitmotiv* and evolved at long last his own more subtle and delicate allusive method.

Ironically, too, *Capriccio* is irrelevant to the development of music. It is a mixture of eighteenth- and nineteenth-century styles written in the twentieth century. When La Roche says: 'I guard the old, patiently awaiting the fruitful new, expecting the works of genius of our time! But where are they? I cannot find them,' Strauss himself is addressing us. He knew that genius chooses its time and medium and he must have known that in *Capriccio* it had again chosen him. How apt, too, that his last opera, stylistic prelude to the relaxed transparency of his final instrumental works, should also epitomize in its leading rôle the vocal and physical beauty of the great sopranos, past, present and future, for whom his operas are a *raison d'être*.

So he completed his fifteen operas, a contribution to the lyric theatre which ranks him among the six greatest opera-composers. Yet more than half of them are rarely performed, and most of that half are still undervalued. If, before the end of the twentieth century, *Daphne*, *Friedenstag* and *Die Liebe der Danae* can be rehabilitated as *Die Frau ohne Schatten* has been, then the general appreciation of Strauss will be more proportionate to the magnitude of his achievements. Far from declining since 1918, he steadily and patiently, with varying degrees of success, explored diverse subjects for opera without needing a new musical vocabulary or system of composition. He believed that his operas would retain 'an honourable place in world history in relation to all earlier creations for the theatre (Wagner excepted) at "the end of the rainbow"'. It is a belief that the passage of time is showing to be abundantly justified.

19 Ballets and other orchestral works

Interspersed among Strauss's operas between 1903 and 1940 are several instrumental compositions, of which the largest in scale and conception was the Diaghilev ballet score *Josephs-legende*. A major point about Strauss, affecting both his music and his attitude to politics, is that he was, and essentially remained, a German Court composer of the old school. He could turn his hand to anything with the certainty that the result would never be less than competent—and, when his heart was in it, very much more. He undertook *Josephslegende* against his inclination, but was urged on by Hofmannsthal's hectoring, the attraction of a large fee, and the undoubted prestige of composing for Diaghilev. The resulting score is better than is usually suggested. If ever a work was a symptom of its period, this is. The scenario is a pretentious mixture of erotic, sadistic and religious symbolism with none of the distinction of *Salome*; the Biblical story, translated into a sixteenth-century Venetian setting of the most lavish kind, is typical of the extravagance of the Russian Ballet at its zenith; the vast orchestra, with threefold division of the violins as in *Elektra*, a double-bass clarinet in the woodwind, and exotic percussion, belongs to the era of Stravinsky's *Le Sacre du printemps*.

What saves the work is the quality of Strauss's music. After a few initial set dances, he abandoned the traditional ballet design and turned the score into another symphonic poem, with a waltz-tune, several splendid 'effects' and a beautiful episode of two-part polyphony melodizing round the tonic key in the style of the great orchestral passage in *Die Frau ohne Schatten*. The music for Joseph, which Strauss eventually borrowed from his discarded ballet *Kythere*, is choreographically effective; and indeed much of the score—notably the 'mourning' scene—sounds today like high-quality film music written before its time. Associations with many a Hollywood fade-out have rendered unbearable Strauss's harp-celesta-pianoforte tinklings which depict Joseph's innocence and purity and which lead, in the finale, to a banal peroration only too indicative of Strauss's total inability to invoke celestial visions of a spiritual kind—one has to go to Vaughan Williams's *Job* to find music to match this kind of theme. Yet long stretches of the score are beautiful and imaginative; to attribute its comparative failure, as Norman Del Mar does, to 'mental lethargy' is too sweeping. Perhaps Strauss would have been wiser to refuse the commission, but he gave the subject more than it deserved.

The scoring entitles him to be regarded as one of the leading trade unionists of orchestral music—providing plenty of jobs for the boys. Not only is the double-bass clarinet employed (when Potiphar's Wife creeps in to find Joseph asleep), but four harps, four pairs of castanets, a wind-machine and much besides are demanded. He was almost as extravagant in his next ballet, *Schlagobers (Whipped Cream)* of 1924—his attempt to create a *Casse-Noisette* out of Viennese confectionery (the characters have names like Prince Coffee, Princess Prâlinée and Marianne Chartreuse) and to write a conventional ballet of set numbers. In 1924 he made the remark—which I have taken as motto for this book—about wanting to write the music he pleased in order 'to create joy'. Unfortunately, in indulging himself so wantonly, he failed to deliver the goods or, in this case, the goodies. It is impossible to make out a case for *Schlagobers* because it is so uninspired. Its ineptness supports the view that Strauss at his best was not a sugar-and-spice-and-all-things-nice composer. The success of *Rosenkavalier* lies in the fact that the icing on that great cake is hard and there is a bitter tang to its filling.

He recovered his form later in 1924 with the left-hand piano concerto written for Paul Wittgenstein to which he gave the cumbersome title *Parergon ʒur Symphonia Domestica,* a clue to the programmatic basis of the work: his son Franz (Bubi) had nearly died from typhus contracted on honeymoon in Egypt and the music reflects the deep anxiety Richard and Pauline underwent, followed by their relief. The anxiety is expressed at the start of the *Parergon* by a C sharp on muted brass which stabs and nags at the Child theme from *Domestica,* presented in F sharp minor in harmonies that toss and turn like a man in a fever. The atmosphere of gloom is extraordinarily vivid. Even the pianoforte's introductory flourishes are darkened by the spectral C sharp, and despite brilliant and stormy episodes for soloist and orchestra, it is a long time before the crisis is passed and a bassoon converts C sharp into the convalescent key of F major, while the clarinet plays this *gemütlich* theme:

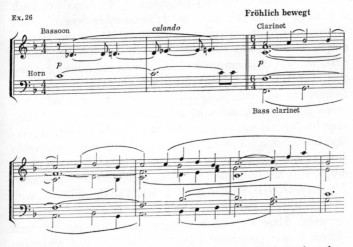

The remainder of the work is a joyous *scherʒando,* with waltz-like interpolations and something of the sparkle of the *Burleske.*

Richard Strauss

Probably its form is against it, for two-handed pianists do not particularly relish playing a one-hand work, but the *Parergon* is such attractive music that it is a pity so few people know it. Wittgenstein, with (he said) the composer's approval, made various additions and alterations and recorded this version in 1959—an historical rarity.[1] In 1926, Strauss wrote a second work for him: symphonic studies in the form of a passacaglia called *Panathenäenzug* (Panathenaea was the ancient Greek festival procession in honour of Athene). This is in four sections— introduction, two interludes and coda—like Liszt's B minor sonata, and in the attractive slow section Strauss uses the lyra (a form of glockenspiel) with harp, celesta and the pianoforte to produce some magical sound-patterns. But the work is less compelling than the *Parergon*, though far from negligible.

In 1922–3 Strauss arranged several Couperin keyboard pieces for a Vienna ballet, later publishing it as an eight-movement *Tanzsuite*. To purists these arrangements, like Elgar's of Bach and Harty's of Handel, are no doubt insufferable. Strauss's small orchestra, with its succulent string tone, is a world away— despite the use of a harpsichord—from the pungent clarity of the originals. Yet his arrangements fail to hold the listener because they fall between two stools: they are neither sufficiently Straussified nor sufficiently pure. Stravinsky's *Pulcinella* is a masterpiece because every note is pure Stravinsky. The *Tanzsuite* has intermittent elegance and wit, but the general impression is of prolonged pious homage. In 1941 Strauss returned to Couperin, whose music he undoubtedly loved, when he added six pieces to the *Tanzsuite* for a 'dance vision from two centuries', *Verklungene Feste*, produced at Munich. The six additions, with two more, were published in 1943 as a *Divertimento* for small orchestra. Here there is a stronger Straussian flavour, with elaborate new contrapuntal treatment of the inner parts, but

[1] The recording was made for Boston Records, B-412.

198

forty minutes of this kind of thing is about twenty-five too many. In the remaining fifteen there are appealing moments, but neither work is likely, nor deserves, to supplant the wonderful *Bourgeois Gentilhomme* suite in the public's affections.

No Strauss survey can avert its gaze from the occasional pieces, tedious though they are. He provided four items for the golden-wedding celebrations of the Grand Duke of Saxe-Weimar-Eisenach at Weimar in 1892. One of them described the Battle of Lützen in 1692 and Strauss twice more pressed it into service, for the *Rosenkavalier* film in 1925 and, re-titled *Kampf und Sieg*, for the Vienna Philharmonic Ball in 1931. In 1906–7, as a good obedient court composer, he obliged the Kaiser's growing taste for militarism in all forms by composing several military marches, of which only the *Königsmarsch* has any intrinsic musical value. These marches are sheer 'duty'; they sowed no seeds in his great works as Elgar's vastly more accomplished *Pomp and Circumstance* marches did in his.

The pre-1914 Teutonic propensity for bombast and size is reflected in the scoring of these works—there were plenty of military bandsmen, so Strauss gave them work. His sombre and impressive *Feierlicher Einzug*, written in 1909 for the Order of St John, requires fifteen trumpets, four horns, four trombones and two tubas, and his *Festliches Präludium*, Op. 61, of 1913, composed for the opening of the Vienna Konzerthaus, is scored for ninety-six strings, quadruple woodwind, eight horns, six trumpets and twelve distant trumpets, four trombones, tuba, percussion and organ. Alas that this array should be given such banal music to play, though the Brahmsian *sehr lebhaft* tune in C major has a glimmer of inspiration. Without a programme, without the impulse derived from words, Strauss was lost at this time, as he freely admitted.

After 1914 his output of this type of music diminished to a few fanfares. In 1940 he accepted a commission from the Japanese to contribute a work to celebrate the 2,600th anniversary (fictitious) of the Mikado's dynasty. This was the *Japanische Festmusik*, his last composition for a very large orchestra. It begins promisingly, with themes and orchestration which show traces of *Danae* and *Capriccio*, but inspiration and, one suspects, Strauss's interest soon peter out and the music makes meaningless and empty gestures in extravagant fashion.

Before turning with a sigh of relief to the post-1942 instrumental works, mention should be made of the odds-and-ends of *Der Rosenkavalier*. Some of these belong to the silent film of 1924–5, about which the then penurious Hofmannsthal was enthusiastic. Strauss had no interest in it. There was no question of singing: a theatre orchestra played music to accompany the action on the screen. Strauss realized a new score was needed. He refused to provide it, leaving adaptation of the opera to Otto Singer and Karl Alwin. But the film interpolated new material. (Ochs was shown at home, the Marschallin's girlhood was depicted, as well as her meeting with her husband, who was seen on the battlefield. There was also a spectacular supper-party in the gardens of the Marschallin's Palace.) For these extra scenes Strauss provided, unaltered, two of his Berlin marches, a movement from his 1892 Weimar *Festmusik* and the *Wirbeltanz* from the first Couperin suite, and for the scene at the Feldmarschall's battle headquarters he wrote a new march in F. Various concert arrangements of the waltzes have been published [1] but only the 1944 *Waltz Sequence* is Strauss's work. This contains new development of the themes, but is only marginally more satisfactory than the anonymous *Suite* (1945) which he approved. It is difficult to believe that anyone who loves the opera can enjoy these concert-hall versions, which merely emphasize that the music belongs to the theatre and nowhere else. If conductors want a good Strauss waltz for their concerts they should try

[1] The earliest dates from 1911 and was played at the Promenade Concerts in London on 23rd August of that year, seventeen months before the opera was heard in England.

München, which is in the *Rosenkavalier* mould but has the advantage of being a concert piece.

After the 1941 opera *Capriccio* Strauss's work moved into what is called its 'Indian summer'. This is a true description if it is not interpreted as emergence from a decline that never was. It is easy to see how this impression arose. Strauss's almost total immersion in opera from 1920 to 1940 meant that his concert-hall reputation rested on the pre-1914 tone poems. In opera houses outside Germany there was little inclination to explore beyond *Rosenkavalier*, which was box-office gold. In Britain up to 1939 *Rosenkavalier* was performed 99 times compared with *Elektra* 28 times, *Salome* 17, *Ariadne auf Naxos* (original version) 8, *Ariadne II* 3, *Feuersnot* 5 and *Arabella* 4. Since 1945 *Rosenkavalier* has easily led the field and *Die Frau ohne Schatten*, *Arabella* and *Capriccio* have been taken into reasonably regular repertory. *Die schweigsame Frau* has had seven performances, *Die Liebe der Danae* four (by a visiting company), and *Intermezzo* was taken up by Glyndebourne in 1974, having been introduced to Britain in 1965 at the Edinburgh Festival. At the time of writing, *Guntram*, *Die ägyptische Helena*, *Friedenstag* and *Daphne* have never been performed in Britain (apart from a BBC studio production of *Friedenstag*). No wonder that, at any rate up to 1945, Strauss was regarded as having 'died', as a composer, thirty years earlier; and no wonder that when, in the years immediately after 1945, it was discovered that Strauss had since 1942 been writing a series of accessible small instrumental works of high quality, it was considered that he had miraculously come to life again.

The last-period works are so successful, so filled with a slender elegance of style and manner, that one is bound to ask why Strauss turned back after fifty years to the classical instrumental forms he had abandoned when he composed *Macbeth*. We know from his operas that he was a nostalgist. In 1942 he must have been well aware of his isolated position: a last link with the noblest period of German and Austrian art. Isolated, too, politically, living in fear, watching Germany's cultural heritage perverted and destroyed. I have no doubt that he re-lived his youth as a form of escape and recaptured the buoyant spirit of his own past. Many will remember the astonishment with which they heard these works for the first time in the 1940s—that such music should still be composed in our time!

The first of these compositions is the Second Horn Concerto (1942), compact, witty and skilful. The rhapsodic opening to the first movement is balanced by the tender link with the *Andante* in which the solo horn is used primarily as a member of the wind ensemble that dominates this idyll. The finale, very difficult for the soloist, is joyously Mozartian in its combination of grace and exuberance. Strauss's pleasure at discovering that he could still write music of this kind overspilled into the two Sonatinas for sixteen wind instruments, No. 1 in F (1943) and No. 2 in E flat (1945). These were scored for two each of flutes, oboes and bassoons, four horns, a contra-bassoon, two B flat clarinets, a C clarinet, bass clarinet and basset horn. It is difficult to know which to admire more, the technical ingenuity of the writing or the bubbling good nature of the music. No. 1 is possibly the better constructed, but No. 2 is stronger thematically; it had been conceived as a one-movement Introduction and Allegro, but this movement is now the finale. Its theme sounds like an allusion to Wagner's Rhinemaidens, and this is probably intentional for there is, despite their lightheartedness, an elegiac streak in all these works which reflects what Strauss wrote in a letter about this time: 'Germany has fulfilled its last and highest cultural mission with the creation of German music, and I shall keep this thought in mind until I am called to my gods in Olympus.'

In fact, this sonatina finale was sketched shortly before Strauss revised his *München* waltz to include a section in memory of the Munich opera house. In the spring of 1945 he composed the weightiest and greatest of his last works, the study for twenty-three solo strings, *Metamorphosen*. This long adagio, which unfolds and proliferates in a complex texture of astoundingly rich and varied polyphony, is a sublimated tone-poem, its main theme a reminiscence (unintentional at first) of the Funeral March in Beethoven's *Eroica* Symphony. There seem also to be allusions to motifs from *Tristan*, and these merely intensify the obvious message of the music: 'Richard III' mourning the physical and spiritual destruction of the world which nurtured him. The music is genuinely tragic and devoid of self-pity because it is governed by a rigorous classical technique. A conductor must have the measure both of its emotional pulse and of its difficult ensemble, for if over-pressed the clear lines of the meticulously adjusted structure become obscured. Any charge that Strauss's protective armour of self-esteem could not be penetrated fails when confronted with *Metamorphosen*, a masterpiece of romanticism in its death-agony which Mahler would surely have applauded. Its last bars, where the Beethoven theme is quoted in the bass, deserve illustration:

Ex. 27

IN MEMORIAM

The Oboe Concerto dates from the autumn of 1945 and has been well described as an essay in rococo chromaticism. This delightful work was eagerly welcomed by solo oboists even though their first entry involves them in fifty-six bars of uninterrupted playing. The short themes flow one from the other rhapsodically and with the familiar harmonic side-slips, while in the slow movement the long cantabile melody breathes the spirit of another age. It was followed two years later by the *Duett Concertino* for clarinet and bassoon, which has been much less frequently heard, perhaps because the long and slightly garrulous finale tends to nullify the effect of the two ravishing short movements, each of which is dominated by one of the solo instruments. The work opens with this superb melody for the clarinet following a prelude for strings which belongs to the world of *Capriccio*:

The work has a programmatic basis. Strauss told Burghauser, the bassoonist for whom it was written, that he had in mind a dancing princess (clarinet) alarmed by the grotesque cavortings of a bear (bassoon). But at last she dances with it and it becomes a prince. It is obvious from Ex. 28 that the princess's name must have been Daphne. As in the sonatinas for wind, Strauss's fertile mind led him into the prolixity of the finale. He confessed on more than one occasion that he spoilt his works by 'putting far too much in them . . . I write in too complex a way. It's because I have a complicated brain'. But one can forgive this flaw, if such it be, for the sake of the beauty he created in a lifetime as a master of the orchestra.

With this too-rarely heard concerto Strauss ended his instrumental work. 'Mozart,' he told Burghauser, 'was the one to have all the most beautiful thoughts, coming straight down from the skies!' Some came down to Richard Strauss, too, in those years of his old age.

20 Songs and choral music

Strauss's choral works are too rarely heard. The first of them, *Wandrers Sturmlied*, to words by Goethe, was composed in 1884 for six-part chorus and orchestra and, as is obvious from almost every bar, was inspired by a hearing of Brahms's *Gesang der Parzen*. Its rich harmonic scheme and elaborate contrapuntal texture are admirable in themselves, the serene coda being especially fine. In 1897 he published his first large-scale work for unaccompanied mixed chorus, two settings of poems by Schiller and Rückert in which the voices are divided into sixteen parts. The resulting antiphonal effects and the splendid description of sunset in *Der Abend* are the choral equivalent of the pulsing ardour and perfect proportion of *Don Juan*. These settings are difficult to sing, requiring extremes of range from the chorus and the utmost professional skill in negotiating the chromatic modulations and flowing decorative figures. It is astonishing that such masterpieces of choral music should have remained unperformed in London until 1975, for they rank among Strauss's great works.

An astonishing *pièce d'occasion* is *Taillefer*, composed in 1902–1903 for the centenary of Heidelberg University, which then conferred an honorary degree on Strauss. The text is a ballad by Uhland about the Battle of Hastings and the courage of Taillefer, minstrel to Duke William of Normandy. Strauss wrote for a colossal orchestra (145 players) and as large a choir as could be mustered. Big effects are therefore the order of the day, including a battle scene which outdoes *Heldenleben* in noise, but some of the music is heroic and frankly enjoyable, with effective solos for soprano, tenor and baritone and clear, lyrical writing for the chorus. On a similar scale is the Klopstock *Bardengesang* of 1905, an offering to Kaiser Wilhelm, of interest only because one can detect in embryo methods more worthily applied in *Elektra*.

Strauss returned to Rückert in 1913 for the words of his *Deutsche Motette*, for four solo voices and *a cappella* mixed chorus again divided into sixteen parts, another example of the amazing range—top D flat for sopranos and bottom B for basses—and of the variety of colour he could create even without an orchestra. Few of Strauss's works could be called ecclesiastical; this is one. Nearer to his usual mood are the atmospheric and romantic Eichendorff settings, *Die Tageszeiten*, for male chorus and orchestra, written in the mid-1920s, and using the orchestra as the principal medium for evoking the sights and sounds of the times of day. That Strauss also relished choral virtuosity for its own sake is delightfully demonstrated in his 1935 setting for double mixed chorus of Rückert's *Die Göttin im Putzzimmer*.

The last and most substantial of his choral works is the elaborate setting for unaccompanied mixed chorus of Gregor's discarded cantata-ending for *Daphne*, published in 1943 as *An den Baum Daphne*. Some of the opera's choicest themes recur, but the work is self-contained. A boys' chorus is effectively used and lovers of the opera will relish this epilogue, which none the less shows how wise Strauss was to detach it from the original scheme.

Strauss's large output of *Lieder* is still perhaps generally underrated and largely unexplored. It requires a book to itself and Alan Jefferson has written an excellent one.[1] Purists reject Strauss *Lieder* because they are not exclusively for voice and pianoforte—a stultifying attitude. Strauss's major contribution to the *Lied* was in his development of orchestral accompani-

[1] A. Jefferson, *The Lieder of Richard Strauss* (London, 1971).

ments, extending the achievements of Berlioz and Mahler. He orchestrated many of his songs which originally had pianoforte accompaniments, and it is in this form that they are most popular. It is curious how he kept his composition of songs in a separate compartment, as it were: there are few links with the operas, few quotations and little relevance to his other works of the same periods. The fact that many of the poems he set are of inferior quality is of little account and is even advantageous.

Most of the songs are for soprano, for Strauss composed many of them for Pauline, who from all accounts sang them incomparably in her heyday, even Hanslick referring to her as her husband's 'better half'. For over twenty years, up to the end of the First World War, Strauss accompanied his wife in recitals throughout Europe, England and the United States. As she grew older and technically less secure, she became more eccentric, wearing extravagant dresses, making operatic gestures and up-staging her husband by inviting applause when her contribution was over even if the composer was playing a piano postlude. But they had a unique mutual understanding, because Strauss would often vary the accompaniments, possibly because he was bored with the 'old favourites' and also because his active brain could never resist the chance of re-composing them. They became improvisations. Later Strauss found another ideal interpreter in Elisabeth Schumann, whom he often accompanied in the inter-war years, and he also gave recitals with Elena Gerhardt.

If one includes his *juvenilia*, Strauss's career as a writer of songs stretched over seventy-eight years: a sketch for a song was on his desk the day he died. Of the more than 200 *Lieder* in his catalogue of works only a handful can be mentioned here. His childhood songs amounted to forty-two, many written for his aunt Johanna Pschorr, who greatly encouraged his early ambitions. A good many have been lost. It is interesting to note that at the age of thirteen he wrote two songs with orchestra, the setting of *Der Spielmann und sein Kind* (*The Minstrel and his*

Child) being almost a *scena* in its ambitious length and scope. The 1878 *Ein Alphorn* is noteworthy, too, because it was one of only three songs in which Strauss used an extra *obbligato* instrument, in this case a horn, for the song was dedicated to his father.

Strauss's song-writing maturity dates from his settings of Gilm published as Op. 10 and previously attributed to 1882–3. It has now been discovered that August to November 1885 is the correct date. The group contains three of his best-loved songs, the impulsive *Zueignung* (*Dedication*), the restrained yet intense *Allerseelen* (*All Souls' Day*) and the superbly accomplished *Die Nacht* (*Night*), its first phrase an anticipation of the oboe solo in *Don Juan*. The song reflects, with mature skill, the lover's fear that night, which takes away the colours and shapes of flowers, rivers and buildings, will also steal his beloved—'sie stehle dich mir auch'—and on the word 'auch' the key changes dramatically from D major to B flat major and the pianoforte postlude struggles with difficulty back to D.

His Op. 15 and 17 groups, to words by Schack, contain the excellent *Heimkehr* (*Homecoming*), its consecutive thirds a typical Strauss feature, and the extremely popular *Ständchen* (*Serenade*). If the latter song has become hackneyed, that should not anaesthetize our response to its delicate *vivace e dolce* accompaniment of the tender and shapely melody. The Op. 19 settings are also of Schack and open with the masterly *Wozu noch, Mädchen?* (*Why must you, girl?*), its lovers' banter a foretaste of the operas' conversational style. Placed centrally is the energetic *Wie sollten wir geheim sie halten?* (*How should we keep it secret?*) with vocal *portamenti* and an exuberant sense of the union of love and Nature in which German songwriters excel—a strong contrast to the closing song, *Mein Herz ist stumm* (*My heart is mute*), a gloomy but powerful vision of old age. For his Op. 21 Strauss set five poems by Felix Dahn, opening with the jolly and Brahmsian *All mein Gedanken* (*All my thoughts*) and the G flat major love-song, *Du meines Herzens Krönelein* (*You, the crown of my heart*), charming in its conventional simplicity of melody and Schubertian accompaniment.

With the four songs of Op. 27, his wedding present to Pauline, Strauss produced a quartet of winners. Three of the poems are by two Socialist-radicals, Karl Henckell and the Scots-born J. H. Mackay, but Strauss selected examples of their Romantic love-poetry. The first song, *Ruhe, meine Seele* (*Rest, my soul*), is a dark, mysterious, tranquil setting, the voice floating hypnotically above sustained chords. Fifty-four years later Strauss orchestrated it, making it a gloomier, more tragic, even more beautiful song. In 1948, evidently, its last verse—'These are sorely troubled times, disturbing to heart and mind; rest, rest, my soul, and forget what threatens you'—had deeper significance for the tired, world-weary composer. *Cäcilie*, composed in a brilliant E major, is the most impassioned and joyous love-song Strauss wrote, rhapsodic and ecstatic. The same intensity of mood, but in a more flowing, transparent sound-texture, is found in *Heimliche Aufforderung* (*Secret Invitation*) where the voice's rapture is supported by a pianoforte accompaniment which Strauss made no attempt to transpose into orchestral terms. The last of the group is the wondrous *Morgen* (*Morning*) which custom can never stale, if the singer is an artist. It opens with a pianoforte statement of the melody, the voice stealing in, as if in mid-sentence, to begin a long arching variation of the melody. The impression is of rapt and timeless wonder, sustained when the voice stops and a long pianoforte coda brings the song to an end that is no end. The voice-and-piano version is the best, but Strauss's orchestration for solo violin, three horns, strings and harp miraculously keeps the delicate atmosphere.

The nostalgic poignancy of *Morgen* is again present in *Traum durch die Dämmerung* (*Dream in the Twilight*), the first of three Otto Bierbaum poems which constitute Op. 29. This is the song said to have been composed in twenty minutes, the time allotted to Strauss by Pauline before she insisted that they should go for a walk. Strauss admitted that some poems immediately suggested music to him, and this was obviously one such. Op. 31, composed in 1895–6, contains *Blauer Sommer* (*Blue Summer*) and is of interest for its chromatic modulations of a five-bar melodic phrase, each statement falling a minor third until the original key (B major) is reached again. The fourth song of this set, *Stiller Gang* (*Silent Walk*), employs a viola *obbligato* and was his first setting of verses by Richard Dehmel, author of the poem which inspires Schoenberg's *Verklärte Nacht*. There is, in fact, a Schoenbergian tonal and harmonic waywardness in this melancholy and descriptive song.[1]

Henckell is the poet of three of the five Op. 32 songs, though the best known of them, *Sehnsucht* (*Yearning*), is a setting of Liliencron. When it was new, this ambitious song led critics to declare that Strauss had abolished rhythm. They were puzzled by the effect, in the accompaniment, of the long minim and the tied crotchet which is sustained by pedal into the next bar. The key-signature of the voice-part is also ambiguous. *Ich trage meine Minne* (*I bear my Love*) is in an unequivocal D flat, always a fruitful Strauss key, a light-hearted song which has overshadowed the even more sparkling *Himmelsboten* (*Heavenly Messengers*), Strauss's first setting of a poem from *Des Knaben Wunderhorn* (*Youth's Magic Horn*).

His first song-cycle composed with orchestral accompaniment (and no alternative pianoforte) was the *Vier Gesänge*, Op. 33, of 1896–7. These emulations of Mahler's example are rarely heard, perhaps because they require two singers, high baritone and soprano. No. 1, *Verführung* (*Seduction*), is another passionate Mackay poem and is provided with an elaborate and imaginative

---

[1] This rare, beautiful and unusual song should be restored to singers. The alternative version with viola was not included in the Complete Edition of the Songs, and the condensed version of the voice-and-piano setting is not accurate because it omits to mention the altered vocal line in the latter part of the song.

instrumental texture. The first song of Op. 36, Klopstock's *Das Rosenband* (*The Rose Garland*), was also composed for orchestra. Undeterred by Schubert's setting, Strauss here wrote one of his most gorgeous songs, its final cadenza on the word '*Elysium*' being an early example of the soprano cantilena that he was to make into a speciality. A magnificent song; and in the same opus is the humorous *Wunderhorn* song, *Hat gesagt*.

Next in this astonishing flood of lyrical invention which followed Strauss's marriage is Op. 37, six songs which include the most touching of his cradle-songs, the intimate, crooning *Meinem Kinde* (*To my child*); the most heroic of his love-songs, in a *Heldenleben* E flat, *Ich liebe dich* (*I love you*); and one of his most enigmatic compositions, *Mein Auge* (*My Eye*), its mood of devotion made more explicit in the 1933 orchestration. Four poems by Dehmel and one by Bierbaum make up Op. 39. The Bierbaum song is *Jung Hexenlied* (*Young Witch*), a strange fantasy about a witch's feelings for her children which, Strauss said, was a perfect vehicle for Pauline's wit and imaginative insight as an interpreter. *Leises Lied* (*Gentle Song*) reminds some writers of Debussy, and *Befreit* (*Set free*) is among Strauss's highest achievements, its repeated cry of 'O Glück' being deeply stirring. This group also contains the gritty 'protest song' for a male singer, *Der Arbeitsmann* (*The Workman*), a dramatic and pessimistic composition inspired by the descriptive nature of the poem rather than by any conversion on Strauss's part to Dehmel's radical opinions.

How different is the Dehmel of *Wiegenlied* (*Cradle-song*), the first of the Op. 41 group of 1899 and perhaps the most frequently sung of Strauss's lullabies—though a lullaby, surely, to the mother rather than the child. Its broad-spanned cantilena over an *arpeggiando* accompaniment makes it a certain winner. The other four songs in this set are almost unknown—a pity in the case of the energetic, E flat *In der Campagna* (Mackay). Of the three Op. 43 songs, too, only the delightful *Muttertändelei*

(*Mother's trifling*) has established itself, not surprisingly, for it rivals in frothy whimsy the best of Mahler's *Wunderhorn* settings.

Op. 44, 46 and 47 have found little favour. The two songs with orchestra of Op. 44—*Notturno* (Dehmel) and *Nächtlicher Gang* (*Night Journey*) (Rückert)—require huge forces. In both there are pointers to *Elektra* and, in *Notturno*, further uses of the bitonality found in *Also sprach Zarathustra*, in this case the extreme keys of F sharp minor and G minor. The Rückert setting is a gothic horror-story of a man running for his life— and dying. Strauss's melodramatic powers are fully employed in this exciting curiosity. Singers could well look out the five Rückert settings of Op. 46, notably *Morgenrot* (*Sunrise*), lively and impulsive, and *Ich sehe wie in einem Spiegel* (*I see as in a mirror*), sentimental and old-fashioned but none the worse for that. The Uhland settings of Op. 47 contain the forgotten and radiant *Rückleben* (*Living backwards*), and the better-known *Einkehr* (*Lodging*), a captivating piece.

Op. 48 begins with Bierbaum's poem *Freundliche Vision* (*Friendly Vision*), set by Strauss in his most sensuous manner: ingratiating harmonies, ecstatic soprano voice seemingly detached from the accompaniment, the Strauss most people love. The remaining four Henckell settings include the jovial *Kling!* (*Ring out!*) and the two winter songs, *Winterweihe* (*Winter Consecration*) and *Winterliebe* (*Winter Love*), in which preechoes of themes from *Arabella* and *Die Frau ohne Schatten* are presumably deliberate. The eight songs of Op. 49 are a varied selection, some of them jaunty folk-songs, but containing two superb Dehmel settings, the lyrical *Waldseligkeit* (*Woodland Bliss*), worthy of comparison with the last songs of 1948, and the adorable *Wiegenliedchen* (*Little Cradle-song*). Then follows another Henckell setting, *Lied des Steinklopfers*, an angry, bitter bass song about a starving stone-breaker, the piano accompaniment vividly depicting the clatter of his work. Much of it is non-tonal, the chordal progressions are weird, and the final despairing E minor reflects the poem's sense of the futility of the man's social plight.

With the six songs of Op. 56, composed in 1903–6, we reach the end of Strauss's prolific *Lieder* period. They open with a Goethe setting, *Gefunden* (*Found*), written for Pauline and altogether in his 'domestic' vein, as is the Heine setting, *Mit deinen blauen Augen* (*With your blue eyes*), where the final Sophie-Oktavian duet is not far away. *Im Spätboot* (*On the last boat*), a setting of Meyer, is perhaps Strauss's finest bass song, significantly in his beloved D flat. On a more elaborate scale is another Heine song, *Frühlingsfeier* (*Spring Festival*), which demands virtuoso singing if its pagan erotic turbulence, another piece of Strauss's Hellenism, is to be satisfactorily realized. It is followed by one of Strauss's few religious works, *Die heiligen drei Könige aus Morgenland* (*The three holy kings from the East*), a song of rich beauty conceived with orchestral accompaniment. The familiar scene of the Journey of the Magi offered Strauss some pictorial moments which he illustrated exquisitely, and the long orchestral coda is of a kind to melt the heart of an atheist.

The gap in Strauss's *Lieder* output from 1906 to 1918 is explicable by his immersion in his operas and by a long wrangle with publishers over copyright and performing rights. One of the firms eventually threatened him with legal action if he did not fulfil a contract for a song-cycle. With the spite which was a part of his character—exemplified in *Heldenleben*, *Feuersnot* and *Intermezzo*—he asked the literary critic Alfred Kerr to write him some scurrilous poems introducing the names of various publishers and their managers. He set these—there are twelve—between March and May 1918 and offered them to the litigating publisher (Bote & Bock) who refused them and thereafter won a court injunction against Strauss. Such is the history of the *Krämerspiegel* (*Shopkeeper's Mirror*), which was privately published in 1921 in an edition limited to 120. The songs, which are nothing more than 'in-jokes' full of Strauss self-quotation, are trivial, but the pianoforte introduction to No. 8, recurring as the coda to the cycle, was rescued by Strauss for magical use in *Capriccio*. The songs, Op. 67, with which Strauss eventually fulfilled his contractual obligation are three of Ophelia's nonsense verses in *Hamlet* and three of Goethe's ill-humoured verses from the *Westöstlicher Divan*. All, especially the austere Shakespeare, are worth revival. In the second of the Goethe settings, *Hab' ich euch denn je geraten? (Have I ever advised you?)* Strauss quotes from *Eine Alpensinfonie* and from the just-completed *Die Frau ohne Schatten*.

His next published group, Op. 68, composed early in 1918, is a masterpiece, six glorious settings of poems by Clemens Brentano, joint compiler of *Des Knaben Wunderhorn*. They were written for Elisabeth Schumann, though it is doubtful if she sang them all. The set is notable for its detail, its intricate and adventurous harmonies and its absolute mastery of word-setting. The chromatic *Ich wollt ein Sträusslein binden (I wanted to tie a nosegay)* and the tender love-song *Säusle, liebe Myrthe (Whisper, sweet myrtle)* are among the gems of Strauss's art, but the concluding (and little-known) *Lied der Frauen wenn die Männer im Kriege sind (Song of women when the men are at war)* is the greatest of all, requiring a strong soprano to dominate the stormy opening and also to give full majesty to the poignant ending. A noble song, which shows that Strauss was very far from impervious to the suffering all around him in May 1918. The five settings of Arnim and Heinrich Heine which comprise Op. 69 are also of superior invention, including the fluent *Der Stern (The Star)* which Strauss told Max Marschalk he wrote 'on the spot' when he read the poem, and the enchanting *Einerlei (Sameness)*, pure Strauss sugar, no doubt, but intensely lovable, as is the humorous and witty *Schlechtes Wetter (Wretched Weather)*, which ends as a waltz!

In a necessarily brief survey, there is room only to draw the attention of conductors and singers to the three Hölderlin hymns with orchestra, Op. 71—lyrical Strauss of the kind audiences love—and to plead for revival of the Bethge settings of Op. 77—*Gesänge des Orients* (*Songs of the East*)—composed in 1928. These are the last songs to which Strauss gave opus numbers, but of the nine he wrote between 1929 and 1942 two are of particular biographical interest. The 1933 *Das Bächlein* (*The Brook*) was dedicated to Goebbels to mark Strauss's appointment to the presidency of the Reichsmusikkammer (and probably in an effort to protect Zweig), and it ends with the words 'mein Führer' (in 'wird mein Führer sein') repeated thrice. Forget Hitler as you enjoy this Schubertian song; if you were born after 1945 the reference is merely historical curiosity. Words by Goethe were used two years later in *Zugemessne Rhythmen* (*Formal Rhythms*), which remained unpublished until 1954. Strauss wrote this song in gratitude to Peter Raabe for defending him in print against a Nazi party-line attack on his 'feminine voluptuousness and torpor of sounds padded with fat'. The Goethe poem refers to the need to create new forms, which Strauss had done in his time, and the music quotes not only Strauss works but Brahms and Wagner too, in support of the victory of new ideas over pedantry.

One would say that the apotheosis of all that is best in Strauss *Lieder* is to be found in the Countess's last aria in *Capriccio*, were it not for the existence of the *Vier letzte Lieder* (*Four Last Songs*) of 1948. The genesis of this glorious cycle has been described in Chapter 14. Perhaps I can best sum up its appeal to performers and audiences alike by this informal quotation from a letter to me from one of today's great Strauss sopranos: 'I went to sing the *Four Last Songs* in Vienna with that superb orchestra. I was just in seventh heaven from beginning to end. I couldn't tell them, but I kept asking to repeat them at the rehearsal just to hear the sound!!' The vocal line, floating, curving, soaring in an ecstasy of cantilena, is given a backcloth of Strauss's most glowing, richly harmonized, detailed and evocative orchestration. Indeed, the voice becomes almost a solo instrument. Arabella, Daphne, the Countess, Sophie—all are reincarnated in these wonderful songs. Of course, they are 'escapist'; the old man had turned his back finally on the madness of the world and sent this last message from the mellifluous age of his golden years; of course, they are contrived with superb artifice—the voice in *Beim Schlafengehen* (*Falling Asleep*) entering exactly as in *Morgen*, the long violin solo epitomizing so much of Strauss in similar vein, the trill of larks in *Im Abendrot* (*At Sunset*) like the birdsong at the start of *Rosenkavalier*, the apt quotation from *Tod und Verklärung* at 'Ist dies etwa der Tod?' ('Is this perhaps death?' Strauss having significantly altered 'das 'to 'dies'), the horn solo bringing *September* (composed last) to a valedictory rather than elegiac end. No suggestion of religious consolation, even *in extremis*. The beauty of the world and the beauty of the female voice were uppermost in his thoughts to the end. Has there been so conscious a farewell in music, or one so touchingly effective and artistically so good? He was tired, ready like summer in *September* to close his weary eyes, but there is no unevenness in these four last benedictions on the world of Romantic music, no faltering, not a false or a superfluous note. There was no winter in Strauss's life, only a long and gorgeous-hued autumn.

These songs were the great culmination of a great career. It could be said of Strauss when he died, as Boito said of Verdi: 'He has carried away with him an enormous quantity of light and vital warmth.' Those who refer to 'the tragedy of Richard Strauss' are those who would like him to have been a different kind of composer. If some of his failings stem from an uneasy co-existence of sophistication and naïveté typical of his period, part of his fascination lies in his contradictoriness—the huge orchestra hammering away in *Elektra* should, he said, be like fairy music; the Mozart world of *Rosenkavalier* is presented on the scale of Wagner's *Die Meistersinger*; his operatic heroines are required also to be *Lieder*-singers. He keeps himself aloof. Perhaps his soul was as scarred and flawed as Elgar's and Mahler's, but if it was, he does not tell us in his music or in his letters. He shows us his family album, not his intimate diaries. The court composer always knew his place, after all. But his achievement remains and, like it or not, it is big, for he was a big artist. That is why his detractors will always find him too much of a good thing, whereas those who cannot have too much of a good thing will continue to relish him, warts and all. It has been thus for nearly a century; yet since his death his stature has steadily grown as more of his work has come into perspective, divorced from sterile theories about its 'relevance' to the time he lived in. He wanted to give pleasure, to create joy, for he understood the human heart. That was his greatest strength and it made him a master musician not for an age but for all the time mankind allows itself.

Appendix A   Calendar

(Figures in brackets denote the age reached by the person mentioned during the year in question.)

YEAR	AGE	LIFE	CONTEMPORARY MUSICIANS AND EVENTS
1864		Richard Georg Strauss born June 11 at Munich, Bavaria, Son of Franz Joseph Strauss (42) and Josephine, *née* Pschorr (27).	D'Albert born, April 10; Berlioz 61; Bizet 26; Brahms 31; Dvořák 23; Elgar 7; Janáček 10; Mahler 4; J. Strauss (ii) 39; Wagner 51; Verdi 51. Meyerbeer (72) dies, May 2.
1868	4	Piano lessons from A. Tombo.	Wagner's *Die Meistersinger* first perf. Munich, June 21. Bantock born, Aug 7; Rossini (76) dies, Nov. 13.
1870	6	Composes *Schneiderpolka* and *Weihnachtslied*. Begins schooling. Sees first operas, including *Der Freischütz*.	Lehár born, April 30; Schmitt born, Sept. 28; Pfitzner 1. Franco-Prussian War.
1872	8	Violin lessons from Benno Walter.	Alfvén born, May 1; Zemlinsky born, Oct. 4; Vaughan Williams born, Oct. 12. Bayreuth Festival Theatre foundation stone laid, May 22.
1874	10	Enters Ludwigsgymnasium, Munich, where he remains a pupil until 1882.	Hofmannsthal born, Feb. 1; Holst born Sept. 21; Ives born Oct. 20; Schoenberg born, Sept. 13; Rakhmaninov 1; Reger 1.

Richard Strauss

YEAR	AGE	LIFE	CONTEMPORARY MUSICIANS AND EVENTS
1875	11	Studies musical theory, etc., with F. W. Meyer.	Ravel born, March 7; Bizet (36) dies, June 3.
1876	12	Composes *Festmarsch* in E flat and various songs.	Falla born, Nov. 23; Bruno Walter born, Sept. 15; Götz (35) dies, Dec. 3. First *Ring* cycle, Bayreuth, Aug. 13–17; Brahms's Symphony No. 1 first perf. Carlsruhe, Nov. 6.
1880	16	Composes String Quartet in A, Symphony No. 1 in D minor and Chorus from *Electra* (perf. Munich Ludwigsgymnasium during this year).	Bloch born, July 24; Pizzetti born, Sept. 20; Offenbach (61) dies, Oct. 4. Mahler (20) completed *Das klagende Lied*.
1881	17	String Quartet in A performed in Munich, March 14; *Festmarsch* in E flat performed in Munich, March 26; Symphony No. 1 performed in Munich under H. Levi, March 30. Composes *Five Piano Pieces* and Pianoforte Sonata in B minor. *Festmarsch* published.	Bartók born, March 25; Mussorgsky (42) dies, March 28.
1882	18	Enters Munich University. Visits Bayreuth, August. *Wind Serenade* in E flat performed in Dresden, Nov. 27; Violin Concerto performed in Vienna (violin and piano), Dec. 5.	Kodály born, Dec. 16; Stravinsky born, June 17; Szymanowski born, Oct. 6; Raff (60) dies, June 24. First perf. of *Parsifal*, Bayreuth, July 25; Berlin Philharmonic Orchestra founded.
1883	19	Completes composition of	Bax born, Nov. 6; Casella

YEAR	AGE	LIFE	CONTEMPORARY MUSICIANS AND EVENTS
		First Horn Concerto. Cello Sonata performed in Nuremberg, Dec. 8.	born, July 25; Webern born, Dec. 3; Wagner (69) dies, Feb. 13. First perf. of Brahms's Symphony No. 3, Vienna, Dec. 2.
1884	20	Conducts Meiningen Orchestra in first perf. of *Suite in B flat* for wind instruments, Munich, Nov. 18. Composes *Wandrers Sturmlied*, Piano Quartet and Symphony No. 2 in F minor, which has first perf. in New York, Dec. 13.	Smetana (60) dies, May 12. Bruckner's Symphony No. 7 first perf., Leipzig, Dec. 30.
1885	21	Becomes assistant conductor to Bülow (55) at Meiningen on Oct. 1 and succeeds him as chief conductor on Nov. 1. Meets Brahms (52) at Meiningen. Comes under influence of Wagnerian Alexander Ritter (52). Piano Quartet first perf. on Dec. 8 at Weimar and awarded first prize in Berlin competition. First performance of Horn Concerto at Meiningen, March 4 (Gustav Leinhos soloist, Bülow conductor). Begins to write *Burleske* for piano and orch.	Berg born, Feb. 9; Varèse born, Dec. 22; Wellesz born, Oct. 21. First perf. of Brahms's Symphony No. 4, Meiningen, Oct. 25.
1886	22	Leaves Meiningen post on April 1. Visits Italy in summer and begins composition of *Aus Italien*. Visits Bay-	Liszt (74) dies, July 31.

YEAR	AGE	LIFE	CONTEMPORARY MUSICIANS AND EVENTS
		reuth to hear *Tristan* and *Parsifal*. Becomes third conductor at Munich Court Opera, Aug. 1. Conducts first opera, Boieldieu's *Jean de Paris*.	
1887	23	Conducts first performance of *Aus Italien* at Munich on March 2 and of *Wandrers Sturmlied* at Cologne on March 8. Meets Pauline de Ahna (25) at Feldafing in August. Meets Gustav Mahler (27) in Leipzig in October. Composes Violin Sonata, song *Ständchen* and begins tone-poem *Macbeth*.	Villa-Lobos born, March 5; Borodin (52) dies, Feb. 28. First perf. of Verdi's *Otello*, Milan, Feb. 5.
1888	24	Visits Italy again. Composes *Schlichte Weisen* songs, op. 21. Violin Sonata performed in Elberfeld on Oct. 3. At work on tone-poem *Don Juan*.	Lotte Lehmann born, Feb. 27; Alkan (74) dies, March 29.
1889	25	Assistant conductor to Hermann Levi (50) at Bayreuth and meets Cosima Wagner. Becomes third conductor at Weimar Court Opera, Oct. 1. *Don Juan* has first perf. on Nov. 11 at Weimar. Begins *Tod und Verklärung*.	Elgar's *Salut d'Amour* published in London. First perf. of Mahler's Symphony No. 1, Budapest, Nov. 20.
1890	26	Conducts first perfs. of *Burleske* (soloist Eugen d'Albert) and *Tod und Verklärung* at Eisenach on	Martinů born, Dec. 8; Franck (67) dies, Nov. 8; Gade (73) dies, Dec. 21. First perf. of Elgar's *Frois-*

YEAR	AGE	LIFE	CONTEMPORARY MUSICIANS AND EVENTS
		June 21, and of *Macbeth* at Weimar on Oct. 13. Pauline de Ahna joins Weimar Court Opera as a leading soprano in September.	*sart*, Worcester, Sept. 9.
1891	27	Severely ill with pneumonia in May and June. Attends Bayreuth Festival while convalescing as guest of Cosima Wagner.	Bliss born, Aug. 2; Prokofiev born, April 23; Delibes (54) dies, Jan. 16. Mahler becomes chief conductor at Hamburg Opera.
1892	28	Conducts uncut *Tristan und Isolde* at Weimar on Jan. 17. Ill again (pleurisy and bronchitis) in June. Visits Greece and Egypt in November and December. Begins work on first opera, *Guntram*.	Honegger born, March 10; Milhaud born, Sept. 4; First perf. of Bruckner's Symphony No. 8, Vienna, Dec. 18.
1893	29	In Egypt, Sicily and Corfu until June. Completes *Guntram* at Marquartstein on Sept. 5. Conducts first perf. of Humperdinck's *Hänsel und Gretel* at Weimar on Dec. 23.	C. Krauss born, March 31; Gounod (75) dies, Oct. 18; Tchaikovsky (53) dies, Nov. 6. First perf. of Verdi's *Falstaff*, Milan, Feb. 9.
1894	30	Becomes engaged to Pauline de Ahna at Weimar on May 12 and marries her there on Sept. 10. Conducts first perf. of *Guntram* at Weimar on May 10. First Bayreuth appearance as conductor in *Tannhäuser*, with Pauline as Elisabeth. Composes *Morgen* and other songs for Pauline and begins *Till*	Warlock born, Oct 30; Bülow (63) dies, Feb. 12; Chabrier (53) dies, Sept. 13. First perf. of Bruckner's Symphony No. 5, Graz, April 8.

Richard Strauss

YEAR	AGE	LIFE	CONTEMPORARY MUSICIANS AND EVENTS
		Eulenspiegel. Appointed assistant conductor to Levi at Munich Court Opera from Oct. 1. Conductor of Berlin Philharmonic Orchestra for 1894–5 season.	
1895	31	*Till Eulenspiegel* first performed at Cologne on Nov. 5. S. conducts *Guntram* in Munich on Nov. 16 but it is a failure.	Hindemith born, Nov. 16; Orff born, July 10. First perf. of Mahler's Symphony No. 2, Berlin, Dec. 13.
1896	32	Composes *Also sprach Zarathustra* between February and August and conducts first perf. at Frankfurt on Nov. 27. Becomes chief conductor at Munich Opera. Visits Russia as conductor.	Gerhard born, Sept. 25; Bruckner (72) dies, Oct. 11; Mahler's *Lieder eines fahrenden Gesellen* performed in Berlin, March 16.
1897	33	Son, Franz, born on April 12. S. visits Paris, Brussels, Amsterdam and London for first time. *Enoch Arden* performed in Munich on March 24. S. at work on *Don Quixote.*	Korngold born, May 29; Brahms (63) dies, April 3. Mahler becomes director, Vienna Court Opera, Oct. 8.
1898	34	First performance of *Don Quixote* given in Cologne on March 8. S. founds society to protect German composers' copyrights. Leaves Munich to become conductor of Royal Court Opera in Berlin from Nov. 1. Composes *Ein Heldenleben.*	Eisler born, July 6; Gershwin born, Sept. 26. Elgar's *Caractacus* first perf. at Leeds, Oct. 5.

YEAR	AGE	LIFE	CONTEMPORARY MUSICIANS AND EVENTS
1899	35	S. conducts first perf. of *Ein Heldenleben* in Frankfurt on March 3. Prolific period for composition of songs.	Poulenc born, Jan. 7; Chausson (44) dies, June 10; J. Strauss (ii) (73) dies, June 3. First perf. of Elgar's *Enigma Variations*, London, June 19.
1900	36	Meets Hugo von Hofmannsthal (26) in Paris in March. Begins to sketch opera *Feuersnot* in autumn.	Copland born, Nov. 14; Křenek born, Aug. 23; Weill born, March 2. First perfs. of Puccini's *Tosca*, Rome, Jan. 14, Charpentier's *Louise*, Paris, Feb. 2, and Elgar's *Dream of Gerontius*, Birmingham, Oct. 3.
1901	37	Conducts first all-S. concert in Vienna, including *Heldenleben*, on Jan. 23. *Feuersnot* first performance under Schuch at Dresden on Nov. 21.	Egk born, May 17; Rubbra born, May 23; Verdi (87) dies, Jan. 27; first full perf. of Debussy's *Nocturnes*, Paris, Oct. 27; first perf. of Mahler's Symphony No. 4, Munich, Nov. 25.
1902	38	Mahler conducts *Feuersnot* in Vienna on Jan. 29. S. tours extensively as conductor. Pays tribute to Elgar at Düsseldorf lunch on May 20.	Walton born, March 29; first perfs. of Mahler's Symphony No. 3, Crefeld, June 9, Schoenberg's *Verklärte Nacht*, Vienna, March 18.
1903	39	Strauss Festival in London in June. While staying in Isle of Wight in June and July begins *Symphonia Domestica*. Honorary doctorate of philosophy, Heidelberg University, on Oct. 26, after which S. conducts	Blacher born, Jan. 3; Khachaturian born, June 6; Wolf (42) dies, Feb. 22. First perf. of Bruckner's Symphony No. 9, Vienna, Feb. 11.

YEAR	AGE	LIFE	CONTEMPORARY MUSICIANS AND EVENTS
		Taillefer. Returns to England in December, conducting in London, Glasgow and Birmingham. Moves into new house in Berlin.	
1904	40	First visit to United States from February to April for concerts and recitals with Pauline. S. conducts first perf. of *Symphonia Domestica* in New York on March 21. Begins to compose *Salome*.	Dallapiccola born, Feb. 3; Skalkottas born, March 8; Kabalevsky born, Dec. 30; Dvořák (62) dies, May 1. First perfs. of Janáček's *Jenufa*, Brno, Jan. 21; Puccini's *Madama Butterfly*, Milan, Feb. 17; Mahler's Symphony No. 5, Cologne, Oct. 18.
1905	41	Conducts *Symphonia Domestica* in London in February and in Strasbourg in May. S.'s father Franz Strauss (83) dies on May 31. Triumphant first performance of *Salome* at Dresden, Dec. 9.	Tippett born, Jan. 2; Lambert born, Aug. 23. First perfs. of Schoenberg's *Pelléas et Mélisande*, Vienna, Jan. 26; Debussy's *La Mer*, Paris, Oct. 15 and Lehár's *Merry Widow*, Vienna, Dec. 30.
1906	42	Performances of *Salome* throughout Europe, many of them conducted by S. He conducts Vienna Philharmonic at Salzburg Festival on Aug. 17 in Mozart and Bruckner (Symphony 9). Agrees to compose *Elektra* to Hofmannsthal's libretto.	Lutyens born, July 9; Shostakovich born, Sept. 25. First perfs. of Delius's *Sea-Drift*, Essen, May 24, and Mahler's Symphony No. 6, Essen, May 27.
1907	43	Conducts six performances of *Salome* in Paris in March.	Fortner born, Oct 12; Grieg (64) dies Sept. 4.

YEAR	AGE	LIFE	CONTEMPORARY MUSICIANS AND EVENTS
		Guest conductor of Vienna Philharmonic. At work on *Elektra*. Composes military marches.	First perfs. of Schoenberg's String Quartet No. 1, Vienna, Feb. 15 and Sibelius's Symphony No. 3, Helsinki, Sept. 25. Mahler leaves Vienna for New York.
1908	44	Succeeds Weingartner in May as conductor of the Berlin Court Orchestra. Moves into villa at Garmisch in September. Completes *Elektra* on Sept. 22. Granted year's leave from Berlin Opera.	Messiaen born, Dec. 15; Elliott Carter born, Dec. 11; Rimsky-Korsakov (64) dies, June 21. First perfs. of Mahler's Symphony No. 7, Prague, Sept. 19; Rakhmaninov's Symphony No. 2, Moscow, Nov. 8; Elgar's Symphony No. 1, Manchester, Dec. 3.
1909	45	First performance of *Elektra* at Dresden on Jan. 25, followed by performances in New York, Munich, Berlin, Hamburg, Vienna and Milan, all before April 7. In May, S. begins to compose *Der Rosenkavalier*.	Albéniz (48) dies, May 18. First perf. of Rakhmaninov's Piano Concerto No. 3, New York, Nov. 28. Schoenberg completes *Drei Klavierstücke*, Op. 11, on Aug. 7.
1910	46	Conducts two performances of *Elektra* in London on March 12 and 15. S.'s mother dies, aged 73, on May 16. S. conducts at Vienna Court Opera for first time in June (*Elektra*). Completes *Der Rosenkavalier* at Garmisch on Sept. 26.	Samuel Barber born, March 9; Balakirev (73) dies, May 29. First perfs. of Stravinsky's *Fire-Bird*, Paris, June 25; Mahler's Symphony No. 8, Munich, Sept 12; Vaughan Williams's *Sea Symphony*, Leeds, Oct. 12; Elgar's Violin Concerto, London, Nov. 10.
1911	47	Extremely successful first	Menotti born, July 7;

YEAR	AGE	LIFE	CONTEMPORARY MUSICIANS AND EVENTS
		performance of *Der Rosenkavalier* at Dresden on Jan. 26, followed by productions in Nuremberg, Munich, Hamburg, Milan, Prague, Berlin and other cities. S. begins to compose *Ariadne auf Naxos* and *Eine Alpensinfonie*.	Mahler (50) dies, May 18. First perfs. of Sibelius's Symphony No. 4, Helsinki, April 3; Elgar's Symphony No. 2, London, May 24; Mahler's *Das Lied von der Erde*, Munich, Nov. 20. Webern composes *Five Pieces*, Op. 10.
1912	48	Completes *Ariadne auf Naxos* at Garmisch on April 20 and conducts first performance at Stuttgart on Oct. 25.	Françaix born, May 23; Cage born, Sept. 15; Massenet (70) dies, Aug. 13. First perfs. of Mahler's Symphony No. 9, Vienna, June 26; Schoenberg's *Five Orchestral Pieces*, London, Sept. 3, and his *Pierrot Lunaire*, Berlin, Oct. 16.
1913	49	Conducts *Elektra* in St Petersburg in February. Journey to Italy with Hofmannsthal in April to discuss *Die Frau ohne Schatten* plot. Composes *Festliches Präludium* for dedication of Vienna Konzerthaus, Oct. 19. Begins to compose *Josephslegende*. First London (Jan. 29) and New York (Dec. 9) performances of *Rosenkavalier*.	Lutosławski born, Jan. 5; Britten born, Nov. 22. First perfs. of Schoenberg's *Gurrelieder*, Vienna, Feb. 23; Stravinsky's *Le Sacre du Printemps*, Paris, May 29; Elgar's *Falstaff*, Leeds, Oct. 1.
1914	50	S. conducts first performance of *Josephslegende* in Paris on May 14. In London for his fiftieth birthday on June 11	Mellers born, April 26; Schuch (67) dies, May 10; Liadov (59) dies, Aug. 28; Sgambati (73) dies, Dec. 14.

YEAR	AGE	LIFE	CONTEMPORARY MUSICIANS AND EVENTS
		and receives honorary degree of Doctor of Music at Oxford on June 12. Begins composition of *Die Frau ohne Schatten* just before outbreak of First World War on Aug. 4. His money banked in London is sequestered.	First perf. of Vaughan Williams's *London Symphony,* March 27.
1915	51	Completes Acts I and II of *Die Frau ohne Schatten,* begins Act III. *Eine Alpensinfonie* completed on Feb. 8, receives first performance on Oct. 28 in Berlin.	Searle born. Aug. 26; Waldteufel (77) dies, Feb. 16; Skryabin (43) dies, April 27. First perf. of Sibelius's Symphony No. 5, Helsinki, Dec. 8.
1916	52	Revises *Ariadne auf Naxos,* completing new Prologue on June 20. Meets Hermann Bahr during summer to discuss libretto for domestic comedy which became *Intermezzo.* Second version of *Ariadne* performed in Vienna on Oct. 4, with Lotte Lehmann as the Composer.	Babbitt born, May 10; Granados (48) dies, March 24; Reger (54) dies, May 11; Butterworth (31) dies, Aug. 5; Richter (73) dies, Dec. 5.
1917	53	Visits Switzerland to conduct in February. Becomes co-founder of Salzburg Festival Association to establish festival on annual basis. Conducts hundredth Dresden *Rosenkavalier* on Dec. 13. Works on music for *Der Burger als Edelmann*	First perfs. of Puccini's *La Rondine,* Monte Carlo, March 28; Falla's *Three-Cornered Hat,* Madrid, April 7; Pfitzner's *Palestrina,* Munich, June 12.

YEAR	AGE	LIFE	CONTEMPORARY MUSICIANS AND EVENTS

(*Le Bourgeois Gentilhomme*). While in hospital in Munich in July writes his own libretto for *Intermezzo*.

1918   54   Completes Act III of *Die Frau ohne Schatten* in February. *Der Burger als Edelmann* performed in Berlin on April 9. S. at work on *Intermezzo*. In conflict with Berlin Opera management and considers move to Vienna. Dispute with Bote and Bock over contract for *Lieder* leads to composition of satirical song-cycle *Krämerspiegel* in March.

L. Bernstein born, Aug. 25; Taneiev (68) dies, Feb. 7; Cui (83) dies, March 24; Debussy (55) dies March 25; Boito (76) dies, June 10; Parry (70) dies, Oct. 7. First perfs. of Prokofiev's Classical Symphony, Petrograd, April 21; Puccini's *Trittico*, New York, Dec. 14.

1919   55   First performance of *Die Frau ohne Schatten* in Vienna on Oct. 10. S. becomes joint director of Vienna State Opera from Dec. 1 and moves to Vienna.

Leoncavallo (61) dies, Aug. 9. First perf. of Elgar's Cello Concerto, London, Oct. 26.

1920   56   Visits South America from August to November to conduct his operas and concerts with Vienna Philharmonic.

Maderna born, April 21; Fricker born, Sept. 5; Bruch (82) dies, Oct 2. Mahler Festival, Amsterdam, May 6–21; first perf. of Korngold's *Die tote Stadt*, Hamburg, Dec. 4.

1921   57   Begins to compose ballet *Schlagobers*. Attends first Donaueschingen Festival in August and meets Hinde-

M. Arnold born, Oct. 21; Caruso (48) dies, Aug. 2; Humperdinck (67) dies, Sept. 27; Saint-Saëns (86)

YEAR	AGE	LIFE	CONTEMPORARY MUSICIANS AND EVENTS
		mith (25). Conducts concerts and operas throughout Europe.	dies, Dec. 16. First perf. of Janáček's *Katya Kabanova*, Brno, Oct. 23.
1922	58	Visits London in June for first time since the war. Conducts Mozart opera at Salzburg in August. Completes composition of *Schlagobers* at Garmisch on Oct. 16. Conducts orchestras in North America and accompanies Elisabeth Schumann at *Lieder* recitals in autumn.	Xenakis born, May 29; Lukas Foss born, Aug. 15; Nikisch (66) dies, Jan. 23. Broadcasting of music begins in England.
1923	59	*Dance Suite* from Couperin pieces first performed in Vienna on Feb. 17. Visits South America from July to September with Vienna Opera and completes *Intermezzo* in Buenos Aires on Aug. 21. In October begins composition of *Die ägyptische Helena* to Hofmannsthal libretto.	Ligeti born, May 28. First perf. of Sibelius's Symphony No. 6, Helsinki, Feb. 19.
1924	60	S.'s son Franz marries in Vienna on Jan. 15 and become seriously ill on honeymoon in Egypt. S. conducts first performance of *Schlagobers* in Vienna on May 9. Widespread celebrations of his sixtieth birthday. Conducts his new version (with Hofmannsthal) of Bee-	Nono born, Jan. 29; Busoni (58) dies, July 27; Fauré (79) dies, Nov. 4; Puccini (65) dies, Nov. 29. First perfs. of Sibelius's Symphony No. 7, Stockholm, March 24; Schoenberg's *Erwartung*, Prague, June 6, *Serenade*, Donaueschingen, July 20, *Quintet*, Vienna,

231

YEAR	AGE	LIFE	CONTEMPORARY MUSICIANS AND EVENTS

thoven's *Ruins of Athens in* Vienna on Sept. 20. Moves into house in Belvedere Gardens district of Vienna built on plot of land presented to him by the city. Disagreements with Franz Schalk lead to S.'s 'resignation' from Vienna Opera. Conducts first performance of *Intermezzo* in Dresden on Nov. 4.

Sept. 13, and *Die glückliche Hand*, Vienna, Oct. 14.

1925 61 Visits France and Spain in February. Composes *Parergon zur Symphonia Domestica* which is performed at Dresden on Oct. 16. Visits Italy in November and December. Selection of correspondence with Hofmannsthal published, edited by Franz Strauss.

Boulez born, March 25; Satie (59) dies, July 1. First perf. of Berg's *Wozzeck*, Berlin, Dec. 14.

1926 62 Conducts première of *Rosenkavalier* film in Dresden on Jan. 10 and in London on April 12. Makes electrical recording of extracts from *Rosenkavalier* in London on April 13. Visits Greece in June. *Ariadne* performed at Dresden Festival in August, conducted by Clemens Krauss. Conducts his own works, with Elena Gerhardt as soloist, in Manchester on

Henze born, July 1. First perfs. of Puccini's *Turandot*, Milan, April 25; Shostakovich's Symphony No. 1, Leningrad, May 12; Kodály's *Háry János*, Budapest, Oct. 16; Hindemith's *Cardillac*, Dresden, Nov. 9; Janáček's *Makropoulos Affair*, Brno, Dec. 18; Sibelius's *Tapiola*, New York, Dec. 26.

YEAR	AGE	LIFE	CONTEMPORARY MUSICIANS AND EVENTS

Nov. 14. Reconciliation with Vienna Opera, where he conducts *Elektra* in December.

1927 63 Vienna première of *Intermezzo* on Jan. 15. First Paris production of *Rosenkavalier* on Feb. 8. S. conducts Beethoven's Ninth Symphony in Dresden on March 27, centenary of Beethoven's death. Composes *Panathenäenzug* for piano and orchestra. Completes *Die ägyptische Helena* on Oct 8. Grandson Richard born on Nov. 1.

First perfs. of Křenek's *Jonny spielt auf*, Leipzig, Feb. 11; Berg's *Chamber Concerto*, Berlin, March 27; Stravinsky's *Oedipus Rex*, May 30; Busoni's *Doctor Faustus*, Frankfurt, June 29; Schoenberg's Third String Quartet, Vienna, Sept. 19.

1928 64 First performance of *Panathenäenzug* in Vienna on March 11, Paul Wittgenstein soloist and F. Schalk conducting. Fritz Busch conducts première of *Die ägyptische Helena* at Dresden on June 6 and five days later, on his birthday, S. conducts its Vienna première. Performances in Berlin on Oct 5, Munich on Oct 8, and New York on Nov. 6. S. receives libretto of Act I of *Arabella*.

Barraqué born, Jan. 17; Musgrave born, May 27; T. Baird born, July 26; Stockhausen born, Aug. 28; Janáček (74) dies, Aug. 12. First perfs. of Ravel's *Boléro*, Paris, Nov. 22; Schoenberg's *Variations*, Berlin, Dec. 2.

1929 65 S. ill during early part of year and goes to Italy in April and May to con-

G. Crumb born, Oct. 24; Diaghilev (57) dies, Aug. 19. First perfs. of Proko-

YEAR	AGE	LIFE	CONTEMPORARY MUSICIANS AND EVENTS
		valesce. Suggests revisions in libretto of *Arabella* Act I. After these are completed, Hofmannsthal dies on July 15. S. conducts at Munich Festival in August and works on version of Mozart's *Idomeneo*.	fiev's Symphony No. 3, Paris, May 17; Hindemith's *Neues vom Tage*, Berlin, June 8; Webern's Symphony, New York, Dec. 8.
1931	67	S. conducts *Idomeneo* at Vienna Opera on April 16.	Nielsen (66) dies, Oct. 3; D'Indy (80) dies, Dec. 2.
1932	68	Grandson Christian born on Feb. 27. S. conducts *Fidelio* at Salzburg in August. Completes *Arabella* at Garmisch on Oct. 12. Meets Stefan Zweig on Nov. 20 in Munich.	A. Goehr born Aug. 10; Sousa (77) dies, March 6.
1933	69	S. conducts Berlin concert in place of Bruno Walter on March 16 and *Parsifal* at Bayreuth in place of Toscanini in July. Berlin Radio performance of *Guntram* in June. First performance of *Arabella* conducted by Krauss at Dresden on July 1. First performance of revised version of *Die ägyptische Helena* conducted by Krauss at Salzburg on Aug. 14. Berlin première of *Arabella* conducted by Furtwängler on Oct. 12 and Vienna première with Lehmann in title-rôle on Oct.	Penderecki born, Nov. 23; Duparc (85) dies, Feb. 13; Hitler comes to power in Germany, Jan. 30; Schoenberg arrives in the United States, Oct. 31.

YEAR	AGE	LIFE	CONTEMPORARY MUSICIANS AND EVENTS
		26. S. becomes president of German Reichsmusikkammer on Nov. 15. Throughout the year S. works on *Die schweigsame Frau,* to Zweig libretto.	
1934	70	Widespread celebrations of S.'s seventieth birthday on June 11. Nazis forbid him to conduct at Salzburg and begin campaign against Zweig. S. completes full score of *Die schweigsame Frau* on Oct. 20 and composes *Olympic Hymn* for opening of 1936 Games in Berlin. Increasing Nazi pressure on Jewish musicians and, in December, virulent attack on 'moral decay' of Hindemith's music.	Birtwistle born, July 15; Maxwell Davies born, Sept. 8; Elgar (76) dies, Feb. 23; Schreker (56) dies, March 21; Holst (59) dies, May 25; Delius (72) dies, June 10. First perfs. of Shostakovich's *Lady Macbeth of the Mzensk District,* Moscow, Jan. 22; Hindemith's suite *Mathis der Maler,* Berlin, March 12; Walton's Symphony No. 1 (minus finale), London, Dec. 3.
1935	71	Nazis forbid further collaboration between S. and Zweig, but Zweig agrees to supervise libretti written for S. by Joseph Gregor. S. meets Gregor in April. First performance of *Die schweigsame Frau* at Dresden on June 24, but opera is banned after fourth performance. S. forced to resign presidency of Reichsmusikkammer on July 13. At Garmisch in	Maw born, Nov. 5; Dukas (69) dies, May 17; Berg (50) dies, Dec. 24. First perfs. of Vaughan Williams's Symphony No. 4, London, April 10; Gershwin's *Porgy and Bess,* Boston, Mass., Sept. 30; Prokofiev's Violin Concerto No. 2, Madrid, Dec. 1.

Richard Strauss

YEAR	AGE	LIFE	CONTEMPORARY MUSICIANS AND EVENTS
		autumn, with Gregor, he begins work on *Friedenstag*.	
1936	72	Conducts *Arabella* in Genoa in March and fulfils other conducting engagements in Italy, Belgium and France during March and April. Completes *Friedenstag* in Garmisch on June 16. Conducts *Olympic Hymn* at opening of Games in Berlin on Aug. 1. Begins composition of *Daphne* in late summer. Visits London, receives Gold Medal of Royal Philharmonic Society on on Nov. 5 and conducts *Ariadne* at Covent Garden on Nov. 6. Conducts in Italy during December.	R. Rodney Bennett born, March 29; Cardew born, May 7; Amy born Aug. 29; Stransky (63) (original of 'Stroh' in *Intermezzo*) dies, March 6; Glazunov (70) dies, March 21; Respighi (56) dies, April 18. First perfs. of Berg's Violin Concerto, Barcelona, April 19; Prokofiev's *Peter and the Wolf*, Moscow, May 2.
1937	73	Visits Italy in March. Famous Munich operatic era under Krauss opens with *Salome* on May 18. S. cancels Paris World Fair visit in September because of illness. While convalescing, completes *Daphne* at Taormina on Dec. 24.	Widor (92) dies, March 12; Szymanowski (52) dies, March 28; Gershwin (39) dies, July 11; Pierné (73) dies, July 17; Roussel (68) dies, Aug. 23; Ravel (62) dies, Dec. 28. First perfs. of Berg's *Lulu*, Zürich, June 2; Orff's *Carmina Burana*, Frankfurt, June 8.
1938	74	In Italy until April. Begins to compose *Die Liebe der Danae* in June. First performance of *Friedenstag* on July 24 at Munich, and of	

YEAR	AGE	LIFE	CONTEMPORARY MUSICIANS AND EVENTS
		Daphne on Oct. 15 at Dresden. Returns to Italy in November.	
1939	75	Intensive celebrations of his 75th birthday on June 11 include revised version of *Arabella* conducted by Krauss in Munich on July 16. In Baden-bei-Zürich taking cure for rheumatism at outbreak of war on Sept. 3.	Holliger born, May 21 ; first perf. of Bartók's Violin Concerto No. 2, Amsterdam, March 23.
1940	76	*Daphne* performed in Vienna on April 25. Completes *Japanische Festmusik* in April (first performed in Tokyo on Dec. 11). Completes *Die Liebe der Danae* on June 28. Begins to compose *Capriccio* to Krauss libretto in July. Revised *Guntram* produced at Weimar on Oct. 29.	First perf. of Stravinsky's Symphony in C, Chicago, Nov. 7; Schoenberg's Violin Concerto, Philadelphia, Dec. 6.
1941	77	Ballet *Verklungene Feste,* with more Couperin-Strauss arrangements, performed in Munich on April 5. S. completes *Capriccio* on Aug. 3. Moves to Vienna, where his version of *Idomeneo* is performed in December.	F. Bridge (61) dies, Jan. 10. First perfs. of Rakhmaninov's *Symphonic Dances,* Philadelphia, Jan. 3 ; Hindemith's Cello Concerto, Boston, Feb. 7.
1942	78	Conducts *Daphne* at Munich National Theatre on Oct. 20, his last appearance there as conductor. First perform-	Zweig (60) dies, Feb. 22 ; Zemlinsky (69) dies, March 16.

Richard Strauss

YEAR AGELIFE   CONTEMPORARY MUSICIANS
                                AND EVENTS

ance of *Capriccio* in Munich
on Oct. 28. Completes
Horn Concerto No. 2 in
November.   Awarded
Vienna Beethoven Prize in
December.

1943 79 Composes Wind Sonatina   Rakhmaninov (69) dies,
No. 1. First performance of   March 28; Schillings (75)
Second Horn Concerto at   dies, July 23. First perf. of
Salzburg Festival on Aug.   Vaughan Williams's Sym-
11.   Munich   National   phony No. 5, London, June
Theatre bombed on Oct. 2.   24.
Composes *An den Baum
Daphne* in November.

1944 80 'Strauss weeks' in Dresden   Tavener born, Jan. 28;
and Vienna to mark his 80th   Sinigaglia (75) dies, May
birthday. First performance   16; R. Rolland (78) dies,
of Wind Sonatina in Dres-   Dec. 30. First perfs. of
den on June 18. Dress re-   Hindemith's *Weber Meta-
hearsal performance of *Die   morphoses*, New York, Jan.
Liebe der Danae* at Salz-   20; Schoenberg's Piano
burg Festival on Aug. 16   Concerto, New York, Feb.
before all theatres were   6; Bartók's *Concerto for
closed in view of war situa-   Orchestra*, Boston, Dec. 1.
tion. Golden wedding on
Sept. 10.

1945 81 Dresden and Vienna opera   Mascagni (81) dies, Aug. 2;
houses destroyed in Feb-   Webern (61) dies, Sept. 15;
ruary and March. S. revises   Bartók (64) dies, Sept. 26.
München on Feb. 24 and   First perf. of Prokofiev's
completes *Metamorphosen*   Symphony No. 5, Moscow,
on April 12. Writes artistic   Jan. 13.
testament in letter to Karl
Böhm in April. Completes
Wind Sonatina No. 2 on

YEAR	AGE	LIFE	CONTEMPORARY MUSICIANS AND EVENTS

June 22. Moves to Switzerland in October where he completes Oboe Concerto.

1946 82 In Switzerland. First performances of *Metamorphosen* in Zürich on Jan. 25, of Oboe Concerto in Zürich on Feb. 26 and of Sonatina No. 2 at Winterthur on March 25.

Falla (69) dies, Nov. 14. First perfs. of Stravinsky's *Symphony in Three Movements*, New York, Jan. 24; Bartók's Piano Concerto No. 3, Philadelphia, Feb. 8. Casella (63) dies, March 5.

1947 83 Still living in Switzerland. Visits London from Oct. 4 to 31 for series of concert and opera performances organized by Beecham. He conducts *Till* at Royal Albert Hall on Oct. 29, his last public appearance in England. Completes Duett-Concertino on Dec. 16.

1948 84 First performance of Duett-Concertino in Lugano on April 4. Completes song *Im Abendrot* on May 6. Cleared by Denazification Board in June. Composes *Frühling* (July 18), *Beim Schlafengehen* (Aug. 4) and *September* (Sept. 20). Serious operation in Lausanne in December.

Wolf-Ferrari (72) dies, Jan. 21. First perfs. of Vaughan Williams's Symphony No. 6, London, April 21; Schoenberg's *Survivor from Warsaw*, Albuquerque, Nov. 4.

1949 85 Returns to Garmisch on May 10. Hon. doctor of philosophy, Munich University, hon. freeman of Garmisch and Bayreuth to

Turina (66) dies, Jan. 14; Pfitzner (80) dies, May 22; Skalkottas (45) dies, Sept. 19.

Richard Strauss

YEAR AGE   LIFE

CONTEMPORARY MUSICIANS
AND EVENTS

celebrate his 85th birthday
on June 11. Conducts for
last time on July 13. Heart
attacks in August. Dies at
2.10 p.m. on Sept. 8 in
Garmisch. Cremated, Sept.
11. Memorial concerts in
Vienna (Krauss) on Sept. 18
and Bayreuth (Keilberth)
on Oct. 9.

Appendix B   Catalogue of works

(Dates given are of composition. Dates of major first performances may be found in the text and in Appendix A. Some early unpublished works composed between 1870 and 1880 are omitted.)

OPERAS

1892–3   *Guntram*, Op. 25. Libretto by R. Strauss in three acts. Revised 1940. (Aibl; rev. version Fürstner, 1940)

1900–1   *Feuersnot*, Op. 50. 'Poem for singing' in one act; libretto by Ernst von Wolzogen. (Fürstner)

1904–5   *Salome*, Op. 54. Drama in one act to libretto by Hedwig Lachmann based on Oscar Wilde's play. (Fürstner)

1906–8   *Elektra*, Op. 58. Tragedy in one act to libretto by Hugo von Hofmannsthal. (Fürstner)

1909–10   *Der Rosenkavalier*, Op. 59. Comedy for music in three acts by Hugo von Hofmannsthal. (Fürstner)

1911–12   *Ariadne auf Naxos*, Op. 60. Original version: play *Le Bourgeois Gentilhomme* by Molière and opera in one act by Hugo von Hofmannsthal; second version (1916), Prologue and opera in one act by Hugo von Hofmannsthal. (Fürstner)

1914–18   *Die Frau ohne Schatten*, Op. 65. Opera in three acts by Hugo von Hofmannsthal. (Fürstner)

1917–23   *Intermezzo*, Op. 72. Bourgeois comedy with symphonic interludes in two acts by R. Strauss. (Fürstner)

1923–7   *Die ägyptische Helena*, Op. 75. Opera in two acts by Hugo von Hofmannsthal. Revised 1933. (Fürstner)

1930–2   *Arabella*, Op. 79. Lyrical comedy in three acts by Hugo von Hofmannsthal. Revised 1939. (Fürstner)

1933–4   *Die schweigsame Frau*, Op. 80. Comic opera in three acts freely adapted from Ben Jonson by Stefan Zweig. (Fürstner)

1935–6   *Friedenstag*, Op. 81. Opera in one act by Joseph Gregor. (Oertel)

1936–7   *Daphne*, Op. 82. Bucolic tragedy in one act by Joseph Gregor. (Oertel)

1938–40   *Die Liebe der Danae*, Op. 83. Cheerful mythology in three acts by Joseph Gregor, using a draft by Hugo von Hofmannsthal. (Oertel)

1940–1   *Capriccio*, Op. 85. Conversation piece for music in one act by Clemens Krauss. (Oertel)

BALLETS AND OTHER STAGE WORKS

1892   *Festmusik*, '*Lebende Bilder*' for orchestra. Composed to accompany *tableaux vivants* in celebration of golden wedding of Grand Duke and Duchess of Weimar. Revived as *Kampf und Sieg* in Vienna 1931. (Published Heinrichshofen 1930)

1913–14   *Josephslegende*, Op. 63. Ballet in one act by Count Kessler and H. von Hofmannsthal for full orchestra. (Fürstner)

1917   *Der Bürger als Edelmann* (*Le Bourgeois Gentilhomme*) (incorporating music for original *Ariadne*, 1912), Op. 60. Comedy, with dances, by Molière, freely adapted in three acts by H. von Hofmannsthal. (Fürstner)

1921–2   *Schlagobers*, Op. 70. Gay Viennese ballet in two acts devised by R. Strauss. (Fürstner)

1940–1   *Verklungene Feste*, dance vision from two centuries with music after Couperin.

ARRANGEMENTS OF STAGE WORKS BY OTHER COMPOSERS

1890   Gluck, *Iphigénie en Tauride*, arranged with additional trio in finale. (Performed Weimar, 1900.) (Fürstner)

1922–4   Beethoven, *Die Ruinen von Athen*, music, including parts of ballet *Die Geschöpfe des Prometheus*, edited and arranged by Strauss and Hofmannsthal, with newly composed *mélodrame*. (Fürstner)

1930   Mozart, *Idomeneo*. 'Re-working' in association with L.
       Wallerstein, including altered recitatives, orchestral
       interlude and new Act III ensemble. (Heinrichshofen)

ORCHESTRAL

1876   *Festmarsch No. 1* in E flat, Op. 1. (Breitkopf, 1881)
1880   Symphony No. 1 in D minor. (MS.)
1881–2 *Serenade in E flat* for 13 wind instruments, Op. 7. (J. Aibl)
1883   *Concert Overture* in C minor. (MS.)
1883–4 Symphony No. 2 in F minor, Op. 12. (Aibl)
       Suite in B flat for 13 wind instruments, Op. 4. (Leuckart,
       1911)
1886   *Aus Italien*, symphonic fantasy in G, Op. 16. (Aibl)
1887–8 *Macbeth*, tone-poem, Op. 23. Revised 1889–90. (Aibl)
1888–9 *Don Juan*, tone-poem, Op. 20. (Aibl)
1889   *Festmarsch No. 2* in C. (MS.)
1889–90 *Tod und Verklärung*, tone-poem, Op. 24. (Aibl)
1894–5 *Till Eulenspiegels lustige Streiche*, after the old rogue's tune,
       in rondo form, Op. 28. (Aibl)
1896   *Also sprach Zarathustra*, tone-poem, Op. 30. (Aibl)
1897–8 *Don Quixote*, fantastic variations on a theme of knightly
       character, Op. 35. (Aibl)
1898–9 *Ein Heldenleben*, tone-poem, Op. 40. (Leuckart)
1903   *Symphonia Domestica*, Op. 53. (Bote and Bock)
1906–7 *Two Military Marches*, Op. 57 (*Militärmarsch* in E flat;
       Kriegsmarsch in C minor). (Peters)
       Der Brandenburgsche Mars. (Fürstner)
       Königsmarsch. (Fürstner)
1909   *Two Parade Marches*. (Fürstner)
       Feierlicher Einzug der Ritter des Johanniterordens for brass
       and timpani. (Lienau)
1911–15 *Eine Alpensinfonie*, Op. 64. (Leuckart)
1913   *Festliches Präludium* for orchestra and organ, Op. 61.
       (Fürstner)
1919   *Suite, Le Bourgeois Gentilhomme*, Op. 60. (Leuckart)
1922   *Tanzsuite* after keyboard pieces by Couperin. (Fürstner)

Richard Strauss

1924	*Wiener Philharmoniker Fanfare* for Vienna Philharmonic ball on 4th March 1924, for brass and timpani. (Boosey and Hawkes, 1960)
	Fanfare for wind instruments, for opening of Vienna Music Week, 14th September 1924. (Boosey and Hawkes, 1960)
1933	4 *Sinfonische Zwischenspiele aus Intermezzo*, Op. 72.
1938–9	*München*, waltz for orchestra, first version. See 1945. (MS.)
1940	*Japanische Festmusik*, Op. 84. (Oertel)
1941	*Divertimento* for small orchestra after keyboard pieces by Couperin, Op. 86. (Two new arrangements added to those made for *Verklungene Feste*: see under *Ballets*, 1940–1.) (Oertel)
1943	*Festmusik* for Vienna city trumpeters, for brass and timpani, two versions. (MS.)
	Sonatina No. 1 in F, for 16 wind instruments. ('Aus der Werkstatt eines Invaliden.') (Boosey and Hawkes, 1964)
1944	First Waltz Sequence from *Der Rosenkavalier*, Op. 59, Acts I and II. (Fürstner)
1944–5	*Sonatina* No. 2 in E flat, for 16 wind instruments. ('Fröhliche Werkstatt.') '(Boosey and Hawkes, 1952)
1945	*München*, memorial waltz (revised version). (Boosey and Hawkes, 1951)
	Metamorphosen, Study for 23 solo strings, in C minor. (Boosey and Hawkes, 1946)
1946–7	Symphonic Fantasy from *Die Frau ohne Schatten*, Op. 65. (Fürstner)
	Josephslegende, Op. 63, symphonic fragment. (Fürstner)

SOLO INSTRUMENT(S) AND ORCHESTRA

1881–2	Violin Concerto in D minor, Op. 8. (Aibl)
1882–3	Horn Concerto No. 1 in E flat, Op. 11. (Aibl)
1885–6	*Burleske* in D minor for pianoforte and orchestra. Revised 1890. (Steingräber, 1894)

244

1925	*Parergon zur Symphonia Domestica*, Op. 73, for pianoforte (left hand) and orchestra. (Boosey and Hawkes, 1964)
	Military March in F (for film of *Der Rosenkavalier*). (Fürstner)
1927	*Panathenäenzug*, Op. 74, symphonic studies in form of passacaglia for pianoforte (left hand) and orchestra. (Boosey and Hawkes, 1953)
1942	Horn Concerto No. 2 in E flat. (Boosey and Hawkes, 1950)
1945–6	Oboe Concerto. (Boosey and Hawkes, 1948)
1947	Duett-Concertino for clarinet and bassoon with strings and harp. (Boosey and Hawkes, 1949)

CHAMBER MUSIC

1879–80	String Quartet in A, Op. 2. (Aibl)
1881–3	Sonata in F for violoncello and pianoforte, Op. 6. (Aibl)
1883–4	Quartet in C minor for pianoforte, violin, viola and violoncello, Op. 13. (Aibl)
1887–8	Sonata in E flat for violin and pianoforte, Op. 18. (Aibl)
1924	*Hochzeitspräludium* for two wind instruments. (Vienna, 1948)
1945	*Daphne-Etude* for solo violin. (MS.)
1948	*Allegretto* in E for violin and pianoforte. (MS.)

KEYBOARD WORKS

1881	*Five Piano Pieces*, Op. 3. (Aibl and UE)
	Sonata in B minor, Op. 5. (Aibl and UE)
1883–4	*Stimmungsbilder*, Op. 9. 1. Auf stillem Waldespfad; 2. An einsamer Quelle; 3. Intermezzo; 4. Träumerei; 5. Heidebild. (Aibl and UE)
	Improvisations and Fugue in A minor on an Original Theme. (*Fugue* published by Bruckmann, 1889)
1944	Suite from *Capriccio* for harpsichord. (MS.)

MELODRAMAS

1897   *Enoch Arden* (Tennyson) for voice and pianoforte. (For-
        berg, 1897)
1899   *Das Schloss am Meer* (Uhland) for voice and pianoforte.
        (Fürstner, 1911)

WORKS FOR CHORUS

1880   Third Choral Speech from *Electra* (Sophocles) for male
        chorus and small orchestra. (Breitkopf and Härtel,
        1902)
1884   *Wandrers Sturmlied* (Goethe), Op. 14, for six-part chorus
        and full orchestra. (Aibl)
1885   *Schwäbische Erbschaft* (Loewe), for four-part male chorus.
        (Leuckart, 1950)
        Bardengesang aus der Hermanns-Schlacht (Kleist) for male
        chorus and orchestra. (Lost. See 1905.)
1889   *Scherzquartett* for unacc. male voices. (MS.)
1897   2 *Gesänge,* Op. 34, for unacc. 16-part mixed chorus.
        1. Der Abend (Schiller); 2. Hymne (Rückert). (Aibl)
        Hymne for women's chorus and orchestra, 'Licht, du
        ewiglich eines' (for opening of Secession art exhibi-
        tion, Munich, 1st June 1897). (MS.)
1899   2 *Choruses,* Op. 42, for unacc. male voices, from Herder's
        Stimmen der Völker, 1. Liebe; 2. Altdeutsches
        Schlachtlied. (Leuckart)
        Soldatenlied (Kopisch) ('Wenn man bei Wein sitzt') for
        unacc. male chorus. (Bauer, 1909)
        3 *Choruses,* Op. 45, for unacc. male voices, from Herder's
        Stimmen der Völker, 1. Schlachtgesang; 2. Lied der
        Freundschaft; 3. Der Brauttanz. (Fürstner)
1903   *Taillefer* (Uhland), Op. 52, for soprano, tenor and bari-
        tone soloists, mixed chorus and orchestra. (Fürstner)
        Canon, 'Hans Huber in Vitznau', for four unacc. voices.
        (Atlantis-Verlag, 1944)
1905   *Bardengesang* (Klopstock), Op. 55, aus der *Hermanns-*

Schlacht for three male choruses and orchestra. (Fürstner)

1906   6 *Folk-songs* arranged for unacc. male voices. 1. Christlicher Maien; 2. Misslungene; 3. Tummele; 4. Hüt' du dich; 5. Wächterlied; 6. Kuckuck. (Peters)

1913   *Deutsche Motette* (Rückert), Op. 62, for soprano, alto, tenor and bass soloists and unacc. 16-part mixed chorus. (Fürstner)

1914   *Cantata* (Hofmannsthal), 'Tüchtigen stellt das schnelle Glück', for unacc. male chorus. (Junker & Dünnhaupt, 1935)

1926   *Hymne* auf das Haus Kohorn, for unacc. male chorus. (MS.)

1928   *Die Tageszeiten* (Eichendorff), Op. 76, for male chorus and orchestra. 1. Der Morgen; 2. Mittagsruh; 3. Der Abend; 4. Die Nacht. (Leuckart)

1929   *Austria* (Wildgans), Op. 78, for male chorus and orchestra. (Bote and Bock)

1934   *Olympische Hymne* (Lubahn), for mixed chorus and orchestra. (Fürstner)

1935   *Die Göttin im Putzzimmer* (Rückert), for unacc. eight-part mixed chorus. (Boosey and Hawkes, 1958)

       3 *Choruses* (Rückert), for unacc. male chorus. 1. Vor den Türen; 2. Traumlicht; 3. Fröhlich im Maien. (Boosey and Hawkes, 1958)

1938   *Durch Einsamkeiten* (Wildgans), for unacc. male voices. (MS.)

1943   *An den Baum Daphne* (Gregor), Epilogue to *Daphne*, for unacc. nine-part mixed chorus. (Boosey and Hawkes, 1958)

SONGS

1870–83   *Jugendlieder* for voice and pianoforte.

       1. Weihnachtslied (Schubart, Dec. 1870); 2. Einkehr (Uhland, Aug. 1871); 3. Winterreise (Uhland, 1871); 4. Der müde Wanderer (Fallersleben, 1873); 5. Husarenlied (Fallersleben, 1873); 6. Der Fischer

(Goethe, 1877); 7. Die Drossel (Uhland, 1877); 8. Lass ruhn die Toten (Chimasso, 1877); 9. Lust und Qual (Goethe, 1877); 10. Spielmann und Zither (Körner, 1878); 11. Wiegenlied (Fallersleben, 1878); 12. Abend und Morgenrot (Fallersleben, 1878); 13. Im Walde (Geibel, 1878); 14. Nebel (Lenau, 1878); 15. Soldatenlied (Fallersleben, 1878); 16. Ein Röslein zog ich mir im Garten (Fallersleben, 1878); 17. Alphorn, with horn obbligato (Kerner, 1878); 18. Waldesgesang (Geibel, 1879); 19. In Vaters Garten (Heine, 1879); 20. Die erwächte Rose (Sallet, 1880); 21. Begegnung (Gruppe, 1880); 22. John Anderson, mein Lieb (Burns, 1880); 23. Rote Rosen (Stieler, 1883).

1878   2 *Songs* with orchestra: Aria der Almaide (Goethe); Der Spielmann und sein Kind (Fallersleben). (MS.)

1885   9 *Lieder* aus 'Letzte Blätter' (Gilm), Op. 10, for voice and pianoforte.
1. Zueignung (orch. Heger 1932, Strauss 1940); 2. Nichts; 3, Die Nacht; 4. Die Georgine; 5. Geduld; 6. Wer Hat's gethan?; 7. Die Verschwiegenen; 8. Die Zeitlose; 9. Allerseelen (orch. Heger 1932). (Aibl 1885 except No. 6, which remained unpublished until 1974, Schneider Tutzing). No. 9 arr. as pianoforte solo by Reger, 1904.

1886   5 *Lieder*, Op. 15, for medium voice and pianoforte.
1. Madrigal (Michelangelo); 2. Winternacht; 3. Lob des Leidens; 4. Dem Herzen ähnlich; 5. Heimkehr (orch. L. Weniger). Nos. 2–5 poems by Schack. (Rahter) No. 5 arr. as pianoforte solo by Gieseking.

1887   6 *Lieder* (Schack), Op. 17, for high voice and pianoforte.
1. Seitdem dein Aug' in meines schaute; 2. Ständchen (orch. F. Mottl); 3. Das Geheimnis; 4. Von dunklem Schleier umsponnen; 5. Nur Muth!; 6. Barkarole. (Rahter)

1887–8   6 *Lieder* (Schack's *Lotosblättern*), Op. 19, for voice and pianoforte. 1. Wozu noch, Mädchen; 2. Breit' über mein Haupt; 3. Schön sind, doch Kalt die Himmelssterne; 4. Wie sollten wir geheim sie halten; 5. Hoffen und Wieder verzagen; 6. Mein Herz ist stumm. (Aibl)

1888   5 *Schlichte Weisen* (Dahn), Op. 21, for voice and pianoforte. 1. All mein Gedanken; 2. Du meines Herzens Krönelein; 3. Ach Lieb, ich muss nun scheiden!; 4. Ach weh mir unglückhaftem Mann; 5. Die Frauen. (Aibl)

4 *Mädchenblumen* (Dahn), Op. 22, for voice and pianoforte. 1. Kornblumen; 2. Mohnblumen; 3. Efeu; 4. Wasserrose. (Fürstner)

1891   2 *Lieder* (Lenau), Op. 26, for high voice and pianoforte. 1. Frühlingsgedränge; 2. O wärst du mein. (Aibl)

1894   4 *Lieder*, Op. 27, for high voice and pianoforte. 1. Ruhe, meine Seele! (Henckell) (orch. Strauss, 1948); 2. Cäcilie (Hart) (orch. Strauss, 1897); 3. Heimliche Aufforderung (Mackay) (orch. Heger, 1932); 4. Morgen (Mackay) (orch. Strauss, 1897). (Aibl)

1895   3 *Lieder* (Bierbaum), Op. 29, for high voice and pianoforte. 1. Traum durch die Dämmerung (orch. Heger, 1932); 2. Schlagende Herzen; 3. Nachtgang. (Aibl)

1895–6   4 *Lieder*, Op. 31, for voice and pianoforte. 1. Blauer Sommer; 2. Wenn; 3. Weisser Jasmin (texts of 1, 2 and 3 by Busse); 4. (Dehmel) with viola obbligato, Stiller Gang. (Fürstner)

1896   5 *Lieder*, Op. 32, for voice and pianoforte. 1. Ich trage meine Minne (Henckell) (orch. Heger, 1932); 2. Sehnsucht (Liliencron); 3. Liebeshymnus (Henckell) (orch. Strauss, 1897); 4. O süsser Mai (Henckell); 5. Himmelsboten (*Knaben Wunderhorn*). (Aibl)

Wir beide wollen springen (Bierbaum) for voice and pianoforte. (Boosey and Hawkes, 1964)

1896–7   4 *Gesänge*, Op. 33, for voice(s) and orchestra. 1. Verführung (Mackay); 2. Gesang der Apollopriesterin (Bodman); 3. Hymnus (author unknown); 4. Pilgers Morgenlied (Goethe). (Bote and Bock)

1896–8   6 *Lieder*, Op. 37, for voice and pianoforte. 1. Glückes genug (Liliencron); 2. Ich liebe dich (Liliencron) (orch. Strauss, 1943); 3. Meinem Kinde (Falke) (orch. Strauss, 1897); 4. Mein Auge (Dehmel) (orch. Strauss, 1933); 5. Herr Lenz (Bodman) (composed June 1896); 6. Hochzeitlich Lied (Lindner). (Aibl)

1897–8   4 *Lieder*, Op. 36, for voice and pianoforte. 1. Das Rosenband (Klopstock) (orch. Strauss, 1897); 2 Für funfzehn Pfennige (*Knaben Wunderhorn*); 3. Hat gesagt—bleibt's nicht dabei (*Knaben Wunderhorn*); 4. Anbetung (Rückert). (Aibl)

1898   5 *Lieder*, Op. 39, for voice and pianoforte. 1. Leises Lied (Dehmel); 2. Jung Hexenlied (Bierbaum); 3. Der Arbeitsmann (Dehmel) (orch. Strauss, 1941 [1]); 4. Befreit (Dehmel) (orch. Strauss, 1933 and by H. Stüber); 5. Lied an meinen Sohn (Dehmel). (Forberg)

1899   5 *Lieder*, Op. 41, for voice and pianoforte. 1. Wiegenlied (Dehmel) (orch. Strauss, 1900); 2. In der Campagna (Mackay); 3. Am Ufer (Dehmel); 4 Bruder Liederlich (Liliencron); 5. Leise Lieder (Morgenstern). (Leuckart)

        3 *Lieder*, Op. 43, for voice and pianoforte. 1. An Sie (Klopstock); 2. Muttertändelei (Bürger) (orch. Strauss, 1900); 3. Die Ulme zu Hirsau (Uhland). (Challier)

        2 *grössere Gesänge*, Op. 44, for low voice and orchestra. 1. Notturno (Dehmel); 2. Nächtlicher Gang (Rückert). (Forberg)

        Weihnachtsgefühl (Greif) for voice and pianoforte. (Boosey and Hawkes, 1964) [2]

1899–
1900   5 *Lieder* (Rückert), Op. 46, for voice and pianoforte. 1. Ein Obdach gegen Sturm und Regen; 2. Gestern war ich Atlas; 3. Die sieben Siegel; 4. Morgenrot; 5. Ich sehe wie in einem Spiegel. (Fürstner)

---

[1] Strauss stated in a letter to Hans Hotter in September 1941 that he had scored this song for him and that it was in manuscript in Vienna, but no trace of it has yet been found.

[2] Although included among the *Jugendlieder* in the complete edition of Strauss songs, this *Lied* was composed at Charlottenburg on 8th December 1899.

1900   5 *Lieder* (Uhland), Op. 47, for voice and pianoforte.
1. Auf ein Kind; 2. Des Dichters Abendgang (orig.
version in E flat, but orch. Strauss, 1918, in D flat for
soprano); 3. Rückleben; 4. Einkehr; 5. Von den
sieben Zechbrüdern. (Fürstner)

5 *Lieder*, Op. 48, for voice and pianoforte. 1. Freundliche
Vision (Bierbaum) (orch. Strauss, 1918); 2. Ich
schwebe; 3. Kling!; 4. Winterweihe (orch. Strauss,
1918); 5. Winterliebe (orch. Strauss, 1918). Texts of
2–5 by Henckell. (Fürstner)

1900–1   8 *Lieder*, Op. 49, for voice and pianoforte. 1. Waldseligkeit
(Dehmel) (orch. Strauss, 1918); 2. In goldener Fülle
(Remer); 3. Wiegenliedchen (Dehmel); 4. Lied des
Steinklopfers (Henckell); 5. Sie wissen's nicht
(Panizza); 6. Junggesellenschwur (*Knaben Wunder-
horn*); 7. Wer lieben will, muss leiden (Elsässische
Volkslieder); 8. Ach, was Kummer, Qual und
Schmerzen (ditto). (Fürstner)

1902–6   2 *Lieder*, Op. 51, for low bass voice and orchestra. 1. Das
Thal (Uhland); 2. Der Einsame (Heine). (Fürstner)

1903–6   6 *Lieder*, Op. 56, for voice and pianoforte. 1. Gefunden
(Goethe); 2. Blindenklage (Henckell); 3. Im Spätboot
(Meyer); 4. Mit deinen blauen Augen; 5. Frühlingsfeier (orch. Strauss, 1933); 6. Die heiligen drei
Könige aus Morgenland (composed 1906 for soprano
and orchestra, accompaniment being transcribed for
pianoforte by Strauss for publication in op. 56). Texts
of 4–6 by Heine. (Bote and Bock)

1904   2 *Lieder* for voice and guitar or harps, from Calderón's play
'Der Richter von Zalamea'. 1. Liebesliedchen; 2. Lied
der Chispa. (Boosey and Hawkes, 1954)

1906   Der Graf von Rom, *vocalise* with pianoforte.

1918   *Krämerspiegel* (Kerr), Op. 66, for voice and pianoforte.
1. Es war einmal ein Bock; 2. Einst kam der Bock als
Bote; 3. Es liebte einst ein Hase; 4. Drei Masken sah
ich am Himmel stehn; 5. Hast du ein Tongedicht
vollbracht; 6. O lieber Künstler sei ermahnt; 7. Unser

Feind ist, grosser Gott; 8. Von Händlern wird die
Kunst bedroht; 9. Es war mal eine Wanze; 10. Die
Künstler sind die Schöpfer; 11. Die Händler und die
Macher; 12. O Schöpferschwarm, O Händlerkreis.
(Cassirer, 1921, limited edn of 120)

6 *Lieder*, Op. 67, for voice and pianoforte. 1–3, 3 *Lieder* der
'Ophelia' (Shakespeare): Wie erkenn'ich mein
Treulieb; Guten Morgen, 's ist Sankt Valentinstag;
Sie trugen ihn auf der Bahre bloss; 3 *Lieder* from
Goethe's 'Büchern des Unmuts' (Westöstlicher
Divan): Wer wird von der Welt verlangen; Hab' ich
euch denn je geraten; Wandrers Gemütsruhe. (Bote
and Bock)

6 *Lieder* (Brentano), Op. 68, for high voice and pianoforte.
Nos. 1–5 orch. Strauss, 1940, No. 6 orch. Strauss,
1933. 1. An die Nacht; 2. Ich wollt ein Sträusslein
binden; 3. Säusle, liebe Myrthe; 4. Als mir dein Lied
erklang; 5. Amor; 6 Lied der Frauen. (Fürstner, 1918,
orch. version, 1940)

5 *kleine Lieder*, Op. 69, for voice and pianoforte.
1. Der Stern; 2. Der Pokal; 3. Einerlei, texts of 1–3 by
Arnim; 4. Waldesfahrt; 5. Schlechtes Wetter. Texts
of 4–5 by Heine. (Fürstner)

1919 Sinnspruch (Goethe), for voice and pianoforte. (Mosse)

1921 3 *Hymnen* (Hölderlin), Op. 71, for high voice and orchestra.
1. Hymne an die Liebe; 2. Rückkehr in die Heimat;
3. Die Liebe. (Fürstner)

1922 Erschaffen und Beleben ('Hans Adam war ein Erdenkloss')
(Goethe), for bass voice and pianoforte. (Oertel, 1951)

1925 Durch allen Schall und Klang (Goethe), for voice and
pianoforte. Composed for R. Rolland's 60th birthday
on 29 Jan. 1926. (Boosey and Hawkes, 1959)

1928 5 *Gesänge des Orients* (Bethge), Op. 77, for voice and
pianoforte. 1. Ihre Augen; 2. Schwung; 3. Liebes-
geschenke; 4. Die Allmächtige; 5. Huldigung.
(Leuckart)

1929 2 *Gesänge* (Rückert), for bass voice and pianoforte. 1. Vom künftigen Alter; 2. Und dann nicht mehr. (Universal, 1964)

1930   Wie etwas sei leicht (Goethe), for voice and pianoforte. (Boosey and Hawkes, 1968)

1933   Das Bächlein (author unknown), for voice and pianoforte (orch. Strauss 1935). (Universal, 1951)

1935   Im Sonnenschein (Rückert), for bass voice and pianoforte. (Universal, 1964) [1]

Zugemessne Rhythmen (Goethe), for voice and pianoforte. (Boosey and Hawkes, Strauss Yearbook, 1954)

1939   Hab dank, du gütger Weisheitspender, for bass voice unacc. (MS.)

1940   Nottschrei aus den Gefilden Lapplands, for voice unacc. (MS.)

1942   2 *Lieder* (Weinheber), for voice and pianoforte. 1. Sankt Michael (baritone); 2. Blick vom oberen Belvedere (soprano). (Boosey and Hawkes, 1964) [2]

Xenion (Goethe), for voice and pianoforte. Composed for Gerhart Hauptmann's 80th birthday on 15 Nov. 1942. (Boosey and Hawkes, 1964)

1943   Wer tritt herein, for voice unacc. (MS.)

1948   4 *letzte Lieder* [3] for high voice and orchestra. In order of composition: 1. Im Abendrot (Eichendorff); 2. Frühling; 3. Beim Schlafengehen; 4. September. Texts of 2–4 by Hesse. (Boosey and Hawkes, 1950, in the order 2, 4, 3, 1. Strauss is said to have favoured the order 3, 4, 2, 1.)

NOTE: The 'symphonic fragment' for orchestra of extracts from *Die Liebe der Danae*, published 1952, was devised by Clemens Krauss.

[1] This song, with the two 1929 Rückert songs and the 1922 Goethe song, appear in the 1964 collected edition as *4 Gesänge* for bass voice under the spurious opus number 87.

[2] These songs, with *Das Bächlein* (1933), appear in the collected edition under the spurious opus number 88.

[3] The title *Four Last Songs* was given to this set by Strauss's publisher, Ernest Roth, after the composer's death.

Appendix C   Personalia

Alwin, Karl (1891–1945). Operatic conductor who married the soprano Elisabeth Schumann in 1919. Was on conducting staff of Vienna State Opera from 1921 to 1938. Assisted in arrangement of music for film version of *Der Rosenkavalier*. Conducted first British performance of second version of *Ariadne auf Naxos* (Covent Garden, 27 May 1924).

Bahr, Hermann (1863–1934). Austrian playwright whom Strauss first approached for libretto of *Intermezzo*. Was married to the great Wagnerian soprano Anna von Mildenburg, formerly Mahler's mistress and a notable exponent of Strauss operatic rôles.

Beecham, Sir Thomas (1879–1961). English conductor and impresario who was a leading champion of Strauss's works. Conducted first English performance of *Elektra* (19 Feb. 1910), *Feuersnot* (9 July 1910), *Salome* (8 Dec. 1910), *Rosenkavalier* (29 Jan. 1913) and *Ariadne auf Naxos* (27 May 1913). Organized 1947 London Strauss Festival.

Bierbaum, Otto Julius (1865–1910). Bavarian novelist and poet some of whose verses Strauss set to music, notably *Traum durch die Dämmerung*.

Blech, Leo (1871–1958). Conductor active especially in Berlin. Was assistant to Strauss when Strauss was chief conductor of the opera there up to 1918. Generally credited with suggestion that the Composer in the Prologue to *Ariadne* should be a *travesti* rôle.

Böhm, Karl (b. 1894). Austrian conductor who has held many important posts in Germany and Austria, notably at Dresden from 1934 to 1942. Conducted first performances of *Die schweigsame Frau* and *Daphne*.

Bülow, Hans von (1830–94). Pianist and conductor of immense eminence, notably at Munich, Meiningen and Hamburg. Conducted first performances of Wagner's *Tristan und Isolde* and *Die Meistersinger*. Appointed Strauss as his assistant at Meiningen.

Busch, Fritz (1890–1951). Conductor of Dresden opera from 1922 to 1933, directing first performances of *Intermezzo* and *Die ägyptische Helena*. Joint dedicatee of *Arabella*. Was first conductor of Glyndebourne Opera.

Dehmel, Richard (1863–1920). German author and poet. Strauss set several of his poems.

Del Mar, Norman (b. 1919). English horn-player and conductor and author of three-volume survey of Strauss's music.

Furtwängler, Wilhelm (1886–1954). German conductor, especially of Berlin Philharmonic Orchestra in 1930s. Fell into disfavour with Nazis, but remained in Germany. Conducted first performance of Strauss's *Four Last Songs*, in London in 1950.

Goebbels, Joseph (1897–1945). German Minister of Enlightenment and Propaganda from 1933 to 1945. Appointed Strauss to presidency of Reichsmusikkammer in 1933 and dismissed him in 1935.

Gregor, Joseph (1888–1960). Viennese art historian who compiled three libretti for Strauss, *Friedenstag*, *Daphne* and *Die Liebe der Danae*.

Gutheil-Schoder, Marie (1874–1935). German soprano engaged by Mahler for Vienna Opera in 1900. Exceptional actress. Fine exponent of rôle of Elektra. Sang one performance as Oktavian at Covent Garden in 1913.

Hartmann, Rudolf (b. 1900). Leading operatic producer, especially at Munich during Clemens Krauss's tenure. Expert on Strauss operas.

Hofmannsthal, Hugo von (1874–1929). Austrian dramatist and poet who first contacted Strauss in 1900. They first collaborated on *Elektra*, which was followed by *Rosenkavalier*, *Ariadne auf Naxos*, *Die Frau ohne Schatten*, *Die ägyptische Helena* and

Arabella. Their published correspondence is of the utmost interest.

Jeritza, Maria (b. 1887). Czech soprano of great vocal and personal beauty. First singer of *Ariadne* (1912) and of the Empress in *Die Frau ohne Schatten* (1919).

Kerr, Alfred (1867–1948). Berlin theatre critic who left Germany for England in 1933. Wrote the satirical poems for Strauss's song-cycle *Krämerspiegel* in 1918.

Krauss, Clemens (1893–1945). Austrian conductor and director of Vienna State Opera who was great exponent of Strauss and one of his closest friends. Librettist of *Capriccio.* Conducted first performances of *Arabella, Friedenstag* and *Capriccio.* Husband of Viorica Ursuleac. Noted for his work at Munich opera, 1937–44.

Lehmann, Lotte (b. 1888). German soprano who was the most distinguished Marschallin in *Rosenkavalier* in inter-war years. First Composer in *Ariadne* and first Christine in *Intermezzo.* Has written interesting book about working with Strauss.

Levi, Hermann (1839–1900). Conductor of Munich Court Opera during Strauss's boyhood and youth. Conducted first *Parsifal* in 1882 and first performances of several early Strauss works.

Mahler, Gustav (1860–1911). Composer and conductor who befriended Strauss though he regarded him as his complete opposite. Strauss and Mahler frequently conducted each other's works.

Mayr, Richard (1877–1935). Austrian bass-baritone whose portrayal of Baron Ochs in *Rosenkavalier* is generally regarded as unsurpassable. Was a medical student but became singer on Mahler's advice. Created role of Barak in *Die Frau ohne Schatten* (1919).

Reinhardt, Max (1873–1943). Theatrical producer of genius whose productions in Berlin inspired both Strauss and Hofmannsthal. Supervised first *Rosenkavalier* in 1911. First producer of *Ariadne auf Naxos,* which is dedicated to him. Closely associated with Salzburg Festival. Emigrated to United States in 1933.

Ritter, Alexander (1833–96). Orchestral violinist and composer. A devotee of Wagner, whose niece he married. Persuaded the young Strauss to follow Lisztian methods of composition.

Rolland, Romain (1866–1944). French writer best known for his novel *Jean-Christophe*. Friend and admirer of Strauss for over forty years.

Roller, Alfred (1864–1933). Leading theatrical designer at the Vienna Opera under Mahler and later under Strauss. Designed first *Rosenkavalier* at Dresden in 1911.

Rösch, Friedrich (1862–1925). Became friend of Strauss in their student days. *Tod und Verklärung* is dedicated to him. Co-founder with Strauss of Genossenschaft deutscher Tonsetzer.

Schalk, Franz (1863–1931). Austrian conductor associated for many years with Vienna Opera which he joined as assistant to Mahler. Joint director with Strauss 1919–24 until they quarrelled. Conducted first performance of *Die Frau ohne Schatten*.

Schoenberg, Arnold (1874–1951). Austrian composer and teacher whose 'system of composing with twelve notes' revolutionized music on 1923.

Schuch, Ernst von (1846–1914). Conductor at Dresden Court Opera from 1872 until his death (musical director from 1882). His interpretations of Strauss were deeply admired by the composer, who awarded him the first performances of *Feuersnot, Salome, Elektra* and *Rosenkavalier*.

Schumann, Elisabeth (1885–1952). German soprano who was one of legendary stars of the Vienna Opera between the wars. A marvellous exponent of Strauss; her Sophie in *Rosenkavalier* was particularly memorable.

Schwarzkopf, Elisabeth (b. 1915), German soprano whose performances as the Marschallin and the Countess in *Capriccio* are widely admired. Wife of Walter Legge.

Specht, Richard (1870–1932). Austrian music critic and essayist who wrote biographies of Mahler, Brahms and Puccini and the first biography of Strauss, published in two volumes in Leipzig in 1921.

Stransky, Josef (1872–1936). Conductor who, after holding various posts in Germany, succeeded Mahler in New York in 1911. It was he for whom Mitzi Mücke's note, which is the basis of the *Intermezzo* misunderstanding, was intended.

Strauss, Franz Joseph (1822–1905). Father of Richard Strauss. Famous horn-player and a member of the Munich Court Orchestra for nearly fifty years. Detested Wagner and his music, which he performed magnificently.

Ursuleac, Viorica (b. 1899). Rumanian soprano and wife of Clemens Krauss. Created rôles of Arabella, Commandant's Wife, in *Friedenstag,* Danae and the Countess (*Capriccio*). Was Strauss's favourite soprano in his later years.

Wolzogen, Ernst von (1855–1934). Munich satirist and poet who wrote the libretto of *Feuersnot.*

Wullner, Franz (1832–1902). German conductor and composer who was appointed a court conductor at Munich in 1864 and after Bülow's departure in 1869 conducted the first performances of Wagner's *Rheingold* (1869) and *Walküre* (1870). In 1884 he became conductor of the Gürzenich concerts, Cologne, after seven years in Dresden. He conducted first performances of Strauss's *Serenade* (Dresden, 1882), *Till Eulenspiegel* (Cologne, 1896) and *Don Quixote* (Cologne, 1898).

Zweig, Stefan (1881–1942). Austrian novelist and playwright who wrote libretto of *Die schweigsame Frau* and supervised libretti of *Friedenstag* and *Daphne.* His collaboration with Strauss was forbidden by the Nazis because he was Jewish. Committed suicide in South America.

Appendix D   Select bibliography

Armstrong, Thomas, *Strauss's Tone-Poems* (Oxford, 1931).

Asow, Mueller von, Richard Strauss, *Thematisches Verzeichnis* (Vienna, 1954–68).

Baum, Gunther, *Richard Strauss und Hugo von Hormannsthal* (Berlin, 1962).

Beecham, Thomas, *A Mingled Chime* (London, 1944).

Böhm, Karl, *Begegnung mit Richard Strauss* (Vienna, 1964).

Busch, Fritz, *Aus dem Leben, eines Musikers* (Zürich, 1949).

Cardus, Neville, 'Richard Strauss' in *Ten Composers* (London, 1945).

Del Mar, Norman, *Richard Strauss: a critical commentary on his life and works*. Three volumes. (London, 1962, 1969, 1972.)

Gray, Cecil, 'Richard Strauss' in *Survey of Contemporary Music* (London, 1924).

Gregor, Josef, *Richard Strauss, die Meister der Oper* (Munich, 1939).

Hofmannsthal, Hugo von, *Briefe der Freundschaft*, correspondence with Eberhard von Bodenhausen (Frankfurt, 1953).

Jefferson, Alan, *The Operas of Richard Strauss in Britain, 1910–63* (London, 1963).

The Lieder of Richard Strauss (London, 1971).

The Life of Richard Strauss (Newton Abbot, 1973).

Richard Strauss (London, 1975).

Krause, Ernst, *Richard Strauss: Gestalt und Werk* (Leipzig, 1955). English edition (third German edition 1963), London, 1964.

Lehmann, Lotte, *Singing with Richard Strauss* (London, 1964).

Mahler, Alma, *Gustav Mahler: Memories and Letters*, ed. D. Mitchell. (Third English edition) London, 1973.

Mann, William, *Richard Strauss: a critical study of the operas* (London, 1964).

Marek, George R., *Richard Strauss: the life of a non-hero* (London, 1967).

Newman, Ernest, *Richard Strauss* (London, 1908).

Pander, Oscar von, *Clemens Krauss in München* (Munich, 1955).

Prawy, Marcel, *The Vienna Opera* (London, 1969).

Rolland, Romain, *Richard Strauss: Correspondance et Fragments de Journal* (Paris, 1951); English edition tr. Rollo H. Myers (London, 1968).

Roth, Ernst, *Musik als Kunst und Ware* (Zürich, 1966), in English as *The Business of Music* (1969).

Schuh, Willi, *Uber Opern von Richard Strauss* (Zürich, 1947).
    Hugo von Hofmannsthal und Richard Strauss (Munich, 1964).

Specht, Richard, *Richard Strauss und sein Werk* (Leipzig, 1921).

Strauss, Richard, *Briefe an die Eltern* (Zürich, 1954).
    Betrachtungen und Erinnerungen, ed. W. Schuh (Zürich, 1949). English translation by L. J. Lawrence (London, 1953).
    Briefwechsel mit Hans von Bülow (Bonn, 1953),
        Joseph Gregor (Salzburg, 1955),
        Hugo von Hofmannsthal (Zürich, 1952. English translation, London, 1961).
        Anton Kippenburg (Bonn, 1960),
        Clemens Krauss (Munich, 1964),
        Willi Schuh (Zürich, 1969),
        Franz Wüllner (Cologne, 1963),
        Stefan Zweig (Frankfurt, 1957).

Tenschert, Roland, *Anekdoten von Richard Strauss* (Vienna, 1945).
    Richard Strauss und Wien (Vienna, 1949).

Trenner, Franz, *Richard Strauss: Dokumente seines Lebens und Schaffens* (Munich, 1954).

Wellesz, Egon, 'Hofmannsthal and Strauss', in *Music and Letters*, Vol. XXXIII, 1952.

Wurmser, Leo, 'Richard Strauss as an Opera Conductor', in *Music and Letters*, Vol. XLV, 1964.

Appendix E The self-quotations in *Ein Heldenleben*

Here is a list, in order of their appearance, of the self-quotations in the 'Hero's Works of Peace' section of the tone-poem *Ein Heldenleben* which occur between pp. 105 and 117 of the original Leuckart score:

Don Juan (2 extracts, p. 105)
Also sprach Zarathustra (p. 105)
Tod und Verklärung (2 extracts, p. 110)
Don Quixote (3 extracts, p. 110)
Don Juan (2 extracts, p. 111)
Don Quixote (p. 111)
Till Eulenspiegel (p. 111)
Guntram (p. 111)
Guntram (2 extracts, p. 112)
Guntram (p. 113)
Tod und Verklärung (p. 113)
Also sprach Zarathustra (p. 113)
Guntram (p. 113)
Macbeth (p. 113)
'Befreit' (p. 113)
Macbeth (2 extracts, p. 113)
'Traum durch die Dämmerung' (p. 114)
Guntram (2 extracts, p. 114)
Don Quixote (p. 114)
Guntram (p. 115)
Tod und Verklärung (p. 116)
Also sprach Zarathustra (p. 116)
Guntram (p. 117)

Index

Index

Index

Index